GED® TEST
SCIENCE
REVIEW

Other titles of interest from LearningExpress

GED® Test Preparation
GED® Test Reasoning through Language Arts (RLA) Review
GED® Test Mathematical Reasoning Review
GED® Test Social Studies Review
GED® Test Flash Review: Mathematical Reasoning
GED® Test Flash Review: Reasoning through Language Arts
GED® Test Flash Review: Science
GED® Test Flash Review: Social Studies

GED® TEST SCIENCE REVIEW

NEW YORK

05 - . 2017

Copyright © 2017 LearningExpress.

All rights reserved under International and Pan American Copyright Conventions.
Published in the United States by LearningExpress, New York.

ISBN-13: 978-1-61103-087-7

Printed in the United States of America

9 8 7 6 5 4 3 2 1

For more information on LearningExpress, other LearningExpress products, or bulk sales,
please write to us at:
  224 W. 29th Street
  3rd Floor
  New York, NY 10001

CONTENTS

CONTENTS

1 ▶ INTRODUCTION TO THE GED® SCIENCE TEST

The test of General Education Development, or GED® test, measures how well you understand high-school-level math, reading and writing, science, and social studies. Passing a GED® test in a specific area proves you have a high-school-level education in that subject. If you pass all four of the GED® tests, you will be awarded a GED® diploma, the equivalent of a high school diploma.

The four separate modules of the GED® test include:

1. Reasoning through Language Arts
2. Social Studies
3. Science
4. Mathematical Reasoning

To pass each test, not only will you need to know the basics of each subject, but you'll also need to use critical thinking, writing, and problem-solving skills.

If you would like to receive a high school diploma, but you are unable or do not wish to graduate via the traditional path of attending high school, the GED® test might be a great fit for you.

This book is designed to help you master the skills and concepts required to do well on the GED® Science test. Some of you preparing for this particular GED® test may have not been in a school setting for some time. This means your science knowledge might be a little rusty—or maybe you've forgotten basic science concepts altogether.

Even if you have been in a school setting, you might not have mastered the various essential science concepts you'll face on the GED® test. This book will give you a better grasp of all the science you'll see on the exam. Once you have a good understanding of GED® science, you'll feel much more comfortable with any passage and question that might come your way on test day.

About the GED® Science Test

The GED® Science test focuses on using critical thinking and reasoning skills along with the fundamentals of scientific reasoning and application of science practices in real-world scenarios. This may sound overwhelming, but the following chapters will give you the information and strategies you need for tackling this test.

The test includes reading passages, analyzing graphs and charts, problem solving, and answering questions, all containing science content. There are also some question sets (i.e., more than one question asked about a particular graphic or passage). You will have 90 minutes to complete the test.

The GED® Science test assesses important science ideas in two ways:

1. Every question tests a science practice skill and measures critical thinking and reasoning skills that are key to understanding scientific information.
2. Additionally, each question is drawn from one of the three main content areas in science—life science, physical science, and Earth and space science.

Understanding the science practice skills and reviewing the information covered within the three main content areas will help when preparing for the test.

How Is the Test Delivered?

You will take your GED® test on a computer at an official testing center. Although you do not need to be a computer expert to pass the GED® test, you should be comfortable using a mouse and typing on a keyboard.

The GED® Testing Service has put together a useful GED® Test Tutorial to familiarize test-takers with important aspects of the exam. It's important to watch this tutorial in order to

- learn how to use the computer to navigate the questions on the test,
- learn how to operate the online calculator that will be provided during the GED® test,
- become familiar with the five different styles of questions that will be on the exam, and
- understand how to access and use several different math reference tools that will be available during your GED® Science test.

You can find this useful tutorial here: http://www.gedtestingservice.com/2014cbttutorialview/.

When and Where Can I Take the Test?

Now that the GED® tests are given online, the testing dates are no longer restricted to just three times a year. The first step is to create an account at www.GED.com. Use this account to select an official Testing Center, a date, and the time that you would like to take any of the four different tests. If you do not pass a particular module on your first attempt, you may take that test up to two more times with no waiting period between test dates. If you still do not pass on your third attempt, you will need to wait 60 days before you can retake that particular test.

GED® Science Test Structure

The GED® Science test consists of 35 questions based on a variety of materials, including brief texts, graphics, and tables.

Multiple-Choice Questions

This is the main question type on the GED® Science test, and it is designed to evaluate your ability to apply general science concepts to various problem-solving and critical-thinking questions. Each multiple-choice question is followed by four answer choices labeled **a** through **d**. You will be instructed to select the best answer to the question. There is no penalty for guessing.

Fill-in-the-Blank Questions

For fill-in-the-blank questions, you will be given a sentence or paragraph that includes a blank. You must manually type your answer into this blank. There will be no choices from which to select your answer.

Drag-and-Drop Questions

For drag-and-drop items, you will need to click on the correct object, hold down the mouse, and drag the object to the appropriate place in the problem, diagram, chart, or graph.

Here's what a computerized drag-and-drop question might look like on the GED® test.

Drag-and-Drop

Drag-and-drop questions have two areas—one area shows all of the answer choices, and the other area is where you will move the correct answers. You will need to drag one or more answer(s) from the first area to the second area.

To answer a drag-and-drop question, click and hold the mouse on an answer and move it (drag it) to the correct area of the screen. Then let go of the mouse (drop it). You can remove an answer and switch it with another answer at any time.

Try the practice question below.

Practice

Drag and drop the seasons in the order in which they occur from December to November.

Hot-Spot Questions

Hot-spot questions require you to click on an area of the screen to indicate where the correct answer is located. For instance, you may be asked to plot a point by clicking on a corresponding online graph. You can change your answer by simply clicking on another area.

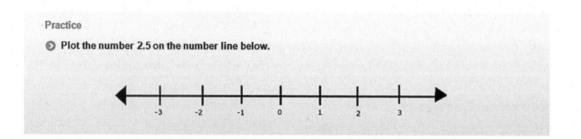

Hot Spot

Hot spot questions ask you to choose a certain place on an image.

To answer the question, click on the correct spot of the image provided. You can change your answer by simply clicking on another area.

Now, you try.

Practice

 Plot the number 2.5 on the number line below.

Drop-Down Questions

These questions will have one or more drop-down menus with options that you can select to complete a sentence or problem. To answer the question, click your mouse on the arrow to show all of the answer choices. Then click on your chosen answer to complete the sentence or paragraph.

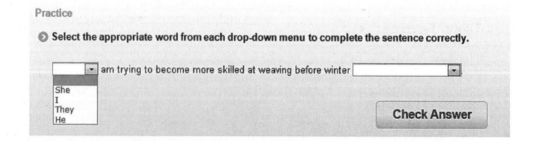

Practice

 Select the appropriate word from each drop-down menu to complete the sentence correctly.

am trying to become more skilled at weaving before winter

She
I
They
He

Check Answer

Answering GED® Science Test Questions

As noted before, the test items may include a scenario that has one question or multiple questions associated with it. For example, you may read a passage about predator-prey population dynamics and review a graph that shows the numbers of rabbits and lynx over time. You then may be asked several questions about the passage and the data in the graph. Other prompts will include charts, diagrams, tables, and brief text passages.

Problem-solving questions will ask you to apply your understanding of information presented as part of the question. Questions of this type could require you to

- interpret results or draw conclusions based on results
- analyze experimental flaws or logical fallacies in arguments
- make a prediction based on information provided in the question
- select the best procedure or method to accomplish a scientific goal
- select a diagram that best illustrates a principle
- apply scientific knowledge to everyday life
- use the work of renowned scientists to explain everyday global issues

Test Topics

The science topics covered on the GED® Science test are:

- Life science—40% of the questions
- Physical science—40% of the questions
- Earth and space science—20% of the questions

On the GED® Science test, life science deals with subjects covered in high school biology classes, physical science includes high school physics and chemistry, and Earth and space science questions cover high school Earth science and astronomy. You should be familiar with the concepts listed and use the content review chapters following to help you refresh your knowledge of them.

NOTE

All the information you will need to answer the questions on the GED® Science test is actually within the passages themselves. The GED® test questions test your ability to read and comprehend scientific information; they do not test your memory or knowledge of science.

The review chapters in this book will give you a solid background of the sciences you must know to succeed on the exam, so you can read the passages with ease and clarity. They will also give you practice reading scientific language, and the practice questions throughout will test your ability to comprehend what you have read, just as the GED® test asks you to do.

How to Use This Book

In addition to this introduction, *GED® Test Science Review* also contains the following:

A Diagnostic Exam. It's always helpful to see where your science skills stand. Therefore, we recommend taking the diagnostic test before starting on the content chapters. By taking the diagnostic test, you should be able to determine the content areas in which you are strongest and the areas in which you might need more help. For example, if you miss most of the physical science questions, then you know that you should pay extra attention to the review and questions in Chapter 5.

The diagnostic test does not count for any score, so don't get caught up on how many you got right or wrong. Instead, use the results of the diagnostic test to help guide your study of the content chapters.

Science Practices. In Chapter 3, we will review the science practice skills in more detail. These skills, as noted previously, are used in each question to measure the critical thinking and reasoning ability necessary for scientific inquiry. These skills include comprehending scientific presentations, designing investigations or experiments, reasoning from data, and using probability and statistics in a scientific context. Reviewing these skills is key to doing well on the GED® Science test.

Content Chapters. Chapters 4, 5, and 6 include a basic review of the three science areas covered on the GED® Science test: life science, physical science, and Earth and space science. These chapters form the heart of the book. Here we cover the basic science concepts discussed earlier. To help you understand all these ideas, every chapter has sample questions, helpful tips, and summaries, as well as explanations of the concepts being discussed. We recommend reading these chapters in order and not skipping around, as many of the concepts in the earlier chapters are built on in the later chapters.

Practice Test. After you've completed your review, take another full-length practice test to assess how much you've learned and what you still need to go over before test day. Every answer has a full-length explanation that tells you why every choice is right or wrong. Don't skip these explanations—they'll give you insight into the types of tricky wrong answers the test maker often uses to steer you in the wrong direction. Then, when you're done, spend the days/weeks/ months before your test reviewing the areas that are giving you the most trouble.

Let's get started with reviewing what you need to do well on the GED® Science test!

GED® SCIENCE DIAGNOSTIC TEST

This practice test is modeled on the format, content, and timing of the official GED® Science test. Like the official exam, the questions focus on your ability to read and comprehend scientific information in the form of text, graphs, charts, diagrams, and more.

Work carefully, but do not spend too much time on any one question. Be sure you answer every question.

Set a timer for 90 minutes, and try to take this test uninterrupted, under quiet conditions.

Complete answer explanations for every test question follow the exam. Good luck!

35 total questions
90 minutes to complete

Please use the following to answer questions 1–3.

A non-predatory relationship between two organisms that benefits at least one of the organisms is called a *symbiotic relationship*. These relationships can be categorized further based on the effect of the relationship on the second organism. The table shows the three types of symbiotic relationships and their effects on each organism.

Symbiotic Relationship	Species 1	Species 2
Mutualism	+	+
Commensalism	+	0
Parasitism	+	−

Key
+ benefits
− harmed
0 no effect

Veterinary clinics often treat pets with illnesses resulting from parasitism. Three common parasites diagnosed in dogs are the dog flea, the deer tick, and *Cheyletiella* mites.

Dog fleas and deer ticks both feed on the host animal's (dog's) blood and can transmit diseases to the host animal through their bites. Dog fleas lay their eggs on the host animal's body and can survive on the host animal or on surfaces the animal comes in contact with, such as bedding. Deer ticks lay their eggs on the ground and attach to the host animal only while feeding.

Cheyletiella mites live within and feed on the keratin layer of the host animal's skin. *Cheyletiella* mites reproduce on the host animal and can survive away from the host animal only for short periods of time.

1. Read the two descriptions of symbiotic relationships that follow, and select the correct term for each relationship from the following list. Write the correct answer in the box after each description.

   commensalism
   mutualism
   parasitism

   Mistletoe attaches to spruce trees. Using specialized structures, mistletoe penetrates into and extracts water and nutrients from the tree's branches.

   _____

   E. coli *bacteria live within the intestinal tract of humans, obtaining nutrients from the food particles that pass through the intestines. Vitamin K produced by the* E. coli *is absorbed through the intestinal walls for use in the human body.*

   _____

2. According to the passage, all of the dog parasites gain which benefit from their symbiotic relationships with the host dogs?
   a. a habitat for living
   b. a vector for disease
   c. a source of nutrients
   d. a site for reproduction

3. A veterinary technician is preparing to examine a dog suspected of having *Cheyletiella* mites. Based on the information in the passage, which precaution would most effectively prevent the transmission of mites to other animals in the clinic?
   a. administering a vaccine to the infected dog
   b. wearing disposable gloves while examining the dog
   c. avoiding contact with open wounds on the dog
   d. sterilizing the exam room before examining the dog

4. The passing of one object in space through the shadow of another object is called an eclipse. The orbits of the moon and Earth in relation to the sun cause both solar and lunar eclipses to occur. During a solar eclipse, the specific alignment of these three objects causes the moon to cast a shadow on Earth. During a lunar eclipse, the alignment causes Earth to cast a shadow on the moon.

The following diagram shows the alignment of the sun, Earth, and moon during a lunar eclipse. Draw an "X" in the correct spot to identify the location of the moon necessary to produce a solar eclipse.

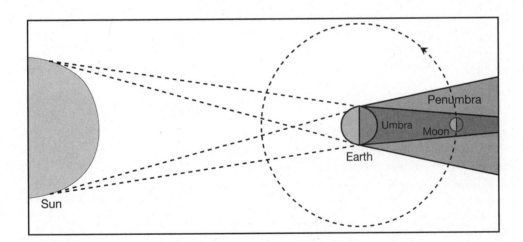

5. The table below compares characteristics for four different groups of plants. A "1" indicates that the characteristic is present, and a "0" indicates that the characteristic is absent.

Plant Type	Vascular Tissue	Seeds	Flowers
Conifers	1	1	0
Ferns	1	0	0
Flowering Plants	1	1	1
Mosses	0	0	0

A cladogram illustrates the relatedness of organisms based on shared characteristics. The group that exhibits the fewest characteristics is listed on the bottom left branch, and the group exhibiting the most characteristics is listed on the top right branch. Branches below a given characteristic represent organisms that do not exhibit that characteristic. Branches above a given characteristic represent organisms that do exhibit that characteristic. Each branch represents one plant type.

Use the information in the table to organize the four plant types onto the appropriate branches in the cladogram.

Write the correct plant type into each box. Select from the choices below.

conifers
ferns
flowering plants
mosses

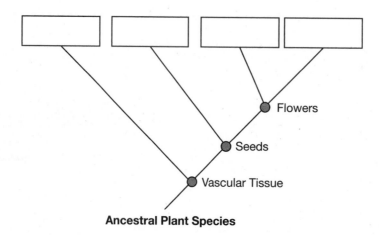

Please use the following to answer questions 6 and 7.

The amount of oxygen gas dissolved in a body of water can provide information about the health of the aquatic ecosystem. In general, the closer the dissolved oxygen level to the maximum level, the more productive and less polluted the ecosystem can be assumed to be.

The table below shows the maximum amount of oxygen gas that can be dissolved in water at various temperatures.

WATER TEMPERATURE (°C)	MAXIMUM OXYGEN SOLUBILITY (mg/L)
0	14.6
10	11.3
20	9.2
30	7.6
40	6.4
100	0

6. The data in the table support which of the following statements about the relationship between water temperature and oxygen solubility?

   a. Bodies of water with a lower average temperature can support a higher concentration of dissolved oxygen.

   b. Bodies of water with an average temperature higher than 40°C contain no dissolved oxygen.

   c. A 10°C increase in water temperature results in an approximately 3 mg/L change in oxygen solubility.

   d. The oxygen solubility of a body of water is affected by many variables, including water temperature.

7. Researchers find that a body of freshwater with an average temperature of 21°C has a dissolved oxygen concentration of 7.2 mg/L. What is a reasonable prediction of the water's dissolved oxygen concentration after the population size of freshwater grasses doubles?

   a. 6.3 mg/L

   b. 7.2 mg/L

   c. 8.5 mg/L

   d. 14.4 mg/L

8. The chart below illustrates how the color of the light emitted by a star is dependent on the star's temperature.

CLASS	COLOR	SURFACE TEMP. (K)
O	Blue	>25,000 K
B	Blue-white	11,000–25,000 K
A	White	7,500–11,000 K
F	White	6,000–7,500 K
G	Yellow	5,000–6,000 K
K	Orange	3,500–5,000 K
M	Red	<3,500 K

Which of the following statements is supported by the data in the table?

   a. In general, white stars are hotter than blue-white stars.

   b. A star with a surface temperature of 3,700 K produces red light.

   c. Yellow light is produced by stars within the narrowest temperature range.

   d. The highest known surface temperature of a star is 25,000 K.

9. The diagram below illustrates the structure of an ocean wave.

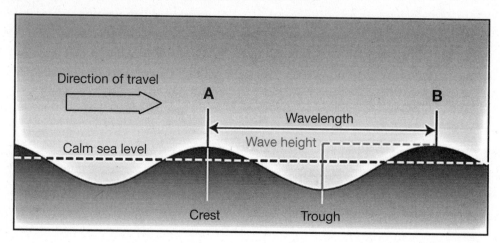

The *period* of a wave is the time required for the wave crest at point A to reach point B. The wave period can also be described as the amount of time required for a wave to do which of the following?

a. reach the shoreline

b. travel one wavelength

c. return to calm sea level

d. travel from crest to trough

Please use the following to answer questions 10 and 11.

The U.S. Geological Survey (USGS) tracks the annual occurrence and effects of natural hazards in the United States. Based on its data, the USGS has calculated the probability of a natural hazard occurring in any given year that would cause 10 or more fatalities. The table below lists the probabilities for the four most commonly occurring natural hazards.

EVENT	PROBABILITY OF AN ANNUAL EVENT WITH ≥10 FATALITIES IN THE UNITED STATES
Earthquake	0.11
Hurricane	0.39
Flood	0.86
Tornado	0.96

0 = no chance of occurring
1 = 100% chance of occurring

10. What is the probability of a hurricane and a tornado, each with 10 or more fatalities, both occurring in the same year?

a. 0

b. 0.37

c. 0.96

d. 1.35

11. Write the appropriate natural hazard from the table in the box below.

A boundary between the Pacific and North American tectonic plates lies along the west coast of the continental United States. The probability of a(n) _____ with 10 or more fatalities is much higher in this region than the probability for the United States as a whole.

12. A marathon runner consumes foods with a high carbohydrate content before and during a race to prevent muscle fatigue. This practice, called *carb loading*, supports which of the following energy transformations within the runner's body?

a. chemical to thermal
b. thermal to kinetic
c. kinetic to thermal
d. chemical to kinetic

Please use the following to answer questions 13–15.

Consumers in an ecosystem are classified by feeding level. Primary consumers feed on producers. Secondary consumers feed on primary consumers, and tertiary consumers feed on secondary consumers. Consumers in a food web are classified according to their highest feeding level.

A consumer's population size is determined largely by the complex relationships that exist within the ecosystem's food web. Population size is most obviously limited by the population size of the consumer's food source(s). An increase or decrease in a food source population often leads to a similar change in the consumer population. The availability of a food source may be limited by other consumer populations competing for the same food source. An increase in a competitor population may lead to a decreased availability of the shared food source. Population size is also limited by the population size of the consumer's predator(s). Predation by higher-level consumers keeps the lower consumer population from growing out of control and upsetting the ecosystem's balance.

The food web for a woodland ecosystem bordering an area of farmland is shown below.

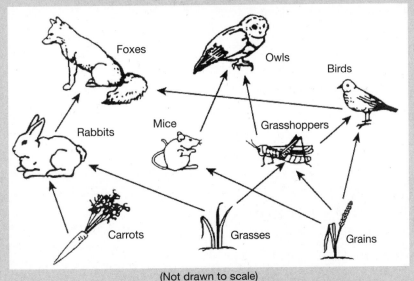

(Not drawn to scale)

13. According to the passage, rabbits are considered primary consumers because they
a. feed on grasses and carrots
b. are consumed by foxes only
c. compete with grasshoppers only
d. are the only consumer of carrots

14. Which three organisms in the food web obtain energy directly or indirectly from grasshoppers?
a. owls, birds, and mice
b. owls, birds, and grains
c. foxes, rabbits, and mice
d. foxes, owls, and birds

15. A bacterial disease has destroyed most of the farm's carrot crop for the past two seasons. As a result, the rabbit population has been forced to rely more heavily on grasses for a food source.

Explain how this disruption is likely to affect the rest of the ecosystem's food web. Include multiple pieces of evidence from the text and discuss specific populations (other than carrots and rabbits) as examples to support your answer.

Write your response on the lines below. This task may take approximately 10 minutes to complete.

_____

_____

_____

_____

_____

_____

_____

_____

_____

_____

_____

16. The table below illustrates the range of normal body temperatures in Fahrenheit for different age-groups.

NORMAL BODY TEMPERATURE	
AGE-GROUP	**TEMPERATURE (IN °FAHRENHEIT)**
Newborn	97.7°F–99.5°F
Infants (1 year or less)	97.0°F–99.0°F
Children (1–17 years)	97.5°F–98.6°F
Adults (above 18 years)	97.6°F–99°F
Elders (above 70 years)	96.8°F–97.5°F

The formula for converting Fahrenheit to Celsius is shown below.

$$(°F - 32) \times \frac{5}{9} = °C$$

The normal body temperature range of a newborn baby is _____ °C to _____ °C. (You may use a calculator to answer this question.)

17. The process of meiosis is depicted in the diagram below.

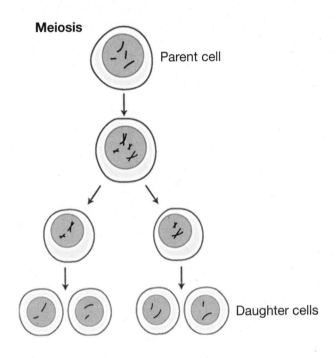

Meiosis

Parent cell

Daughter cells

The daughter cells produced during meiosis are used for what purpose?
a. growth
b. tissue repair
c. differentiation
d. reproduction

18. A highway patrol officer is monitoring the speed of vehicles along a stretch of highway with a speed limit of 55 mph. The results are shown below.

    Vehicle 1: 61 mph
    Vehicle 2: 48 mph
    Vehicle 3: 61 mph
    Vehicle 4: 51 mph
    Vehicle 5: 59 mph

What is the average speed of the five vehicles? (You may use a calculator to answer this question.)

a. 55 miles per hour
b. 56 miles per hour
c. 59 miles per hour
d. 61 miles per hour

19. Meiosis produces cells containing one chromosome from each chromosome pair. The diagram below shows the chromosome combinations that can be produced from a cell containing two pairs of chromosomes.

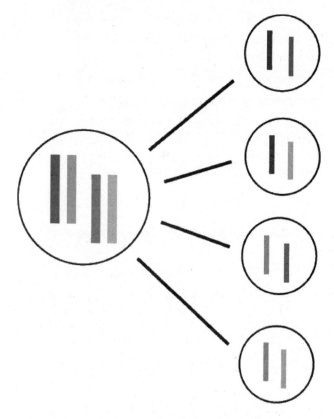

A barley plant has seven pairs of chromosomes. How many unique combinations of chromosomes can result from meiosis in barley?

a. 7
b. 14
c. 49
d. 128

Please use the following to answer questions 20–22.

Respiration is the cellular process used by living things to convert the chemical energy in food to a form that can be used by cells. Adenosine triphosphate (ATP) is the high-energy molecule that all living things use to fuel cellular processes. During respiration, a molecule of glucose is converted to molecules of ATP to be used by the cell.

Depending on the conditions, respiration occurs by two different pathways: aerobic and anaerobic. When a cell has a sufficient supply of oxygen, aerobic respiration occurs. This pathway uses oxygen as a reactant, along with glucose, to produce 36 to 38 molecules of ATP from each molecule of glucose. Aerobic respiration is the preferred pathway in most cells. The general equation for aerobic respiration is shown below.

$$C_6H_{12}O_6 + 6O_2 \rightarrow energy + 6CO_2 + 6H_2O$$

When sufficient oxygen is not available, anaerobic respiration occurs. This pathway produces two molecules of ATP from each molecule of glucose. Anaerobic respiration sometimes occurs in human muscle cells. During exercise, muscle cells use energy faster than the oxygen supply can be replenished, causing the cells to switch temporarily to anaerobic respiration.

20. A student draws the model below to represent the process of aerobic respiration.

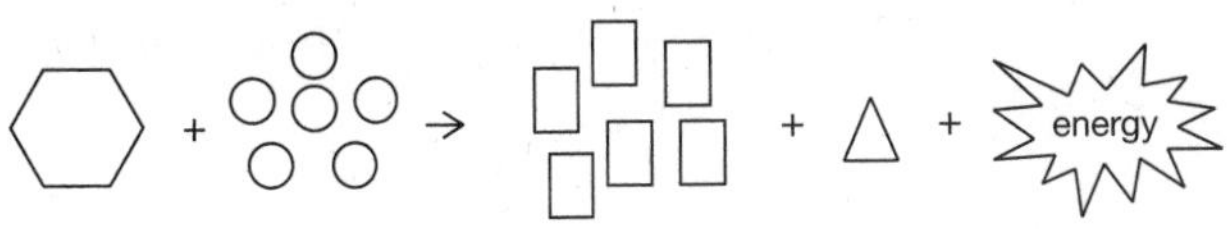

Which change would improve the accuracy of the student's model?

a. connecting all of the circles to each other to show bonds

b. moving the energy symbol to the left side of the equation

c. adding five triangles to balance the right side of the equation

d. making the rectangles smaller to show relative molecular sizes

21. The energy produced by respiration is in what form?

a. ATP

b. oxygen

c. glucose

d. carbon dioxide

22. Explain the benefit of having two pathways for respiration in the human body.

Include multiple pieces of evidence from the text to support your answer.

Write your response on the lines on the following page. This task may take approximately 10 minutes to complete.

_____

_____

_____

_____

_____

_____

_____

_____

_____

_____

_____

_____

_____

_____

_____

_____

_____

_____

Please use the following to answer questions 23 and 24.

Matter exists in solid, liquid, and gas states. A substance may change between these three states. State changes can alter the physical properties of a substance, as depicted in the models below.

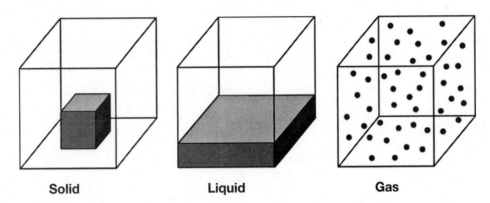

23. Which summary best explains the model of the states of matter?
   a. Liquids have a fixed shape like solids but assume the volume of the container as gases do.
   b. Liquids have a fixed volume and shape like solids. Gases assume the volume and shape of the container.
   c. Liquids have a fixed volume like solids but assume the shape of the container as gases do.
   d. Liquids assume the volume and shape of the container as gases do. Solids have a fixed volume and shape.

24. Based on the model, which state change increases the density of a substance?
   a. gas to liquid
   b. solid to gas
   c. liquid to gas
   d. solid to liquid

Please use the following to answer questions 25 and 26.

Information about five different fuel sources is listed in the table below.

	ENERGY CONTENT (kJ/g)	CO_2 RELEASED (MOL/10^3kJ)
Hydrogen	120	------
Natural gas	51.6	1.2
Petroleum	43.6	1.6
Coal	39.3	2.0
Ethanol	27.3	1.6

25. Which statement represents a fact supported by the data in the table?
   a. All cars will be fueled by hydrogen cells in the future.
   b. Petroleum is a better fuel source for cars than ethanol is.
   c. Natural gas is too expensive to use as a fuel source for cars.
   d. Ethanol fuel provides a car with less energy per gram than petroleum does.

26. Natural gas, petroleum, and coal are fossil fuels. Ethanol is derived from biomass.

Based on the data in the table, what is the best estimate of the energy content of fossil fuels?
a. 40 kJ/g
b. 42 kJ/g
c. 45 kJ/g
d. 50 kJ/g

27. The term *exothermic* describes a process in which energy is released, usually as thermal energy. The term *endothermic* describes a process in which thermal energy is absorbed.

Which of the following is an example of an exothermic process?
a. a candle burning
b. a snow bank melting
c. a loaf of bread baking
d. a plant making sugar

28. The graph below represents the motion of a remote-controlled car. The car's acceleration, or change in velocity, is indicated by the slope of the graph.

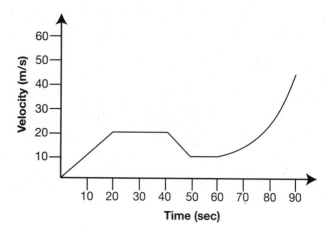

During which period did the car experience a constant positive acceleration?
a. between 0 and 20 seconds
b. between 20 and 40 seconds
c. between 40 and 50 seconds
d. between 50 and 90 seconds

Please use the following to answer questions 29 and 30.

The mechanical advantage (MA) of a machine is a measure of how much the machine multiplies the input force applied to it.

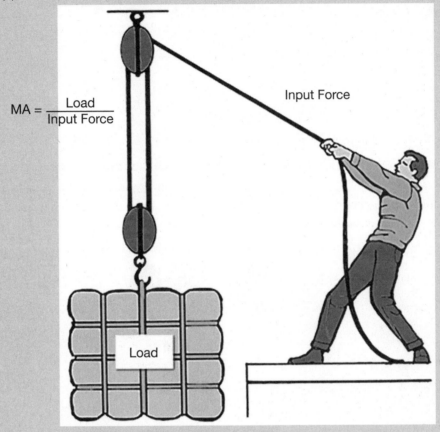

$$MA = \frac{Load}{Input\ Force}$$

The table below shows the input force required to lift different loads using the pulley system shown above.

LOAD (N)	INPUT FORCE (N)
30	10
60	20
90	30
150	50

29. Based on the data in the table, what happens to the mechanical advantage of the pulley system as the load size increases?

a. The mechanical advantage increases at a constant rate.

b. The system's mechanical advantage does not change.

c. The pulley system multiplies the mechanical advantage.

d. The mechanical advantage decreases at a constant rate.

30. A 1 newton load has a mass of 10 grams. According to the table, what is the maximum mass that can be lifted by the pulley system using an input force of 50 newtons?

a. 15 grams

b. 50 grams

c. 150 grams

d. 1,500 grams

31. Artificial selection is the process of breeding plants or animals to increase the occurrence of desired traits. Farmers use artificial selection to produce new crop species from existing plant species. The diagram below illustrates six crop species that have been derived from the common wild mustard plant.

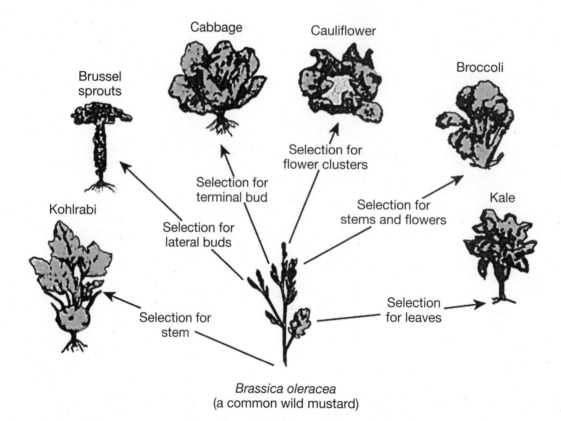

Based on the information in the passage, how did farmers produce kale?

a. Farmers removed the stems and flowers from mustard plants as they grew.

b. Farmers allowed only wild mustard plants with large leaves to reproduce.

c. Farmers bred small-leafed plants with large-leafed plants to increase leaf size.

d. Farmers prevented wild mustard plants with large leaves from reproducing.

32.

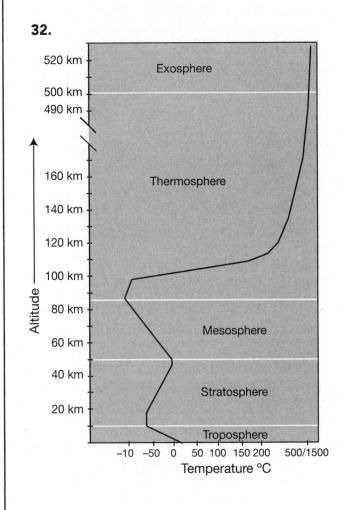

According to the graph, in which atmospheric layers does temperature decrease as altitude increases?

a. mesosphere and exosphere

b. troposphere and thermosphere

c. stratosphere and thermosphere

d. troposphere and mesosphere

33. Surface currents in the ocean are classified as warm or cold currents. In general, warm currents tend to travel from the equator toward the poles along the eastern coast of continents. Cold currents tend to travel from the poles toward the equator along the western coast of continents.

The map below shows the major surface ocean currents of the world.

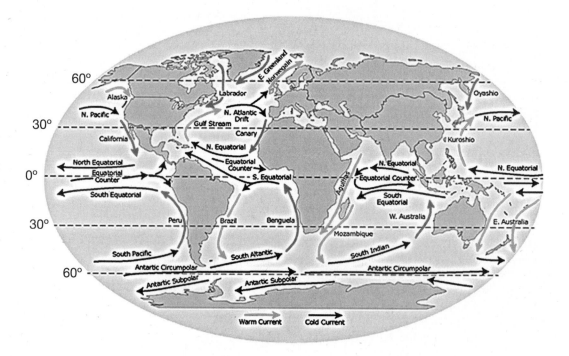

Based on the passage, which of the following statements about the Alaska current is true?
a. The Alaska current is a typical cold current because it travels along the western coast of the continent.
b. The Alaska current is not a true surface current because it does not follow the general pattern of surface currents.
c. The Alaska current is an exception to the general pattern because warm currents typically travel along the eastern coast of continents.
d. The Alaska current transports water from the north pole toward the equator because it travels along the western coast of the continent.

34. Every person has two copies, or alleles, of the ABO blood type gene. A person's ABO blood type is determined by his or her specific combination of alleles. The table below shows the allele combinations that cause the four different ABO blood types.

BLOOD TYPE	GENOTYPE
A	$I^A I^A$ or $I^A i$
B	$I^B I^B$ or $I^B i$
AB	$I^A I^B$
O	ii

Suppose that a mother's allele combination is $I^A i$, and a father's allele combination is $I^A I^B$. Which of the following statements is true about the blood type of their first child?

a. The child will have the same blood type as the mother.

b. The child cannot have the father's blood type.

c. The child will have a blood type different from both parents'.

d. The child cannot have blood type O.

35. Blood glucose levels are tightly regulated in the human body by the hormones insulin and glucagon. When glucose levels become too high or low, the pancreas produces the appropriate hormone to return the body to homeostasis. The diagram below shows the feedback mechanism for regulating blood glucose levels.

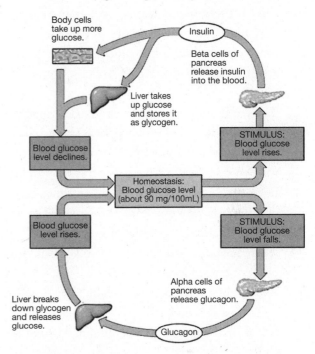

Diabetes mellitus is a disease in which the pancreas is unable to produce the insulin needed to regulate blood glucose levels. What result would occur from providing an insulin injection to a diabetic person with high blood sugar?

a. The insulin travels to the liver, where it binds to and destroys excess glucose in the bloodstream.

b. The insulin signals the pancreas to produce glucagon, which increases the level of glucose in the bloodstream.

c. The insulin causes the liver to convert glucose to glycogen, removing excess glucose from the bloodstream.

d. The insulin breaks down glycogen into glucose, releasing stored glucose into the bloodstream.

Answers and Explanations

You should aim to answer 26+ questions correctly on this practice exam in order to be well-prepared to pass the GED® Science test. If you score between 19–25 items correctly, you are on your way to passing, though you probably need a little more review before you take your test. If you answer fewer than 19 items correctly, take extra time to go over the review chapters and try some additional practice exams before you go in for your official test.

1. The symbiotic relationship exhibited by mistletoe and spruce trees is **parasitism**. The mistletoe receives a benefit in the form of a source of nutrients and water. The spruce tree is harmed because it loses nutrients and water, which can eventually lead to the death of the tree. The table indicates that parasitism is occurring when one organism benefits (mistletoe) and the other organism is harmed (spruce tree).

   The symbiotic relationship exhibited by *E. coli* and humans is **mutualism**. The *E. coli* receive a benefit in the form of nutrients and a habitat in which to live. The human also receives a benefit because the *E. coli* produce vitamin K, which is then used within the human body. The table indicates that mutualism is occurring when both organisms benefit.

   Commensalism is not demonstrated in either of these relationships. The table indicates that commensalism occurs when one organism benefits, but the other organism is neither helped nor harmed.

2. **Choice c is correct.** The fleas and ticks obtain nutrients from the host animal's blood, and the mites obtain nutrients from the host animal's skin.

   Choice **a** is incorrect. Though the fleas and mites may live on the host animal's body, the ticks do not.

   Choice **b** is incorrect. Parasites can transmit diseases to the host animal, but this does not provide a benefit to the parasite.

   Choice **d** is incorrect. Though the fleas and mites reproduce on the host animal's body, the ticks do not.

3. **Choice b is correct.** The passage states that *Cheyletiella* mites live within the outermost layer of the dog's skin and have difficulty surviving away from the host animal's body. A technician wearing gloves during examination of the dog and disposing of them afterward helps to prevent mites that may be on the technician's hands from being transmitted to other animals in the clinic.

   Choice **a** is incorrect. Vaccines can be administered to uninfected individuals to prevent the transmission of diseases caused by viruses. Mites are arthropods that live on the host animal's body and cannot be eliminated with a vaccine.

   Choice **c** is incorrect. Avoiding contact with open wounds would help prevent the transmission of blood-borne pathogens, such as those transmitted by fleas and ticks.

   Choice **d** is incorrect. Sterilizing the exam room after, not before, examination of the infected dog could help prevent the transmission of mites to other animals in the clinic.

4. In order for an eclipse to occur, the sun, Earth, and moon must be aligned in a particular way. When Earth is positioned between the sun and the moon, Earth will prevent sunlight from reaching the moon. This is a lunar eclipse. When the moon is positioned between the sun and Earth, the moon will prevent sunlight from reaching a portion of Earth. This is a solar eclipse.

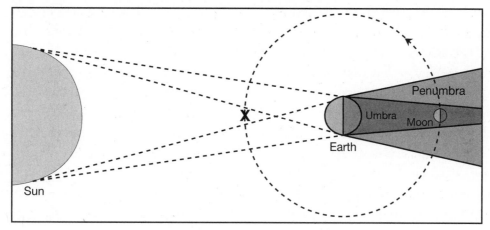

On the diagram, the moon has reached the position in its orbit that is in Earth's shadow, resulting in a lunar eclipse. From its current position on the diagram, the moon would need to travel 180° (or halfway) around its orbit to produce a solar eclipse. In this new position, the moon would cast a shadow on Earth.

5. In a cladogram, the group that exhibits the fewest characteristics is listed on the bottom left branch, and the group exhibiting the most characteristics is listed on the top right branch.

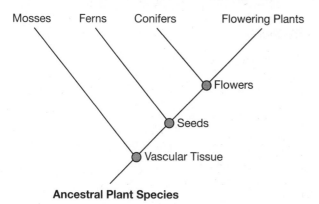

Mosses are placed on the first (lower left) branch because they exhibited none of the characteristics listed in the table. Ferns contain vascular tissue, so are listed on the second branch. Confers are the third branch because they contain vascular tissue and produce seeds. Flowering plants exhibit all three characteristics listed in the table, so are the fourth (highest) branch.

6. Choice a is correct. Describing the pattern in the data allows for the relationship between water temperature and oxygen solubility to be identified. As you look down the table, water temperature increases and maximum oxygen solubility decreases. This shows that water temperature and dissolved oxygen concentration have an inverse relationship, with highest dissolved oxygen concentrations occurring at the lowest temperatures.

Choice **b** is incorrect. According to the table, bodies of water with an average temperature of 40°C have a maximum oxygen solubility of 6.4 mg/L, and bodies of water with an average temperature of 100°C contain no dissolved oxygen. Temperatures between these two should support oxygen concentrations between 6.4 and 0 mg/L.

Choice **c** is incorrect. Though an increase from 0 to 10°C results in a 3 mg/L increase in oxygen solubility, oxygen solubility does not continue to increase by the same increment with each additional 10°C increase in temperature.

Choice **d** is incorrect. Though many variables can affect oxygen solubility, the table focuses only on the relationship between oxygen solubility and water temperature.

7. Choice c is correct. Grasses release oxygen into the environment as a byproduct of photosynthesis. Using this reasoning, it can be predicted that an increase in freshwater grasses will increase the dissolved oxygen concentration. Based on the data in the table, an increase to 8.5 mg/L brings the dissolved oxygen concentration closer to the maximum oxygen solubility for a body of water with an average temperature of 21°C.

Choice **a** is incorrect. Aquatic plants like freshwater grasses release oxygen into the environment. A dissolved oxygen concentration of 6.3 mg/L would result from an event that decreases the amount of dissolved oxygen in the water.

Choice **b** is incorrect. A dissolved oxygen concentration of 7.2 mg/L would indicate no change in the ecosystem. A change in the freshwater grass population would alter the amount of dissolved oxygen in the water.

Choice **d** is incorrect. A doubling of the freshwater grass population would cause an increase in dissolved oxygen concentration but not a doubling. According to the table, a dissolved oxygen concentration of 14.4 mg/L far exceeds the maximum oxygen solubility for a body of water with an average temperature of 21°C.

8. **Choice c is correct.** Range can be determined by calculating the difference between the lowest and highest values in a data set. The table shows that the temperature of a yellow star is between 5,000 K and 6,000 K. This is a range of 1,000 K, which is the smallest (or narrowest) range listed in the table.

Choice **a** is incorrect. White stars have a maximum temperature of 11,000 K. The minimum temperature of blue-white stars is 11,000 K.

Choice **b** is incorrect. Red stars have a maximum temperature of 3,500 K. A star with a temperature of 3,700 K would be within the range of an orange star.

Choice **d** is incorrect. The table does not provide information about the highest surface temperature recorded for a star. The minimum temperature of a blue star is shown to be 25,000 K. This indicates that blue stars can have temperatures higher than 25,000 K.

9. **Choice b is correct.** In the context of this ocean wave diagram, a wavelength is the horizontal distance between two crests (*A* and *B*). Using the given definition of wave period, it can be determined that the wave period is the amount of time required to travel one wavelength.

Choice **a** is incorrect. A shoreline is not shown or mentioned in the diagram.

Choice **c** is incorrect. Wave period relates to the horizontal movement of a wave, while calm sea level is a reference point used to measure the vertical movement of a wave.

Choice **d** is incorrect. In the diagram, points *A* and *B* used to measure wave period are both crests. The time required to travel from crest to trough would be half of a wave period.

10. **Choice b is correct.** A hurricane and tornado occurring in the same year would be considered a compound event because two events are occurring together. The probability of a compound event can be determined by multiplying the probabilities of each event occurring individually. The probability of a hurricane (0.39) multiplied by the probability of a tornado (0.96) provides a compound probability of 0.3744.

Choice **a** is incorrect. A probability of 0 indicates that there is no chance of an event occurring. Since there is a possibility of a hurricane and a possibility of a tornado occurring individually, there is also a possibility of both events occurring in the same year.

Choice **c** is incorrect. This is the probability of a tornado alone occurring during any given year. The probability of both a tornado and a hurricane occurring in the same year would be much lower because the probability of a hurricane is much lower (0.39) than the probability of a tornado (0.96).

Choice **d** is incorrect. A probability greater than 1 indicates that an event is guaranteed to occur. Since the individual probabilities of a hurricane or tornado occurring are both less than 1, the probability of both events occurring in the same year would also be less than 1.

11. The natural hazard that best completes this statement is **earthquake**. The Earth's crust is made up of tectonic plates. The location where two or more tectonic plates meet is called a plate boundary. When the pressure built up at a plate boundary becomes too great, energy is released in the form of an earthquake. Earthquakes can be expected to occur most frequently along plate boundaries. Since the west coast of the continental United States lies on a plate boundary, the probability of an earthquake occurring in this region can be predicted to be much higher than the probability for the United States as a whole, most of which does not lie on plate boundaries.

The occurrence of hurricanes, floods, and tornadoes is not specifically tied to the activity of tectonic plates. An increase in the probability of any of these natural hazards along a plate boundary as compared to the United States as a whole is not a reasonable prediction.

12. Choice d is correct. The runner takes in chemical energy in the form of carbohydrates. This chemical energy is transformed into kinetic energy as the runner's muscles contract and relax, causing the runner to move. Runners carb load to ensure that their bodies have enough chemical energy to be transformed into the kinetic energy required to run a marathon. Choice **a** is incorrect. The runner does take in chemical energy in the form of carbohydrates. Though some of this chemical energy is transformed into thermal energy in the form of body heat, the purpose of carb loading is to improve muscle performance, not increase body heat.

Choice **b** is incorrect. The purpose of carb loading is to increase the amount of energy available for transformation into kinetic energy (motion). Carb loading increases the availability of chemical energy, though, not thermal energy. Carbohydrates contain energy stored in their chemical bonds, not as heat.

Choice **c** is incorrect. The goal of carb loading is to improve muscle performance (motion), not increase body heat. Muscle performance is improved by increasing the chemical energy available for transformation into kinetic energy.

13. Choice a is correct. A primary-level consumer feeds on producers. Producers, such as plants, make their own food using energy from sunlight. Rabbits feed on two producers, carrots and grasses, making rabbits a primary-level consumer.

Choice **b** is incorrect. An organism's feeding level is determined by how it obtains its food, not by the organisms that it provides food for. Though the rabbits in the food web are consumed by foxes, this does not determine the rabbits' feeding level.

Choice **c** is incorrect. Competition with other organisms does not affect how an organism's feeding level is classified.

Choice **d** is incorrect. The presence of other organisms that consume the same food source does not affect how an organism's feeding level is classified.

14. Choice d is correct. An organism provides energy to all organisms above it in the food web. In this food web, the grasshoppers provide energy to the birds, owls, and foxes. The birds and owls obtain energy directly when they consume the grasshoppers. The foxes obtain energy indirectly when they consume birds that previously consumed grasshoppers.

Choice **a** is incorrect. Although owls and birds obtain energy from grasshoppers, mice do not obtain energy from grasshoppers.

Choice **b** is incorrect. Grains provide energy to grasshoppers but do not obtain energy from grasshoppers.

Choice **c** is incorrect. Rabbits and mice do not obtain energy from grasshoppers either directly or indirectly.

15. The highest number of points you can earn on this short-response essay is 3.

A **3-point essay** contains
- a clear and well-developed explanation of how a change in one population effects change in other populations within the food web.
- well-developed examples from the given food web describing the likely effects of change in the rabbit population on other specific populations.
- complete support from the passage.

Sample 3-point response

The interrelatedness of populations in the food web makes it likely that all populations will be affected in some way by the shift in the rabbits' feeding habits. The rabbits' increased reliance on grasses will cause a domino effect on the availability of food for all primary consumers. Since grasshoppers directly compete with rabbits for grasses, the availability of grasses for grasshoppers may be limited. As a result, grasshoppers would likely increase their dependence on grains, decreasing the availability of this food source for birds and mice. The overall increase in competition among primary consumers may cause some decreases in population sizes, which would also limit the population sizes of higher-level consumers.

A **2-point essay** contains
- an adequate or partially articulated explanation of how a change in one population effects change in other populations within the food web.
- partial examples from the given food web describing the likely effects of change in the rabbit population on other specific populations.
- partial support from the passage.

Sample 2-point response

When the rabbits start eating more grasses, the grass-hoppers will have less food because they eat grasses too. This means that the grasshopper population might get smaller, so the owls and birds would have less food. Foxes eat birds, so they would have less food too.

A **1-point essay** contains
- a minimal or implied explanation of how a change in one population effects change in other populations within the food web.
- one or incomplete examples from the given food web describing the likely effects of change in the rabbit population on other specific populations.
- minimal or implied support from the passage.

Sample 1-point response

The rabbits will eat more grass. Grasshoppers will not have as much grass to eat. Some grasshoppers will die because they don't have enough food.

A **0-point essay** contains
- no explanation of how a change in one population effects change in other populations within the food web.
- no examples from the given food web describing the likely effects of change in the rabbit population on other specific populations.
- no support from the passage.

16.

Blank 1:
The appropriate value to complete this statement is **36.5**.
The formula for converting temperature from Fahrenheit to Celsius is given as $(°F - 32) \times \frac{5}{9} = °C$. Replacing the lower variable °F with 97.7 and solving gives $(97.7 - 32) \times \frac{5}{9} = 36.5$.

Blank 2:
The appropriate value to complete this statement is **37.5**.
The formula for converting temperature from Fahrenheit to Celsius is given as $(°F - 32) \times \frac{5}{9} = °C$. Replacing the lower variable °F with 99.5 and solving gives $(99.5 - 32) \times \frac{5}{9} = 37.5$.

17. Choice d is correct. As indicated in the diagram, the daughter cells produced during meiosis each have half the total number of chromosomes as the parent cell does. These daughter cells, called gametes, are used for reproduction. When reproduction occurs, two gametes (egg and sperm) unite to create a cell with a full set of chromosomes.

Choice **a** is incorrect. To allow an organism to grow larger, the daughter cells produced must be identical to the parent cell. Cells used for growth are produced by the process of mitosis.

Choice **b** is incorrect. To allow an organism to repair tissues, the daughter cells produced must be identical to the parent cell. The cells used for tissue repair are produced by the process of mitosis.

Choice **c** is incorrect. Cell differentiation occurs when a single, non-specialized cell is converted to a specialized cell type, like a blood cell or skin cell. No daughter cells are produced during the differentiation process.

18. Choice b is correct. The average speed can be determined by adding the individual vehicle speeds and dividing by the total number of vehicles. This is calculated as $\frac{61 + 48 + 61 + 51 + 59}{5} = 56$ mph.

Choice **a** is incorrect. This is the speed limit for the highway, not the average speed of the five vehicles listed.

Choice **c** is incorrect. This is the median speed of the five vehicles, not the average (mean) speed.

Choice **d** is incorrect. This is the mode for the speed of the five vehicles, not the average (mean) speed.

19. Choice d is correct. Each new cell created by meiosis must contain one chromosome from each of the seven chromosome pairs. As illustrated in the diagram, these single chromosomes can be combined in multiple ways. To determine the total number of unique chromosome combinations, the number of chromosomes in each set (pair) must be multiplied. Seven sets of two chromosomes each means that seven 2's must be multiplied $(2 \times 2 \times 2 \times 2 \times 2 \times 2 \times 2 = 128)$ to determine the total number of unique chromosome combinations possible.

Choice **a** is incorrect. There are seven total chromosomes in a cell produced by meiosis, but the specific chromosome present from each chromosome pair can vary.

Choice **b** is incorrect. Two chromosomes in each of seven pairs provides a total of 14 chromosomes, but the specific chromosome present from each pair can vary.

Choice **c** is incorrect. Multiplying 7×7 does not provide the total number of chromosome combinations possible. To determine this, the number of chromosomes in each pair must be multiplied by the number of chromosomes in each other pair.

20. Choice c is correct. The products of respiration are six molecules of carbon dioxide, six molecules of water, and energy. On the right side of the model, six rectangles are present but only one triangle. To accurately represent a balanced equation, all molecules must be represented in the model.

Choice **a** is incorrect. The circles represent the six molecules of the reactant oxygen. Connecting the circles would not improve the model's accuracy because separate molecules are not bound to each other.

Choice **b** is incorrect. Energy is a product of the respiration reaction and is therefore appropriately placed on the right side of the equation. Moving the energy symbol to the left side of the equation would indicate that energy is a reactant.

Choice **d** is incorrect. Reducing the size of the rectangles is not the most needed change, since the other molecules are not represented to scale.

21. Choice a is correct. The purpose of respiration is to convert energy into a form that is usable by cells. Respiration produces ATP, a high-energy molecule, which the cell can use to carry out cellular functions.

Choice **b** is incorrect. Oxygen is a reactant—not a product—of aerobic respiration and does not provide energy for the cell.

Choice **c** is incorrect. Respiration uses the glucose in food to produce ATP. Respiration does not produce glucose.

Choice **d** is incorrect. Though respiration does produce carbon dioxide, this molecule does not provide energy for the cell.

22. The highest number of points you can earn on this short-response essay is 3.

A **3-point essay** contains
- a clear and well-developed explanation of the benefits of the aerobic respiration pathway in the human body.
- a clear and well-developed explanation of the benefits of the anaerobic respiration pathway in the human body.
- complete support from the passage.

Sample 3-point response
The human body may use two different pathways to carry out respiration. The presence of two different pathways is valuable because it allows a cell to choose the pathway that best meets its current energy needs. Aerobic respiration produces the greatest amount of ATP per glucose molecule. Under normal conditions with adequate oxygen, this pathway provides the greatest possible amount of energy to the cell. Anaerobic respiration produces much less ATP per glucose molecule but does not require oxygen. Under strenuous conditions when the cell demands energy faster than the oxygen supply can be replenished, this pathway provides enough energy to maintain cell functions. The ability to switch between aerobic and anaerobic pathways allows the human body to function properly under varying conditions.

A **2-point essay** contains
- an adequate or partially articulated explanation of the benefits of the aerobic respiration pathway in the human body.
- an adequate or partially articulated explanation of the benefits of the anaerobic respiration pathway in the human body.
- partial support from the passage.

Sample 2-point response
Aerobic respiration produces the most ATP but requires oxygen. Anaerobic respiration produces much less ATP but does not require oxygen. Having two pathways is important because sometimes oxygen is available, and sometimes it is not.

A **1-point essay** contains
- a minimal or implied explanation of the benefits of the aerobic respiration pathway in the human body.
- a minimal or implied explanation of the benefits of the anaerobic respiration pathway in the human body.
- minimal or implied support from the passage.

Sample 1-point response
Cells use aerobic respiration most of the time. Muscle cells use anaerobic respiration when a person is exercising. Both types of respiration are important.

A **0-point essay** contains
- no explanation of the benefits of the aerobic respiration pathway in the human body.
- no explanation of the benefits of the anaerobic respiration pathway in the human body.
- no support from the passage.

23. Choice c is correct. As shown in the model, a solid has a fixed volume and shape. A liquid has a fixed volume but assumes the shape of the container. A gas assumes the volume and shape of the container. A liquid has one property in common with solids, and one property in common with gases.
Choice **a** is incorrect. In this summary, the properties of a liquid are reversed. Liquids have a fixed volume and assume the shape of the container.
Choice **b** is incorrect. Liquids have a fixed volume as solids do but not a fixed shape.
Choice **d** is incorrect. Liquids assume the shape of the container as gases do but not the volume.

24. Choice a is correct. The density of a substance describes how tightly packed the substance's molecules are. As shown in the model, a substance's molecules are most spread out when in the gas state. This means that a substance's density is lowest when in the gas state. The substance's density increases when going from gas to liquid state because the molecules become more tightly packed.

Choice **b** is incorrect. A substance's molecules become more spread out when changing from solid to gas state. This causes the substance's density to decrease.

Choice **c** is incorrect. A substance's molecules become more spread out when changing from liquid to gas state. This causes the substance's density to decrease.

Choice **d** is incorrect. A substance's molecules may become slightly more spread out, or less dense, when changing from solid to liquid state. However, the density of a substance does not change much during this state change.

25. Choice d is correct. Based on the data in the table, this statement can be identified as a fact. The energy content of ethanol is 27.3 kJ/g, about 16 kJ/g less than the energy content of petroleum (43.6 kJ/g).

Choice **a** is incorrect. This statement is speculation based on data from the table. According to the table, hydrogen has the greatest energy content and releases no carbon dioxide. Although this data supports the speculation that cars may be fueled by hydrogen cells in the future, this statement is no guarantee.

Choice **b** is incorrect. This statement is a judgment based on data from the table. According to the table, petroleum has a higher energy content than ethanol. Although this data can be used to support the judgment that petroleum is the better fuel source, this statement is an opinion rather than a fact.

Choice **c** is incorrect. This statement is speculation based on data from the table. Although the data in the table suggests that natural gas is a relatively efficient and clean fuel source, the statement is speculation because no information is provided about the cost of natural gas.

26. **Choice c is correct.** The passage identifies natural gas, petroleum, and coal as fossil fuels, because each is derived from the fossil remains of organisms. The energy content of each fossil fuel can be approximated to 50 kJ/g, 45 kJ/g, and 40 kJ/g, respectively. This provides an estimated average energy content of 45 kJ/g. Choice **a** is incorrect. This would be an appropriate estimate for the energy content of coal, not for the energy content of all three fossil fuels.
Choice **b** is incorrect. This would be an appropriate estimate for the energy content of petroleum and coal, but natural gas is also a fossil fuel.
Choice **d** is incorrect. This would be an appropriate estimate for the energy content of natural gas, not for the energy content of all three fossil fuels.

27. **Choice a is correct.** Burning a candle is an exothermic process because thermal energy, or heat, is released as a result of the process. Choice **b** is incorrect. Melting a snow bank is an endothermic process because the input of heat is required to melt the snow. This means that thermal energy is absorbed during the process, not released.
Choice **c** is incorrect. Baking a loaf of bread is an endothermic process because the input of heat is required to convert the ingredients to bread. This means that thermal energy is absorbed during the process, not released.
Choice **d** is incorrect. Photosynthesis is an endothermic process because the input of energy (sunlight) is required for plants to make sugar. This means that energy is absorbed during the process, not released.

28. **Choice a is correct.** The car has a constant positive acceleration when the car's velocity is increasing at a steady, or constant, rate. Between 0 and 20 seconds, the graph moves upward in a straight diagonal line, indicating that the velocity is increasing at a constant rate. Choice **b** is incorrect. Between 20 and 40 seconds, the car is maintaining a constant velocity of 20 m/s. Since the velocity is constant within this time period, the car is not accelerating (has an acceleration of 0 m/s^2).
Choice **c** is incorrect. Between 40 and 50 seconds, the car's velocity is decreasing at a constant rate. This indicates a constant negative acceleration.
Choice **d** is incorrect. Between 50 and 90 seconds, the car's velocity is increasing but not at a constant rate. The graph moves upward in a curved line within this time period, indicating that the velocity is increasing at a variable rate.

29. **Choice b is correct.** The mechanical advantage of a pulley system does not change with the load. Mechanical advantage is calculated as load divided by input force. In the data table, dividing each load by its corresponding input force produces a mechanical advantage of three. Choice **a** is incorrect. As the load size increases, the input force required to lift the load increases at a constant rate. The mechanical advantage of the pulley system does not change.
Choice **c** is incorrect. A pulley system multiplies the input force, not the mechanical advantage, applied to a load.
Choice **d** is incorrect. No decrease in mechanical advantage occurs with an increase in load. The mechanical advantage of a pulley system is constant regardless of the size of the load.

30. Choice d is correct. According to the table, an input force of 50 N can lift a 150 N load. If a 1 N load has a mass of 10 grams, the mass of a load can be determined by multiplying the force of the load by 10. A 150 N load therefore has a mass of 1,500 grams.

Choice **a** is incorrect. This value is the result of dividing the force of the load (150 N) by 10. The mass of the load is determined by multiplying, not dividing, the force of the load by 10.

Choice **b** is incorrect. This is the value of the input force, not the mass of the load.

Choice **c** is incorrect. This is the value of the force of the load in newtons, not the mass of the load in grams.

31. Choice b is correct. Kale is a leafy crop species. According to the diagram, wild mustard plants were selected for leaves to produce kale. This means that wild mustard plants that had large leaves were specifically bred together to increase leaf size. This selective breeding over multiple generations led to a new species (kale) characterized by large leaves.

Choice **a** is incorrect. Plants with desired characteristics (large leaves for kale) must be bred together to produce offspring plants with those characteristics. Removing stems and flowers from existing mustard plants will not increase leaf size in subsequent generations.

Choice **c** is incorrect. Breeding small-leafed plants and large-leafed plants allows the possibility that offspring will have either small or large leaves. To ensure offspring have the best chances of large leaves, large-leafed plants should be bred together.

Choice **d** is incorrect. Preventing plants with large leaves from growing works to remove the large-leaf trait from subsequent generations rather than increase its appearance.

32. Choice d is correct. In the graph, temperature increases to the right and altitude increases upward. Any portion of the graph that has a negative slope, or slopes to the left, indicates a decrease in temperature. The graph has a negative slope in the troposphere and mesosphere layers.

Choice **a** is incorrect. The graph has a negative slope within the mesosphere but a slight positive slope in the exosphere. This means that temperature decreases as altitude increases in the mesosphere but increases with altitude in the exosphere.

Choice **b** is incorrect. The graph has a negative slope within the troposphere but a positive slope in the thermosphere. Even though the slope is not constant within the thermosphere, the slope remains positive within this layer. This means that temperature decreases in the troposphere but increases in the thermosphere.

Choice **c** is incorrect. The graph has a positive slope within both the stratosphere and the thermosphere. This means that temperature increases with altitude in both layers.

33. Choice c is correct. The Alaska current is a warm current. The passage states that warm currents typically travel along the eastern coast of continents, but the Alaska current travels along the western coast of North America.

Choice **a** is incorrect. Although the Alaska current does travel along the western coast of the continent, the map key indicates that it is a warm current.

Choice **b** is incorrect. The Alaska current does not follow the typical pattern for a warm current but is identified as a surface current on the map.

Choice **d** is incorrect. The map key identifies the Alaska current as a warm current. Warm currents transport warm water originating near the equator toward the poles.

34. Choice d is correct. The blood type O can be produced only by the allele combination ii. A child receives one allele from each parent. Since the mother has an i but the father does not, the allele combination ii is not possible for their children.

Choice **a** is incorrect. Based on the table, the mother's blood type is A. The child can receive I^A or i from the mother and I^A from the father, resulting in type A blood caused by the possible allele combinations I^AI^A or I^Ai. However, the child could receive I^B from the father, which would result in a blood type different from the mother's.

Choice **b** is incorrect. Based on the table, the father has blood type AB. The child can receive I^A from the mother and I^B from the father, resulting in the possible allele combination I^AI^B. This allele combination will produce the same blood type as the father's.

Choice **c** is incorrect. Based on the table, the mother's blood type is A, and the father's is AB. The child can receive I^A or i from the mother and I^A from the father, resulting in type A blood caused by the possible allele combinations I^AI^A or I^Ai. The child can receive I^A from the mother and I^B from the father, resulting in the blood type AB caused by the possible allele combination I^AI^B. This means it is possible for the child to have the same blood type as one of the parents'.

35. Choice c is correct. According to the diagram, when a person's blood glucose level rises, the pancreas secretes insulin. The insulin signals body cells to absorb glucose from the blood and signals the liver to convert excess glucose into the storage molecule glycogen. These processes remove excess glucose from the blood, returning the blood glucose level to homeostasis. Insulin injected into a diabetic person initiates the same pathway as insulin produced in the pancreas of a healthy person.

Choice **a** is incorrect. Insulin signals the liver to convert and store excess glucose to glycogen, not to destroy the glucose.

Choice **b** is incorrect. Insulin and glucagon do not signal each other but perform opposite functions. Insulin works to decrease blood glucose levels, while glucagon works to increase these levels.

Choice **d** is incorrect. Glucagon signals the breakdown of glycogen into glucose when blood glucose levels are low. Insulin signals the conversion of glucose to glycogen when blood glucose levels are high.

3 ▶ SCIENCE PRACTICES

Science practices can be best described as the skills necessary for understanding scientific concepts using critical thinking and reasoning, as well as reading comprehension and quantitative analysis, or mathematical comprehension. In short, you can think of them as comprehension, analysis, and solving skills.

While it's relatively easy to simply describe these skills, it is also still necessary for you to review them in preparation for the test in the same way that runners train their muscles in preparation for a marathon. So let's start doing some laps or reviewing some of these specific skills! All answers and explanations for the practice questions throughout are at the end of the chapter.

Comprehending Scientific Presentations

Scientific data and presentations are encountered every day in life, as well as on the GED® Science test. You might find scientific concepts and data in a newspaper or magazine article, a TV program, or an advertisement. Regardless, there are several important things that you must be able to do so that you can understand what is being presented:

- *Understand the textual information being presented.* What is the presenter trying to say by his or her words or language? Do you know the meaning of the scientific terms (jargon) being used?
- *Understand any symbolic or mathematical representations.* Scientists often use symbols or abbreviations to represent scientific quantities (e.g., forces, chemical formulas, biological quantities). In many presentations, they use mathematical equations that represent the relationships between scientific phenomena.
- *Understand visual information.* Do you remember the saying that "a picture is worth a thousand words"? Scientists often present information visually in the form of graphs, tables, and diagrams. Visual representations shorten the amount of text or spoken words necessary to convey information and can clearly show relationships between scientific phenomena.

These three skills encompass comprehending a scientific presentation as a whole and are necessary for understanding the questions you may be asked in the GED® Science test.

Let's look at these in detail.

Understand the Textual Information Being Presented

In life and on the GED® Science test, scientific information is often presented in written form. On the test, you will be asked to read short passages full of scientific information. Within these passages, there will be a wealth of important ideas that you must be able to recognize. There may be obstacles to recognizing the ideas (such as unfamiliar vocabulary terms); however, there will also often be clues to help you navigate around these obstacles.

As an example, read the following passage and consider how you would analyze the information in it.

ANATOMY OF MUSCLES

Muscles are made of bundles of cells wrapped in connective tissue called *fascicles*. Each bundle contains many cylindrical muscle cells or muscle fibers. Like other cells, muscle fibers have mitochondria that provide energy, a plasma membrane that separates the inside and outside of the cell, and endoplasmic reticulum, where proteins are made. However, muscle cells are different from other cells in several ways. First, muscle cells have more than one nucleus. Second, the muscle cell's plasma membrane surrounds bundles of cylindrical myofibrils that contain protein filaments and regularly folds into the deep parts of the fiber to form a transverse tubule or T-tubule. Third, the muscle cell's endoplasmic reticulum is called *sarcoplasmic reticulum*; it is regularly structured, envelops the myofibrils, and ends near the T-tubule in sacs called *terminal cisternae*.

Here are some tips to help you with analyzing this information:

1. **Look at the title.**
   The title tells us that the passage is going to be about the *structure or anatomy of muscles*.
2. **Look at patterns in the information, such as patterns in the subjects.**
   The subjects of the sentences all have *muscle* in common. The pattern of *muscle* as the subject of each sentence also provides a clue as to the subject of the entire passage. So, what do you think is the main purpose of this passage?
   The main purpose of this passage is to *describe the structure of muscles*.

3. **Look for details in the sentences and note them on scratch paper.**

   One detail is that the second sentence mentions that bundles contain many *cylindrical* cells.

4. **Look for similarities and differences in the information.**

   The fifth sentence of the passage states, *First, muscle cells have more than one nucleus.* This sentence shows one of the differences between muscle cells and other cells.

5. **Use context clues (*called, or*) to define unfamiliar terms.**

   . . . *bundles of cells wrapped in connective tissue called fascicles.* The word *called* connects the term with its definition.

   . . . *many cylindrical muscle cells or muscle fibers.* The word *or* connects the term *fibers* with another more familiar term, *cells.*

6. **Note information set off by commas and by *that* clauses.**

   For example, *a plasma membrane that separates the inside and outside of the cell* reveals that the function of the plasma membrane is to separate the inside from the outside of the cell.

Note that each sentence provides more details about the subject. You may need to write details down on scratch paper, especially for long reading passages. By looking at details in each sentence, you can gather important information. GED® test questions often focus on details to assess your comprehension of the passage.

Practice

1. According to the passage, what is the shape of a muscle cell?
   a. sphere
   b. cylinder
   c. disc
   d. cube

Notice that the passage also describes both how muscle cells are like other cells and how they are different from other cells. There are clues in the sentences:

- *Like other cells, muscle fibers have mitochondria . . . , plasma membrane . . . , and endoplasmic reticulum.*
- *However, muscle cells are different from other cells in several ways.* (The next sentences detail the ways that muscle cells are different.)

Looking at how the information is similar and how it is different can help you interpret the main ideas of the information presented. The GED® Science test often assesses whether you can distinguish differences stated in scientific presentations.

Practice

2. Which is a difference between a muscle cell and another type of cell?
   a. Only muscle cells have mitochondria.
   b. The plasma membrane separates the inside from the outside of the cell.
   c. Muscle cells have more than one nucleus.
   d. Muscle cells do not have endoplasmic reticulum.

Understand Symbols, Terms, and Phrases in Scientific Presentations

The GED® Science test also uses symbols (scientific and mathematical), chemical formulas, and equations (mathematical, chemical) to present information. Since you won't be supplied with a science formula sheet on test day, any mathematical equations will have to be defined in context. Let's look at an example.

LIGHT WAVES AND THEIR PROPERTIES

In the late seventeenth century, Isaac Newton explained light as consisting of particles. But in the early twentieth century, physicists began explaining light not as a particle but rather as a wave. A wave is a periodic oscillation. The shape of a wave starts from a zero level and increases to the highest point or crest. Then it decreases past zero to its lowest level or trough. From the trough, it rises again to zero and another crest. This wave pattern repeats itself over time.

The wave has three properties that describe it: amplitude, wavelength, and frequency.

Amplitude (A) is the distance from the zero point to the crest of the wave and has the International System of Units (SI) unit of meters (m). Wavelength (λ) is the distance from the peak of one wave to the peak of the next wave or the trough of one wave to the trough of the next wave; λ has the SI unit of meters (m). The frequency (v) is the number of wave cycles per unit time; the SI unit of frequency is the hertz (Hz). The speed of a wave is the product of the wavelength and the frequency. In the case of a light wave, the speed of light (c) is a constant (3×10^8 m/s) and is described by this formula: $c = \lambda v$. The wavelengths of light vary from extremely short gamma rays ($\lambda < 10^{-12}$ m) to very long radio waves ($\lambda > 1$ m).

This passage is loaded with many concepts, terms, and symbols, and an equation:

- **New terms:** *wave, periodic, oscillation, crest, trough, amplitude, wavelength, frequency*
- **Symbols:** A, λ, v, c
- **Units:** m, Hz, m/s
- **Equation:** $c = \lambda v$

Most of the terms are clearly defined in sentences of the passage. For example, we are told the specific meanings of *wave, amplitude, wavelength,* and *frequency*. The terms *crest* and *trough* we can get by the word *or*, which relates the term to its meaning—for example, *to the highest point or crest* and *to its lowest level or trough*. The terms *periodic* and *oscillation* you will either know or have to think about or deduce from the reading and the sentence that states, *This wave pattern repeats itself over time.*

Symbols and units are often shown in parentheses after their first mention.

Notice that the formula is stated in words (*The speed of a wave is the product of the wavelength and the frequency*) and in mathematical symbols ($c = \lambda v$).

Let's look at another example.

COMBINATION REACTION

Oxygen is a very corrosive substance and will combine with many other substances or oxidize other substances. A common example is that of a piece of iron left out in the air. Over time, the iron rusts. The rust is a chemical change and can be described by a chemical reaction. Four atoms of solid iron (Fe) combine with three molecules of gaseous oxygen (O_2) from the air to form two molecules of solid iron oxide (Fe_2O_3). The chemical reaction can be written by this chemical equation:

$$4Fe(s) + 3O_2(g) \rightarrow 2Fe_2O_3(s)$$

This class of chemical reaction is called a *combination reaction.*

The terms *oxidize* and *combination reaction* may be unfamiliar. You can get the meaning of *oxidize* from the first sentence, *Oxygen is a very corrosive substance and will combine with many other substances or oxidize other substances*. *Oxidize* thus means to combine with oxygen, and the two words sound similar.

Similarly, a *combination reaction* is one where molecules combine together. You can get this from the word *combine* in the fifth sentence, where the chemical reaction is described.

Practice

3. Using the information presented in the passage, write each substance's symbol below its name in the table.

- Fe_2O_3
- Fe
- O_2

IRON	OXYGEN	IRON OXIDE

Understand and Explain Visual Scientific Presentations

Humans are visual animals, and many of us learn difficult concepts more easily by visual means. Visual scientific presentations often take the form of charts and graphs. On the GED® Science test, you may be required to understand a graphic like a diagram or table and put its meaning into words. You need to be able to restate or translate information into different formats. When you see this type of presentation, first determine the purpose. What is it trying to illustrate or convey?

Graphs

Simply put, a **graph** is a diagram that shows a relationship between two or more things. For example:

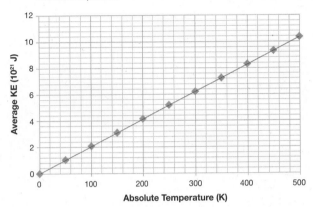

The change in the average kinetic energy of gas molecules versus absolute temperature

Using the title and headings, you should be able to identify that this graph represents the relationship between the *average kinetic energy (KE) of gas molecules* and *absolute temperature*. What do you think the numbers on the graph represent?

In this graph, the numbers on the horizontal (left-to-right) axis, or **x-axis**, represent the temperature in degrees Kelvin (K), and the numbers on the vertical (down-to-up) axis, or **y-axis**, represent the average kinetic energy (KE) of gas molecules.

It's important to note the axis labels. Looking at the vertical or *y*-axis, for example, you see that the numbers are labeled 2, 4, 6, 8, 10, and 12. But if you look at the axis label, each number represents 10^{21} joules (J), not whole numbers. This distinction could be very important if you were asked to answer questions based on the graph. The points are plotted on the graph and connected by a line to show the linear, or direct, relationship between these two factors.

The graph in this example correlates just two things. However, a graph can correlate more than two things at a time. When this happens, the additional data sets are usually graphed in another color or pattern to avoid confusion. If there is more than one data set or more than one variable, a **legend** will help you interpret the graph. It will list the symbols, colors, or patterns used to label a particular data set.

For example, in the following graph the legend lists atmospheric CO_2, seawater pCO_2, and seawater pH.

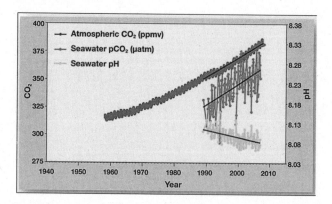

A look at the vertical axes and the legend tells you that this graph shows the correlation between the changes in carbon dioxide (CO_2) levels in the atmosphere and the ocean over time, as well as the pH of seawater over time.

There are a number of graph types you might come across on the exam, but the four graph types most commonly encountered in science are bar graphs, line graphs, scatterplots, and pie graphs.

Bar Graphs

Bar graphs provide a simple way to compare and contrast numerical data. You can tell if a graph is a bar graph right away because bar graphs have rectangular bars as their visual means of representing data. Bars in a bar graph usually start at the *x*-axis, which is labeled with the **independent variable**. The independent variable in an experiment is the variable that the scientist changes in the experiment. On the *y*-axis is the **dependent variable**, the variable that the scientist is measuring. The height of the bar along the *y*-axis gives the value of the dependent variable.

For example, if a scientist wants to compare the plant heights of a plant that receives water and a plant that does not receive water, the presence of water is

the independent variable, and the plant height is the dependent variable. A bar graph for the results of this experiment is shown below:

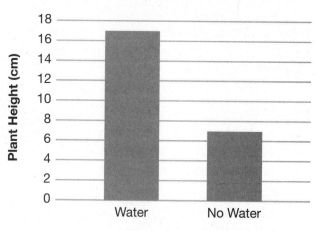

Based on this bar graph, the plant that received water grew to a height of 17 cm, while the plant that received no water grew to a height of 7 cm. From this bar graph, we can conclude that watering plants helps them to grow taller.

Line Graphs

Line graphs are similar to bar graphs in that, like most graphs, they have their independent variable on the *x*-axis and their dependent variable on the *y*-axis. The key difference between a bar graph and a line graph is in the way the data is visualized. Rather than using a bar, a line graph uses a point to represent a data point. Then, the data points for each independent variable value are connected with a line. Line graphs are especially useful for showing changes over time, so the *x*-axis will often be some form of time.

For example, think back to the scientist who wants to compare the heights of the plants that were and were not watered. If the scientist measures the plants' heights every day, a line graph would be a great choice for displaying these data:

Change in Heights of Watered and Unwatered Plants Over the Course of One Week

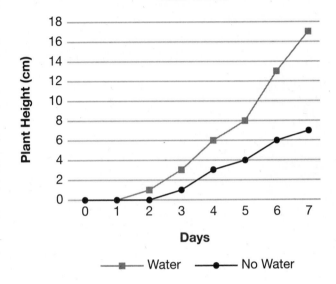

For example, a scientist has ten plants and wants to measure all of their heights and longest root lengths to see if there is any correlation between the two variables. The following scatterplot shows the data she collected:

Correlation between Plant Height and Longest Root Length

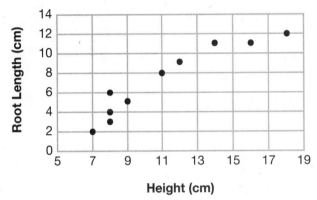

The independent variable is a unit of time, the number of days. The dependent variable is the plant height, in centimeters. The points represent the actual collected data, and the lines that connect the points predict the values in between the collected data points. For example, at 3 days, the watered plant was approximately 3 cm tall, and at 4 days, the watered plant was approximately 6 cm tall. From the line connecting these two points, we might predict that the plant height was approximately 4.5 cm after 3.5 days. Most importantly, however, the lines make the trend in data clear, as they help to show whether the numbers increase, decrease, or stay the same.

Scatterplots

Scatterplots look just like line graphs, except they do not have lines that connect the points. The independent variable is usually still on the *x*-axis and the dependent variable is usually still on the *y*-axis. Scatterplots are useful when there are a lot of data points that may be difficult to organize, or if a particular independent variable has multiple values you want to display on the graph.

According to this scatterplot, three plants had the same height, 8 cm, but different root lengths. The scatterplot accounts for all three with separate points. The three root lengths are 3, 4, and 6 cm. If you were analyzing this graph, you might say that in general, taller plants have longer roots.

Pie Graphs

When you want to display parts of a whole in the form of percentages, you might use a **pie graph**. Pie graphs are circular in shape, and each "slice" of the pie represents a different category, sized according to the percentage of the total represented by the associated category. There are no axes in a pie graph, and sometimes there isn't even a boxed legend. Pie graphs are usually labeled directly to indicate the percentage represented by each slice. Pie graphs are therefore especially useful for a visual comparison of different percentages in a data set.

For example, a scientist may use a pie graph to display the different kinds of flowering plants in her garden plot:

Types of Flowering Plants in the Garden

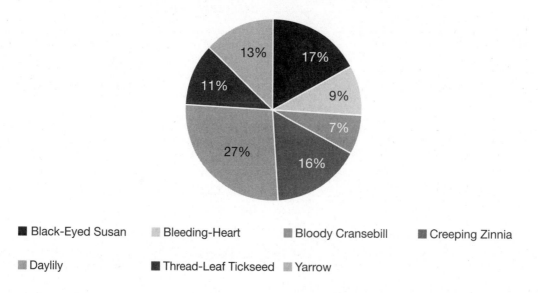

■ Black-Eyed Susan   ■ Bleeding-Heart   ■ Bloody Cransebill   ■ Creeping Zinnia

■ Daylily   ■ Thread-Leaf Tickseed ■ Yarrow

Based on the pie graph, the slice for the daylily is clearly the largest, and this correctly reflects that the daylily was the type of flowering plant that was the most abundant in this garden plot. On the other hand, the slice for the bloody cranesbill is the smallest, indicating that this was the least abundant flowering plant in this garden plot.

Tables and Charts

Tables have horizontal rows and vertical columns. The data entries in a single row of a table or chart usually have something in common. The same is true for the data entries in a single column. **Charts** are often used to show trends. Look for changes in numerical values to spot those trends.

The following chart detailing the pH scale uses images and numbers to demonstrate what the different pH numbers actually mean. The chart has an arrow that describes a continuum of conditions from acidic through neutral to basic, and there is a scale that shows this continuum. There are three columns of numbers. One shows the pH of a substance. The other two show the concentrations of hydrogen ions (H^+), one with numbers in scientific notation and the other in actual decimal numbers. Note that the symbol for hydrogen ions (H^+) is used but not defined. Some abbreviations, like chemical symbols, are often assumed.

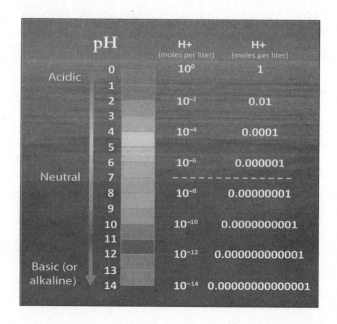

pH		H+ (moles per liter)	H+ (moles per liter)
Acidic	0	10^0	1
	1		
	2	10^{-2}	0.01
	3		
	4	10^{-4}	0.0001
	5		
	6	10^{-6}	0.000001
Neutral	7	- - - - - - - - - -	- - - - - - - - - -
	8	10^{-8}	0.00000001
	9		
	10	10^{-10}	0.0000000001
	11		
	12	10^{-12}	0.000000000001
Basic (or alkaline)	13		
	14	10^{-14}	0.00000000000001

Practice

4. Look at the pH scale. What is its range?

_____

5. Notice that the concentrations of hydrogen ions correspond to values of pH. If a chemist measures a solution with a pH value of 9, what is the hydrogen ion concentration?
   a. 10^{-9} moles per liter
   b. 10^9 moles per liter
   c. $\frac{1}{9}$ mole per liter
   d. 9.0 moles per liter

6. From the arrow on the left, notice that acidic substances have pH values less than 7, while basic substances have pH values greater than 7. If a chemist measures that a solution has a pH value of 5.5, this indicates the solution is
   a. acidic.
   b. alkaline.
   c. neutral.

Diagrams

Diagrams are often used to show processes on the GED® Science test. In the following diagram of the water cycle, you can see that there are three main places for water to be exchanged: among the oceans and rivers, in the atmosphere, and on the ground. Pay attention to any labeled features and arrows. Generally, arrows connect processes. In this case, arrows show the direction of water flow, and the terms name the processes.

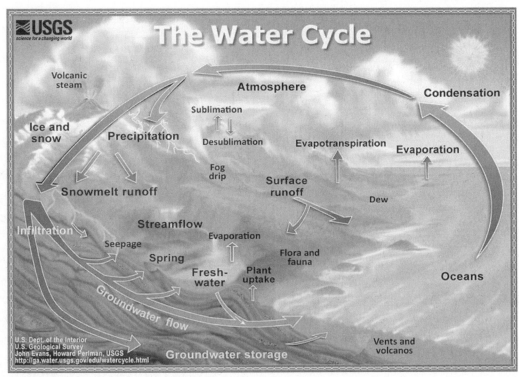

Source: http://water.usgs.gov/edu/watercycle.html.

Practice

7. In this diagram, what is the name of the process that moves water directly from bodies of water into the atmosphere? _____

8. Which way does water move during infiltration?
  a. from air into the ground
  b. from ground up to the surface
  c. from surface down into the ground
  d. from surface into the air

The key to understanding any type of scientific presentation is reading and looking carefully and critically. This type of careful evaluation will allow you to interpret which pieces of information go together, to determine relationships, and to clarify explanations.

Designing Investigations

Good scientific investigations begin with a question that often asks *What if?*, *How?*, or *What effect will something have?* The question should be one that can be investigated through experimentation and will then yield data. The experiment should also be repeatable. This allows other people to replicate the experiment to verify that the results stay the same.

On the GED® Science test, you will be provided descriptions of an experiment in a reading passage and the results in a table or in graph form. From the description, you will be asked to evaluate the design of the experiment. You will also be asked about the results and conclusions from the experiment based on the results. So, it is important that you know how scientific investigations work.

Scientific investigations are hypothesis driven. A **hypothesis** is a predictive answer to a question. It is an explanation on trial, one that can be tested. Deductive reasoning is used to test a hypothesis. The test is

accomplished by designing and conducting an experiment. The experiment yields results (data). If the experiment was designed and conducted correctly and the data fit what was predicted by the hypothesis, then the experimenter must conclude that the hypothesis was correct. Otherwise, the experimenter must reject the current hypothesis and change it or form a new one. This scientific method is the basis of science. No hypothesis is accepted just because the scientist or others believe it is true; it must be testable and withstand experimental trial by many experiments conducted by different scientists before it is accepted.

To evaluate these scientific investigations, ask these questions:

- What was the hypothesis?
- What was the independent variable?
- What was/were the dependent variable(s)?
- What were the other variables, and were they controlled?
- Were the measurement methods appropriate to what was being measured?
- Was the number of samples adequate?
- Overall, was the experimental design appropriate to test the hypothesis?

Let's look at the scientific method as it applies to experiments and experimental design topics on the GED® Science test.

Identify Possible Sources of Error and Change an Investigation to Remove the Error

In science, the word *error* doesn't always mean *mistake*; it might mean that there is uncertainty in the design. A source of error is any factor that could affect the outcome of the investigation. There are numerous possibilities for error in any experiment, so you will want to focus on the factors that matter the most.

When evaluating the design of an experiment for errors, ask yourself these questions:

- *Is the hypothesis of the experiment testable?* For example, a teenage student wants to assess a claim that a new acne product improves the condition of the skin. If the student merely takes the word of celebrity endorsers, does that mean the product works well? If the student conducts an experiment to measure the incidence of acne upon treatment with the product, then that is a way to test the hypothesis.

- *Does what the experimenter measured reflect what is predicted by the hypothesis?* For example, if the hypothesis predicts that a treatment for acne reduces the incidence of blemishes, then does the investigator measure the number of blemishes over an area of the skin with time or the rate at which blemishes disappear?

- *Does the experiment have a control group?* A control is an experimental treatment where all the variables that affect the experimental group are the same except one—the one that is testing the hypothesis. For example, in an experiment to test acne medication, there might be a group of people who do not receive the acne medication but who are studied for the same amount of time, eat the same type of foods, are the same age and sex, and so on. The results from the experimental group are compared to those of the control group to test the hypothesis.

- *Is the experimental method specified in enough detail so that another investigator could repeat the experiment?* Remember that experiments must be able to be repeated by others and must produce the same results so that the hypothesis can be evaluated. In the example of acne medication, does the experimental procedure specify how much medication should be applied to the skin and how often? Does the procedure mention anything about how often the subjects should wash their faces?

- *Are there enough subjects or samples in each group to represent a more general population?* For example, if the acne medication study looks at only four people (one teenage male and three teenage girls), are these groups sufficient to represent the larger population of teenagers?

- *Is the data gathered accurately and precisely?* **Accuracy** is defined as the closeness of a measured value to the actual value. You can only truly determine if a measurement is accurate if you have a known number to which the measured value can be compared. **Precision** is the closeness of data points to one another for multiple trials. High precision means that the values are close to one another, while low precision means that the values are far from one another.

  In the acne study example, if two investigators separately count the number of blemishes on each subject's face, how similar are the numbers they come up with?

When identifying errors on the GED® test, or in any experimental procedure, you should assume that the scientist performing the experiment is competent; in other words, avoid indicating errors that might have been caused by the scientist doing something incorrectly.

For example, if a scientist is doing an experiment in which she needs to transfer a small amount of liquid from a test tube into a sample in a beaker using a graduated cylinder, do not state that a possible source of error is that the scientist could spill the contents of the test tube or the beaker. Instead, look for procedural flaws that are inherently part of the protocol. In this example, a procedural flaw could be that the scientist should use a pipette rather than a graduated cylinder to transfer liquid because a graduated cylinder is not ideal for accurate small liquid transfers.

Practice

Read the following experimental design carefully. Critically review it to identify possible sources of error. Then, explain how that source of error would have affected the results. Think about specific things that can change the end result of the experiment.

MEAT TENDERIZER EXPERIMENT

A group of students wants to know what effect meat tenderizer will have on starches, fats, and proteins.

The group hypothesizes that meat tenderizer will break down proteins but not starches or fats.

They formulate the following experimental design:

1. Add water to six jars.
2. Add 9 grams of meat tenderizer to three of the jars of water, and stir until dissolved.
3. Place one sample of starch, of fat, and of protein in each of the three jars that contain meat tenderizer.
4. Place one sample of starch, of fat, and of protein in the three remaining jars.
5. Put lids on all six jars.
6. Observe changes after 24 hours.

9. What possible sources of errors do you see in this design? Is the hypothesis stated adequately to make a predictable result? Write your response on the lines below.

_____

_____

_____

10. Look at the first step of the experimental design. Is there something not specified?

_____

_____

_____

11. What about step 2? Is there something not specified?

_____

_____

_____

12. What is unclear about steps 3 and 4?

_____

_____

_____

13. What is unclear about step 6?

_____

_____

_____

Identify and Refine Hypotheses for Investigation

Asking questions and defining problems are essential to the investigative process. Once those questions have been asked, the next step is trying to find and investigate the answer.

A **hypothesis** is a prediction, an attempted answer to the question being investigated. A hypothesis attempts to predict the outcome of the experiment and suggests one or more possible reasons for the results. A good hypothesis should be based on observations and prior knowledge.

Consider this example:

SLEEPINESS EXPERIMENT

Ruby and Mary are identical twins. They are often sleepy at noontime while attending their science class. They want to know why they frequently fall asleep at this time of day. Possible explanations might include:

- Eating a big lunch right before science class every day makes the twins sleepy.
- The classroom is too warm.
- The twins are less engaged in this class because they sit at the back of the room, instead of at the front as in the rest of their classes.
- The science teacher has a monotonous voice that Mary and Ruby find boring.
- Ruby and Mary become tired at noontime every day.

Each of these possible explanations for the twins falling asleep in class is a potential hypothesis. A hypothesis should be stated in a way that allows you to make a prediction that can be investigated by experiments or more observation. Proposing more than one hypothesis can be a good scientific practice.

Last, hypotheses can be eliminated—but not confirmed—with 100% certainty.

Let's rephrase two of the possible explanations into questions to show how they might be tested.

Possible Explanation: *Eating a big lunch right before science class every day makes the twins sleepy.*

Question 1:	Does eating a big lunch before science class make them sleepy?
Hypothesis 1:	If the twins become sleepy because they eat a big lunch before the noon class, then postponing lunch should make them less sleepy.
Suggested Experiment:	Ruby postpones lunch until science is over at 1 P.M., whereas Mary still eats lunch at 11 A.M.
Predicted Result:	Ruby should be less tired and Mary should still be sleepy in science class.

Possible Explanation: *The twins are less engaged in this class because they sit at the back of the room, instead of at the front as in the rest of their classes.*

Question 2:	Are Mary and Ruby less engaged in this class because they sit at the back of the room, instead of at the front as in the rest of their classes?
Hypothesis 2:	If the twins become sleepy in the noon class because they sit in the back of the room, then moving to the front of the room should make them less sleepy.
Suggested Experiment:	Ruby moves to the front of the room, while Mary remains in the back.
Predicted Result:	Ruby should be less tired and more alert than Mary, and Mary should be sleepy during the science class.

Notice the *If . . . then . . .* format of the two hypotheses. It is not required that you format a hypothesis this way. However, it can provide you with a simple way to make sure that your hypothesis fits the criteria of a testable prediction.

Practice

Try this example.

DOG FOOD EXPERIMENT

Jim has two overweight dachshunds. He sees an advertisement for a new reduced-calorie dog food that claims to allow the dogs to eat normally but still lose weight.

14. Propose a hypothesis to test the claim in the advertisement. What is the hypothesis, suggested experiment, and predicted result?
Hypothesis:

_____

_____

_____

_____

Suggested experiment:

_____

_____

Predicted result:

_____

_____

Identify and Interpret Variables in Investigations

On the GED® Science test you might be asked to identify the different variables in an investigation, so understanding and being able to spot these variables is an important skill. **Variables** are factors in an experiment that can be *changed*, *measured*, or *controlled*:

- **Independent variables** are the manipulated variables. They are the factors that will be intentionally changed during the investigation to find out what effect they have on something else. Usually, time is an independent variable because the investigator can always decide how long to look at something.
- **Dependent variables** are the responding variables. These are the factors that are observed and measured to see if they are affected by the change made in the independent variable.
- **Controls** are variables that must be kept exactly the same to make sure that they do not affect the dependent variable.
- Controls are also runs for which the researcher knows the expected outcome. A **positive control** shows what would happen if the expected phenomenon occurred in an experimental run, and a **negative control** shows what would happen if the expected phenomenon did not occur in an experimental run. For example, if a scientist is testing the effect of an unknown antibiotic on bacterial growth, a negative control would be a run without any antibiotics because this would show how bacteria behave in the absence of antibiotics. In contrast, a positive control would be a run with an antibiotic known to hinder bacterial growth because this would show how bacteria behave in the presence of an effective antibiotic.
- **Constants**, or **controlled variables**, are conditions that are kept exactly the same in order to make sure they do not affect the dependent variable.

WEED KILLER EXPERIMENT

James wants to know how effective a weed killer is in preventing the growth of dandelions. James sets up an experiment with the following procedures to test the effectiveness of the weed killer.

1. Take two identical areas of grass and label them 1 and 2.
2. Apply the weed killer to area 2.
3. Seed both areas with the same number of dandelion seeds.
4. Water the areas daily with the same amount of water.
5. Expose the areas to the same amount of sunlight and temperature.
6. Once they bloom, count the number of dandelions in each area once a day for one week.
7. Record the results.

In this experiment:

- The **independent variable** is the weed killer. It is the manipulated factor that is being tested because James wants to find out what effect it has on something else.
- The **dependent variable** is the number of dandelions growing in the areas of grass. The number of dandelions is the responding variable, the factor that is observed and measured to see if it is affected by the changes made by the presence or absence of the weed killer.

- There are six **controlled variables**—the identical areas of grass, amount of dandelion seed, amounts of water used daily, lighting and temperature, and time of investigation.

Identify Strengths and Weaknesses of Investigation Designs

Experimental designs are not just about a list of procedures. It is important to understand the weaknesses and the strengths of a design. While a well-written list of procedures can be a strength in a scientific investigation, there are more factors at work. For example:

- Does the investigation have a clear purpose?
- Can the stated problem really be investigated using the designed procedures?
- Are the objectives measurable?
- Are the planned procedures appropriate to the project?
- Can the data be analyzed in a meaningful way?
- What are the financial and time costs involved in the experiment and analysis?
- Is there any potential harm to the subjects?
- Is the investigation repeatable by others?
- Are there safeguards to minimize bias and invalidity?

Here is a description of a student's scientific investigation. Read it to identify the strengths and weaknesses of the design. Look at each sentence and try to analyze what might help or hurt the investigation.

VITAMINS AND GROWTH EXPERIMENT

Andrew is studying the effect of vitamins on the growth of mice. His hypothesis is that mice receiving a daily vitamin will grow faster than those not receiving the vitamin. To test his hypothesis, he follows these procedures. He obtains two identical mice and places them in the same cage. He feeds them the same food and the same amount of water. One mouse gets 5 milligrams of vitamin powder sprinkled on its food every day, while the other does not. He weighs the mice daily, giving them an edible treat if they cooperate during the handling and weighing.

First, the strengths of this experimental design:

- The hypothesis is measurable and testable.
- The independent variable is clearly identified as the vitamin. The dependent variable is identified as the growth of the mice as measured by changes in weight.

Now, some of the weaknesses:

- Are only two mice (one control, one experimental) sufficient to represent a larger population?
- The mice are identical, but there is no mention of a way to identify which mouse gets the vitamin and which does not.
- The mice are placed in the same cage, meaning that they both have access to the food sprinkled with the vitamin. This may invalidate the data.
- Has the vitamin been approved for use in mice? Can the mice be harmed by ingesting the vitamin?

- Giving the mice an edible treat at unspecified intervals introduces another independent variable.

Practice

Use the passage to answer the questions that follow.

PAINT DURABILITY EXPERIMENT

A paint company has developed a new brand of outdoor latex paint (Brand X) that it thinks might be more durable than another company's brand (Brand Y). To save money, the company paints boards of different scrap wood with Brand X and Brand Y paints. Employees paint boards with the same number of coats of paint and measure the paint thickness of each board. They place matched boards painted with Brand X and Brand Y in different environments (desert, temperate forest, arctic tundra) for 12 months. After 12 months, they measure the paint thickness of each board again. They find that the boards painted with Brand Y have thinner coats of paint than those painted with Brand X. They conclude that Brand X is more durable than Brand Y.

15. What is the hypothesis of this experiment?

_____

_____

_____

16. Is this hypothesis testable? _____

17. Identify the controlled and uncontrolled factors in the experiment. Write each of the experiment factors in the correct table column.

Controlled	Uncontrolled

- The boards were painted with the same number of coats to the same paint thickness.
- The boards were matched in size.
- Weather conditions varied.
- The boards were made of different woods.
- The boards were exposed to the same weather conditions for the same amount of time.

Design a Scientific Investigation

Planning and designing scientific investigations requires the ability to test a hypothesis that has been formed. As you've learned, the investigator needs to identify the important variables and determine how they might be observed, measured, and controlled. In fact, being able to control factors in the experiment is critical to the investigation. In many instances, especially investigations that take place outside of the laboratory, there are often conditions that are outside the control of the investigator.

The investigator must also make decisions about what measurements will be taken and what instruments are best suited to making those measurements. Because precision is a key issue, it is important to measure the variable as accurately as possible. This will reduce sources of error in the experimental design.

An important part of the investigation is the data that is produced. Selecting an appropriate format in which to record data is also part of good experimental design.

Now let's design an experiment. Here's the question:

> **Does Fertilizer A help plants grow faster than Fertilizer B?**

First, identify what variables will be tested and what variables should be controlled. Fertilizers A and B should be applied to the same type of plant. This makes the type of plant one of your controls.

Should all the plants be fertilized?
No, there should be a control that has no fertilizer for comparison to make sure that both types of fertilizer are working. For the plants that are being fertilized, the amount of fertilizer being applied should be the same.

Should one plant get more sunlight or water or be exposed to different temperatures than the other experimental plant?
No. Water, temperature, and amount of light should also be controls, as well as the length of the experiment (time).

What will be the independent variable?
The type of fertilizer

What will be the dependent variable?
The plant growth

Now that these decisions have been made, writing a set of procedures for the investigative design will allow you to follow the guidelines and carry out the experiment.

The scientific investigative procedures might look something like this when you are finished:

FERTILIZERS AND GROWTH EXPERIMENT

1. Take 30 bean sprouts of equal height and weight, potted in identical containers with identical types and amounts of soil. Label the bean sprouts: Plant 1, Plant 2, Plant 3, . . . Plant 30.
2. Place each of the plants on the window-sill of a room with controlled temperature.
3. Treat Plants 1–10 with 4 grams of Fertilizer A every day at 7:30 A.M.
4. Treat Plants 11–20 with 4 grams of Fertilizer B every day at 7:30 A.M.
5. Do not fertilize Plants 21–30.
6. Water each plant at 8 A.M. daily. Give each plant 20 milliliters of water.
7. Measure the height of each plant with a metric ruler daily at 5 P.M.
8. Record the measurements.

Reasoning from Data

On the GED® Science test, you will be expected to evaluate and verify various sources of data to form a hypothesis, come to a conclusion, or answer a question. You should be prepared to make sense of information from a variety of texts, data sets, and models. Applying scientific reasoning to this process will help you link evidence to claims and assess how data supports conclusions. You may also be asked to use statistical data in mathematical ways to determine probabilities or statistical variance. For each of these expectations, you should be able to interpret tables, diagrams, charts, and other texts; to explain and predict causal relationships; and to arrive at conclusions. This section will help you review and practice these important skills.

Use Evidence to Support a Finding or Conclusion

On test day, you may be asked to gather information to support a finding or conclusion. In these cases, you will be provided with a written source—some sort of scientific literature or technical information. Now, what do you do with it?

First, critically read the source to determine the central, or main, ideas. Look for any conclusions the author may have made based on evidence presented in the source. Compare and evaluate the sources of information to see if they support the finding or conclusion with which you have been presented.

What specifically are you looking for? Here are some suggestions:

- Look for valid and reliable claims that are verified with data.
- Examine the method or design of the investigation that produced the data. Remember that if the investigation that produced the data is flawed, then the data itself is flawed.
- Evaluate the reliability of the sources of information. Reliable sources may include government institutions, universities, and some non-profit institutions.
- When possible, combine information from a variety of sources to establish evidence and resolve any conflicting information.

Read the following excerpt.

ARE BIOFUELS THE ANSWER?

As the world searches for alternatives to petroleum, corn-based ethanol and other biofuels derived from organic material have been considered as the perfect answer to transportation fuel problems. In fact, a U.S. government energy bill mandates that over 30 billion gallons of biofuels a year be used by the year 2020. However, separate studies released by the Nature Conservancy and Ivy League institutions reveal that ethanol may not be the best answer in the fight against global warming. They say using biofuels could make things worse.

Biofuel crops, such as corn and sugar cane, remove carbon from Earth's atmosphere while they are growing. When biofuels are burned, they emit fewer greenhouse gases than fossil fuels like coal or oil. This makes biofuels almost carbon-neutral. However, studies are showing that ethanol could be even more dangerous for the environment than fossil fuels. The Ivy League study noted that clearing previously untouched land to grow biofuel crops releases long-contained carbon into the atmosphere. While planting biofuel crops in already tilled land is acceptable, the problem arises when farmers disturb new land to grow more sugar cane or corn. Additionally, food and feed crops are being displaced by biofuel crops. The Nature Conservancy warns that "converting rainforests, peat lands, savannas, or grasslands to produce biofuels in Brazil, Southeast Asia, and the United States creates a 'biofuel carbon debt' by releasing 17 to 420 times more carbon dioxide than the fossil fuels they replace." Other negative effects include the extreme amounts of water needed for irrigation, runoffs from pesticides and fertilizers, and the natural gas used to make the fertilizers that adds to the carbon deficit.

Your task is to gather information that supports the conclusion that corn-based ethanol is not a sustainable source of transportation fuel for the future. Let's look at information in the passage and address the points mentioned earlier.

Are the claims in the article from reliable sources?
The article mentions studies released by the Nature Conservancy and Ivy League institutions. These institutions generally count as reliable and valid sources.

Are they verified with supporting data?
This article excerpt does not include copies of the data from the studies it mentions. However, the quote from the Nature Conservancy does provide some supporting data for the answer: "converting rainforests, peat lands, savannas, or grasslands to produce biofuels in Brazil, Southeast Asia, and the United States creates a 'biofuel carbon debt' by releasing 17 to 420 times more carbon dioxide than the fossil fuels they replace."

Are there various sources to help establish evidence and resolve conflicting information?
Yes, the article cites reports from the Nature Conservancy, Ivy League institutions, and a U.S. government energy bill.

Let's combine the evidence supporting the claims that ethanol is not a sustainable source of transportation fuel:

- Clearing previously untouched land to grow biofuel crops releases long-contained carbon into the atmosphere.
- Growing biofuel crops displaces food and feed crops.
- Biofuel crops need extreme amounts of water for irrigation.
- Treating fields of biofuel crops with pesticides and fertilizers creates pollution when these chemicals run off into waterways.
- Making fertilizers for growing biofuel crops requires natural gas, which adds to the carbon deficit.

Taken together, all of these points support the idea that growing biofuel crops for fuel for transportation is not sustainable and may be worse than burning the fossil fuels that they are intended to replace.

Use Data to Arrive at a Conclusion

Another important scientific practice skill is that of using data or evidence to arrive at a conclusion. To do this well on the GED® Science test, you need to synthesize information from the sources with which you are provided. The sources might include texts, experimental results, models, or data sets. Critically read the information provided to you. You will need to interpret the tables, diagrams, charts, and any coordinating information. Then, apply scientific reasoning to arrive at a conclusion. Take a look at the following example.

AVOIDING VITAMIN D DEFICIENCY

Approximately one billion people worldwide have vitamin D deficiency. This deficiency is thought to be largely due to insufficient exposure to the sun. In some cases, poor diet can also play a role. There is increasing evidence that vitamin D deficiency also increases a person's susceptibility to autoimmune conditions. Additionally, a lack of vitamin D can impact bone development.

The main source of vitamin D in the body comes from exposing the skin to sunlight. Just 10 minutes of exposure to ultraviolet B radiation wavelengths between 280 and 315 nm, five days a week, will give most people enough vitamin D. However, extended exposure to ultraviolet radiation from the sun is known to increase the risk of skin cancer. Widespread campaigns for the use of sunscreen and sun avoidance have reduced the incidences of skin cancers. However, sunscreens with sun protection factors of 15 or higher also decrease the body's ability to synthesize vitamin D by 99%.

RADIATION TYPE	UVA	UVB	UVC
linked to	aging	burning	
wavelength	400 nm to 315 nm	315 nm to 280 nm	280 nm to 100 nm
% reaching Earth at noon	0.95	0.05	0%—absorbed by ozone, molecular oxygen, and water vapor in the upper atmosphere
% reaching Earth before 10 A.M. and after 2 P.M.	0.99	0.01	0
% reaching Earth (average)	0.97	0.03	0

What are the consequences of vitamin D deficiency?

Poor bone development and autoimmune disease

How do we make vitamin D?

Exposure to ultraviolet radiation

What type of radiation is necessary to make vitamin D?

UVB radiation (315 to 280 nm)

How much daily sunlight exposure is necessary to make vitamin D?

10 minutes

From information in the passage, what are the apparent contradictions regarding vitamin D deficiency and sunlight exposure?

While exposure to ultraviolet radiation is important for your body to make vitamin D, it also puts you at risk for cancer.

So, how can we resolve this contradiction and come to a conclusion? Let's look at the information further.

When does the amount of UVA reaching the Earth peak?

Before 10 A.M. and after 2 P.M.

When does the amount of UVB reaching the Earth peak?

Noon

Does wearing sunscreen reduce UV exposure?

Yes, when the SPF value is greater than 15.

Now, let's put all the information together to draw a conclusion about how we can safely expose our skin to ultraviolet radiation to make vitamin D but minimally risk skin cancer:

SYNTHESIZING VITAMIN D SAFELY

A daily exposure of ten minutes of UVB sunlight therapy at noon has been shown to reduce risks of autoimmune disease and improve bone health. UVB peaks at noon, while UVA peaks before 10 A.M. and after 2 P.M. So, by going outside for 10 minutes around noon and wearing a sunscreen with an SPF factor less than 15, we can have beneficial sunlight therapy for vitamin D synthesis with a relatively low risk of skin cancer associated with exposure to ultraviolet radiation.

Note that we used multiple pieces of scientific information in the passage and the data table to come to a conclusion regarding the risks and benefits of exposure to sunlight for vitamin D therapy.

Practice

Use the following information to answer questions 18 and 19.

WOLVES AND MOOSE POPULATIONS

Wolves originally crossed an ice bridge from Canada to Isle Royale, MI, and the wolf population was established. Moose were native to the island. Since the 1950s, ecologists have studied the moose and wolf populations on the island. The population data are shown in the graph.

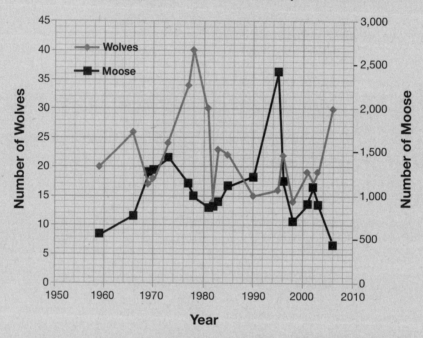

Isle Royale Moose and Wolf Populations

Ecologists noted several events, which are summarized in the table:

YEAR	EVENT
1964–1972	Mild winters
1972–1980	Severe winters
1981–1984	Humans' inadvertent introduction of canine parvovirus to the island
1997	Severe winter, outbreak of moose ticks, new world emigration from Canada

18. Does a stable relationship hold after 1995? Why or why not?

_____

_____

19. Based on the information, what can you conclude about the relationship between moose (prey) and wolves (predator) between 1959 and 1995?

_____

_____

_____

_____

_____

Formulating a hypothesis—a testable prediction—involves asking questions about data and claims that are made. You can ask a question about data that will lead you to analyze more evidence and make interpretations about that evidence. On the GED® Science test, you may be asked to make a prediction based on a given data set or textual evidence. As always, reading and analyzing the information critically and carefully are key.

Use Sampling Techniques to Answer Scientific Questions

Scientific questions involving sampling techniques often use statistics and probability to explain concepts such as variation and distribution in populations. To be well prepared to answer questions using this science practice, you should become familiar with the following types of statistical and probability concepts:

- **Mean** ($\overline{X}$)—the average, computed as the sum of all the observed outcomes from the sample divided by the total number of events.

- **Median**—the middle value or score. If you have an even number of values in a set, take the average of the two middle values. The median is better for describing the typical value and is often used for income or home prices.
- **Mode**—the number of a set of data with the highest frequency (i.e., that occurs more often than any of the other numbers in the set).
- **Variance** (σ^2)—a measure of how far the data is spread apart.
- **Standard deviation** (σ)—the square root of the variance, which can be thought of as measuring how far the data values lie from the mean.
- **Probability**—the likelihood of one or more events happening divided by the number of possible outcomes. If you have ever used percentages, fractions, or ratios to describe or predict the likelihood of an outcome, you have measured probability.

Here's how you'd find the mean, median, and mode for a list of values:

12, 17, 12, 13, 12, 15, 13, 20, 12

Mean
To find the mean, take the values, add them up, and divide by how many values you have.

1. Add the values. The sum is 126 (12 + 17 + 12 + 13 + 12 + 15 + 13 + 20 + 12 = 126).
2. Count up how many items or values you have added: 9.
3. Divide the sum of the values (126) by the number of values (9), and you get 14 (126 ÷ 9 = 14).

The mean, or average, is 14.

Median

To find the median, reorder the values from lowest to highest. The median will be the number in the middle. If you have an even number of values, the median will be the average of the two numbers in the middle.

1. First, put the values in order from smallest to largest: 12, 12, 12, 12, 13, 13, 15, 17, 20.
2. Then, find the number in the middle of this list. There are nine numbers in the list, so the middle one will be the fifth number: 12, 12, 12, 12, **13**, 13, 15, 17, 20.

The median is 13.

Mode

The mode refers to the value that occurs most frequently in the list. If you have a list of three numbers and one occurs twice, that will be the mode. In longer lists, it will again help to put the values in order. From then on, it's simple! Just look for the number that occurs most often:

1. Put in order from smallest to largest: 12, 12, 12, 12, 13, 13, 15, 17, 20.
2. Look for the number that occurs most often: **12, 12, 12, 12**, 13, 13, 15, 17, 20.

There are four 12s, more than any other number. The mode is 12.

Here's another example.

A restaurant owner wants to know how much customers spend at the establishment. She randomly selects 10 receipts from groups of four diners and records the following data: 44, 50, 38, 96, 42, 47, 40, 39, 46, 50

What is the average amount of money that a group of four spends at the restaurant? You learned previously that to calculate the mean, add all the numbers and divide by the number of values, in this case 10. The mean (or average) of the values is 49.2 or $49.20.

To get the variance and standard deviation of this data, you must perform the following steps:

1. First, find the mean of your given values. This step is complete—49.2. Now that you know this number, set up a table that subtracts the mean from each observed value.

Value	–	Mean	=
44	–	49.2	–5.2
50	–	49.2	0.8
38	–	49.2	–11.2
96	–	49.2	46.8
42	–	49.2	–7.2
47	–	49.2	–2.2
40	–	49.2	–9.2
39	–	49.2	–10.2
46	–	49.2	–3.2
50	–	49.2	0.8

2. Square each of the differences, and then add up all those values.

Value	–	Mean	=	x^2	=
44	–	49.2	–5.2	–5.2 × –5.2	27.04
50	–	49.2	0.8	0.8 × 0.8	0.64
38	–	49.2	–11.2	–11.2 × –11.2	125.44
96	–	49.2	46.8	46.8 × 46.8	2,190.24
42	–	49.2	–7.2	–7.2 × –7.2	51.84
47	–	49.2	–2.2	–2.2 × –2.2	4.84
40	–	49.2	–9.2	–9.2 × –9.2	84.64
39	–	49.2	–10.2	–10.2 × –10.2	104.04
46	–	49.2	–3.2	–3.2 × –3.2	10.24
50	–	49.2	0.8	0.8 × 0.8	0.64
				Total:	2,599.60

3. Divide by $n-1$, where n is the number of items in the sample (10). This is the variance.

$$\sigma_x^2 = \frac{2,599.60}{n-1}$$
$$\sigma_x^2 = \frac{2,599.60}{10-1}$$
$$\sigma_x^2 = \frac{2,599.60}{9}$$
$$\sigma_x^2 = 288.8 \text{ or } 289 \text{ rounded}$$

4. To get the standard deviation, take the square root of the variance:
$$\sigma_x = \sqrt{289}$$
$$\sigma_x = 17$$

The standard deviation can be thought of as measuring how far the data values lie from the mean, so take the mean and move one standard deviation in either direction.

The mean of the values was 49.2 and the standard deviation is 17.

- 49.2 – 17 = 32.2
- 49.2 + 17 = 66.2

Therefore, most groups of four customers spend between $32.20 and $66.20.

Now, let's look at an example of probability:

The seven days of the week are written on scraps of paper and placed into a hat. What is the probability of picking a weekend day out of the hat?

The desired outcome is choosing a day that falls on the weekend. This is what you want to answer:

1. The number of outcomes is the total number of days in a week, 7.
2. There are 2 weekend days.
3. 2 ÷ 7 = 0.2857

Practice

Use a calculator for the following questions, if needed.

In an experiment, Jan records the heights in centimeters of five plants:

10.1, 9.8, 10.0, 10.1, 9.9

20. The mean height of the plants is _____ cm.

21. The median height of the plants is _____ cm.

22. The mode height of the plants is _____ cm.

Whether you are using data to form a hypothesis or a conclusion, or to support findings or probabilities, critically reading and analyzing the information is important. Take the time to identify the main idea and logically interpret the data. Do not be intimidated by large sets of data or wordy texts. Look for coordinating information. Then, evaluate how that information supports your task and use it to answer the necessary questions.

Evaluating Conclusions and Evidence

On the GED® Science test, as in life, you will have to evaluate theories, conclusions, and claims. For example, as you are viewing some page on the Internet, an advertisement might pop up and make a claim such as this: "Revolutionary new fruit lets you shed pounds!" Accompanying the claim, there may be a testimonial from some man or woman who claims to have lost 40 pounds while eating this fruit; before-and-after photos are often included. There may even be an endorsement by some celebrity as to the fruit's effectiveness for losing weight. The advertisement might link to another web page

for you to buy the fruit or some extract from it. So, you must then draw some conclusion or make a judgment based on the information presented. Is there enough information? Is the information scientifically valid? Is it worth spending money on the product? Is it safe?

Evaluating scientific findings, drawing conclusions, and making judgments are what scientists do. They evaluate experiments, analyze scientific data (data obtained by themselves and others), draw conclusions, and make judgments. The conclusions and judgments help them accept or reject hypotheses and modify theories. In this section, we examine and practice such skills.

Making Judgments about Whether Theories or Conclusions Are Supported or Challenged by Data or Evidence

In any scientific experiment, the hypothesis makes some sort of testable prediction. The investigator designs an experiment to test the hypothesis and gathers data. The investigator must then examine the data to determine whether the data supports or refutes the prediction made by the hypothesis. The data must be scrutinized thoroughly with a skeptical eye. As you learned previously, critical questions must be asked about the methods used in the investigation. For example, was the experimental design adequate to test the hypothesis? Were the technologies used appropriate? Were all the variables identified and properly controlled, except for the independent and dependent variables? Was the control group appropriate? Were there enough samples taken? Once such questions have been answered satisfactorily, then we have confidence about the data obtained and whether it can support or refute the hypothesis.

Let's look at an example.

BRAND X VERSUS BRAND Y FERTILIZER EXPERIMENT

A company claims that its new fertilizer, Brand X, will make plants, such as tomato plants, grow faster and produce more fruit than a leading brand by another company, Brand Y. The directions for each fertilizer indicate that they are used at the same concentration (50 g/kg soil). A scientist uses 150 tomato plant seedlings. He divides the seedlings into three groups of 50 plants. Each seedling is 10 to 12 cm high at the start of the study and is planted in a pot containing 1 kg of potting soil; the soil is identical for all groups. To one group (control), nothing is added to the soil. To a second group, 50 g of Brand Y is added to the soil of each plant. To a third group, 50 g of Brand X is added to the soil. All of the plants are grouped together in the same greenhouse at a constant temperature of 25°C. The greenhouse is uniformly illuminated and all plants are exposed to a 12-hour on/off cycle. The plants are carefully watered each day with 200 mL of water each. The height of each plant is measured and recorded weekly for 20 weeks. In addition, the number of tomatoes produced by each plant is noted at the end of the experiment (week 20).

Before we examine the data, review the experimental design:

What was the hypothesis?
If tomato plants are treated with Brand X, then they should grow faster and produce more tomatoes than those treated with Brand Y or untreated.

What was the independent variable?
The amount of time that growth was measured (weeks).

What was/were the dependent variable(s)?
The average height of the tomato plants and the number of tomatoes produced per plant.

What were the other variables, and were they controlled?
Other variables were the temperature of the greenhouse as well as the amounts of soil, water, and sunlight. All of these variables were controlled.

Was the number of samples adequate?
Yes, 50 samples in each group were adequate.

Overall, was the experimental design appropriate to test the hypothesis?
Yes, the experimental design was adequate and appropriate.

Look at the data obtained from the experiment. The average height of the plants in each group is shown in the graph.

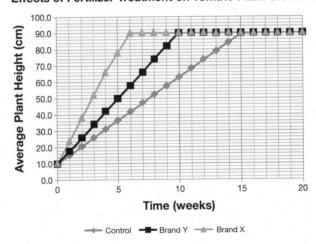

Effects of Fertilizer Treatment on Tomato Plant Growth

Here are some questions to consider when looking at the graph:

What was the maximum height of tomato plants in each group?

The maximum height was 90 cm in each group.

How long did it take each group to reach the maximum height?

The control plants took 15 weeks to reach the maximum height, while plants treated with Brand Y and Brand X took 10 weeks and 6 weeks, respectively.

Which plants grew the fastest?

Brand X grew fastest (about 13.3 cm/week). Brand Y grew the next fastest (about 8 cm/week). The control plants grew the slowest (about 5.3 cm/week).

Consider the hypothesis. Did the growth results support the prediction made in the hypothesis?

Yes, as predicted, the plants treated with Brand X fertilizer grew faster than the control plants and the Brand Y–treated plants.

Now, look at the number of tomatoes produced by the plants, as shown in the table.

EFFECT OF FERTILIZER ON TOMATO PLANT PRODUCTION	
TREATMENT	**AVERAGE NUMBER OF TOMATOES PER PLANT**
Control	3.5
Brand Y	7.2
Brand X	6.1

Use this data to answer the following questions.

Practice

23. Did treating the plants with fertilizers increase the fruit production?
   a. Yes
   b. No

24. Consider the hypothesis. Did the plants treated with Brand X produce more tomatoes than those treated with Brand Y?
   a. Yes
   b. No

25. Now that you have all this data, what would you conclude about the company's claims regarding Brand X? Remember that the company claimed Brand X would cause plants to grow faster *and* produce more fruit.

_____

_____

_____

In this example, we were able to use data to evaluate a claim (hypothesis or theory) by examining the experimental procedure and then the data obtained from that experiment. Once we were convinced that the experiment was sound, we were confident that the data could be used. In this case, there were multiple findings: The data supported one claim (faster growth) but challenged another (increased tomato production).

Often, the details of the experimental design and procedures may not be available, so you must look at the data only. Always keep in mind what predictions are made by the hypothesis, claim, or theory. Does the data address those predictions? What can you conclude from the data? How does the data relate to the predictions? Does the data support the hypothesis? Does the data refute the hypothesis? If the data refutes the hypothesis, then how should the hypothesis be modified?

Bring Together and Make Sense of Multiple Findings, Conclusions, or Theories

On the GED® Science test you will be asked to examine multiple pieces of information to come to conclusions and make judgments. Consider the following example.

EFFECTS OF TEMPERATURE AND PRESSURE

The Haber process is a chemical reaction where nitrogen and hydrogen gases are combined to form ammonia gas. The reaction is represented by this chemical equation:

$$N_2(g) + 3H_2(g) \xleftrightarrow{\text{exothermic}}_{\text{endothermic}} 2NH_3(g)$$

Chemists studied the effects of increasing pressure on the gases in the reaction. The same amounts of nitrogen and hydrogen gases were combined in a fixed chamber. They increased the pressure of the chamber from 0 to 400 atmospheres (atm). They repeated the experiment at several fixed temperatures from 350°C to 550°C. In each case, they measured the percent yield of ammonia produced in the reaction. The data are shown in the graph:

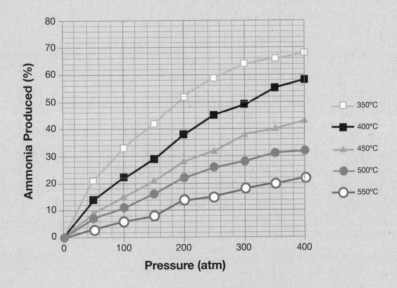

As you can see, the results contain more than one piece of information. Don't get confused by the multiple lines. Let's look at each individually:

- How does the percent yield of ammonia change with increasing pressure at 350°C?
- How does the percent yield of ammonia change with increasing pressure at 400°C?
- How does the percent yield of ammonia change with increasing pressure at 450°C?
- How does the percent yield of ammonia change with increasing pressure at 500°C?
- How does the percent yield of ammonia change with increasing pressure at 550°C?

The answer to all these questions is—*it increases*. So, generally, if you increase the pressure of the reaction at a fixed temperature, you will increase the production of ammonia.

Now, let's look at the effects of temperature by examining the graph:

- How does the percent yield of ammonia change with increasing temperature at a pressure of 50 atm?
- How does the percent yield of ammonia change with increasing temperature at a pressure of 100 atm?
- How does the percent yield of ammonia change with increasing temperature at a pressure of 200 atm?
- How does the percent yield of ammonia change with increasing temperature at a pressure of 300 atm?
- How does the percent yield of ammonia change with increasing temperature at a pressure of 400 atm?

The answer to all these questions is—*it decreases*. So, generally, if you increase the temperature of the reaction at a fixed pressure, you will decrease the production of ammonia.

From a practical industrial standpoint, there are costs associated with building an apparatus that can increase pressures and temperatures. The changes in costs of increasing pressure and temperature are shown in the graphs:

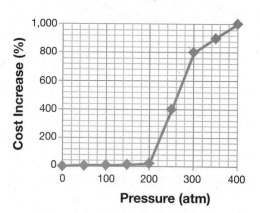

Cost Increases Associated with Increasing Pressure

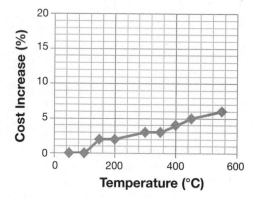

Cost Increases Associated with Increasing Temperature

By this example, you can see how decision makers (e.g., scientists, engineers, project managers, etc.) can integrate multiple pieces of information to make conclusions and judgments.

Use this information to answer the following questions.

Practice

26. Suppose that you are a chemical engineer and must make a facility that will produce large amounts of ammonia using the Haber process. The best conditions to produce the greatest percent yield of ammonia would be:

_____ atm at _____°C.

27. Which is the highest pressure that the reaction can be run at without significantly increasing the costs (significant increase is defined as greater than 25%)?
   a. 100 atm
   b. 200 atm
   c. 300 atm
   d. 400 atm

28. Which is the highest temperature that the reaction can be run at without significantly increasing the costs (significant increase is defined as greater than 25%)?
   a. 350°C
   b. 400°C
   c. 500°C
   d. 550°C

On the GED® test, you will be asked to evaluate conclusions, theories, and judgments based on data. In some cases, you may have the experimental designs available to you. If so, look at the experimental design and ask these questions:

- What was the hypothesis?
- What was the independent variable?
- What was/were the dependent variable(s)?
- What were the other variables, and were they controlled?
- Were the measurement methods appropriate to what was being measured?

- Was the number of samples adequate?
- Overall, was the experimental design appropriate to test the hypothesis?

If you are satisfied with the answers to these questions, then you can be confident that the data is appropriate to address the hypothesis. You can then draw conclusions from the data. In doing so, you may look at the patterns in the data. Once you have drawn conclusions, you can then ask, "Do the conclusions from the data support or refute the hypothesis?"

In many cases, you may not have details of the experimental design available. So, you need to assess whether the data is appropriate to evaluate the hypothesis. For example, a hypothesis dealing with growth of an organism might be appropriately assessed with height or weight data, but not temperature measurements.

In some instances, you may have multiple pieces of information available and must integrate them into conclusions, judgments, or theories. For example, what is the most cost-effective way to produce ammonia?

Expressing Scientific Information

When carrying out experiments, scientists gather data. The data can be **qualitative data**. For example, the color of the solution changes from clear to dark purple as the chemical reaction proceeds. Most often, the data is **quantitative data**—the data are numbers. The numbers may be described verbally, as in a sentence. Numerical data is most often expressed in graphs, tables, or other charts, where it can easily be analyzed for patterns. This section examines various ways of expressing scientific data.

Express Scientific Information or Findings Visually

Numerical data can be either categorical data or continuous data. **Categorical data** has the numbers broken up into groups or categories. **Continuous data** has numbers expressed on a continuous number line. Both categorical and continuous data can be expressed visually in tables, charts, or graphs. Let's look at some examples.

RATING A CEREAL

A survey asks 100 respondents to rate how well they like a particular brand of cereal on a scale of 1 to 4. The number 1 represented "Did not like at all," 2 represented "Did not like or dislike," 3 represented "Liked," and 4 represented "Liked very much." The responses were 10, 25, 30, and 35 for responses 1, 2, 3, and 4, respectively. You see that the responses are grouped into distinct categories (1, 2, 3, or 4), so this is categorical data. One way to express this data visually is to organize it into a table. The first column contains the categories of responses. This column is usually the independent variable. In contrast, the second column contains the total number of respondents in each category, which is the dependent variable. The table would look like this:

CONSUMER OPINION OF CEREAL BRAND X	
RESPONSE	**NUMBER**
1. Did not like at all	10
2. Did not like or dislike	25
3. Liked	30
4. Liked very much	35

Another way to express categorical data is by using a **pie chart**. Here, the number of each category is converted to a percentage. Each category is represented by a "slice" that corresponds to that category's percentage of the whole.

Here, you can more easily see that more respondents had a favorable opinion (*Liked very much* and *Liked*):

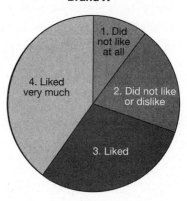

Consumer Opinion of Cereal Brand X

A third way to visualize this data is by using a **bar graph**. In this type of graph, the categories are plotted on the *x*-axis, while the number of respondents in each category is plotted on the *y*-axis. The bar graph of this data looks like this:

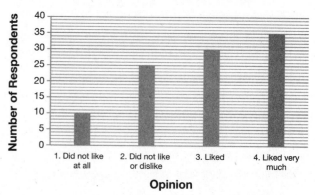

Consumer Opinion of Cereal Brand X

Consider an example of continuous data. Jamie is doing an experiment in physics class. In the experiment, he is trying to answer the question "How does the velocity of a ball rolling down a ramp change with time?"

Distances along the ramp are marked at 0.1, 0.2, 0.3, 0.4, and 0.5 m. He rolls a ball down the ramp. He starts a stopwatch when he releases the ball at the top of the ramp and stops it when the ball passes the first mark. He repeats this four times and records the average time. He repeats the experiment again, but this time he stops the watch at the second mark and records the time. He continues with the procedure until he records the average time to the last mark. He then calculates the velocities. The data are shown in the table.

DISTANCE (m)	TIME (s)	VELOCITY (m/s)
0	0	0
0.1	0.20	0.50
0.2	0.28	0.70
0.3	0.35	0.88
0.4	0.40	1.00
0.5	0.45	1.13

To visualize how the velocity changes, Jamie decides to make a graph. The variables are time and velocity. First, he must determine the independent and dependent variables.

- **Which is the independent variable?** *Time is the independent variable. Ask yourself: Is time changed by the velocity of the ball? No. Therefore, time must be the independent variable.*
- **Which is the dependent variable?** *If the velocity of the ball does not change time, then time may change the velocity of the ball. Therefore, the velocity of the ball is the dependent variable.*

In a graph, the independent variable gets plotted on the horizontal axis, or *x*-axis. The dependent variable gets plotted on the vertical axis, or *y*-axis. In this example, time gets plotted on the *x*-axis and velocity gets plotted on the *y*-axis. We choose a scale on each axis that will include all the values and is divided evenly. The *x*-axis and the *y*-axis do not need to have the same values.

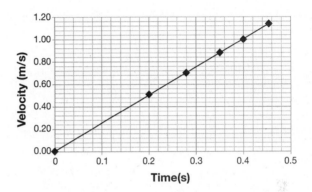

This graph is an example of a **linear line graph**; it is perhaps the most common type of line graph that you will see. Other types of line graphs may be **non-linear**. For example, if Jamie plotted the distance versus time, he would get a graph like this:

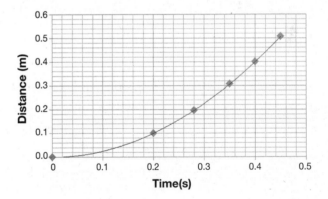

This is an example of a non-linear line graph. Note that the distance that the ball rolls down the ramp increases with time, but not at a constant rate.

Express Scientific Information or Findings Using Numbers or Symbols

Scientific data can be **quantitative** (expressed with numbers) or **qualitative** (expressed verbally or with symbols). Such data may be organized into a table. Let's look at an example.

Cindy is conducting an experiment on human hearing and musical notes. She blindfolds a subject and plays a reference note like middle C (C_4). Next, she plays another note and asks the subject whether the note was higher or lower relative to the reference note. She indicates a higher pitch with one or more "+" signs and a lower note with one or more "−" signs. She organizes her subject's responses in a table like this:

MUSICAL NOTE	RELATIVE PITCH
G_3	− −
A_3	−
Middle C (C_4)	0
D_4	+
E_4	+ +

Suppose that Cindy had a microphone hooked up to an oscilloscope where she could measure the frequency of each musical note. She could then add quantitative data (frequencies) to her table:

MUSICAL NOTE	RELATIVE PITCH	FREQUENCY (Hz)
G_3	− −	196
A_3	−	220
Middle C (C_4)	0	262
D_4	+	294
E_4	+ +	330

Note that the quantitative data still shows the notes in the same order from lowest to highest as the qualitative data does. However, Cindy can now answer the question that an E_4 musical note is 134 Hz higher than a G_3 musical note.

Practice

Jill is watching the development of red color in a solution over time during a chemical reaction. She notes the time and rates the color on a scale of 1 to 10 with 1 being light red (almost pink) and 10 being dark red (almost purple). She expresses her data in a table:

TIME (MINUTES)	RELATIVE RED COLOR
1	1
2	3
3	5
4	6
5	6

29. After 1 minute, what color is the solution?

_____

30. What color does the solution finally develop?

_____

Express Scientific Information or Findings in Words

When publishing scientific papers or reports, space may be limited. Producing graphs or tables may be expensive. Therefore, some data may need to be summarized verbally. In addition, some information may be noteworthy but not important enough to justify its own table, graph, or chart. Consider this example:

DROPPED BALL EXPERIMENT

A student drops a ball from a tall building, while another student videotapes the ball's path. They repeat the experiment 10 times. From the videotape, they measure the distance and calculate the velocities and accelerations with time. They average the values and plot them on graphs:

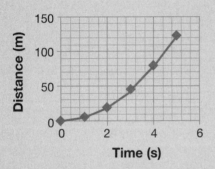

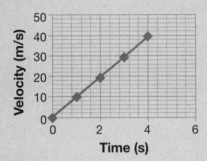

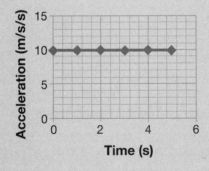

How could we simplify the description of these results? First, look at the graph of acceleration. Note that acceleration does not change; it is constant at 10 m/s/s. So, one way to simplify the presentation might be to eliminate that graph and verbally state the result:

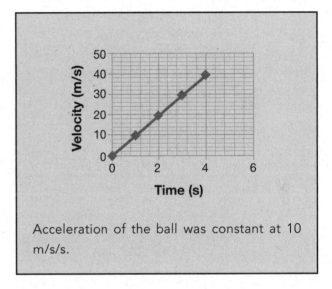

Acceleration of the ball was constant at 10 m/s/s.

How might the students simplify the presentation of the results even further?

The velocity graph could also be described verbally. For example, the velocity of the ball *increased linearly from zero at a constant rate of 10 m/s.* (*Note:* The rate of a linear graph is the slope of the line.) Pick any two points on the line and use the slope formula. For example, use (4,40) and (0,0). The slope becomes:

$$m = \frac{(y_2 - y_1)}{(x_2 - x_1)}$$

$$m = \frac{(40 - 0)}{(4 - 0)}$$

$$m = \frac{40}{4}$$

$$m = 10$$

Plus, we already know that the acceleration of the ball was constant at 10 m/s/s. So, the only graph that needs to be displayed is the graph of distance versus time.

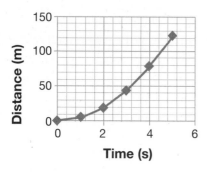

You will learn more about calculating acceleration and velocity later on in this chapter.

Practice

A biochemist conducts an experiment in which she measures the rate of a reaction as a function of temperature. The reaction is conducted in the presence and in the absence of an enzyme. She also monitors the pH of the reaction. Here are the data:

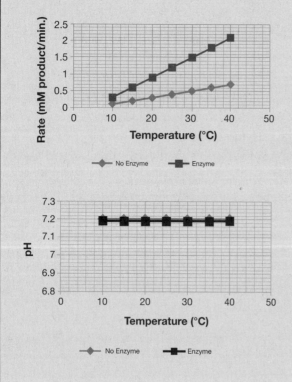

31. Which data is the most important?
  a. rate versus temperature
  b. pH versus temperature

32. How would you simplify this presentation?

_____

_____

Scientific Theories and Probabilities and Statistics

We've learned that scientists and others must often present information and data, and that the information may be qualitative data or quantitative data. Most often, qualitative data may be expressed verbally or in tables using symbols or numbers. Quantitative data is best presented visually so that one can see the patterns in the data to draw conclusions.

To understand the world around us, scientists carry out experiments, gather data, draw conclusions, and form theories and models. The theories and models lead to new predictions that can be tested by experiments. Thus, the cycle continues as new discoveries are made and old ideas are either discarded or modified into new ones that better explain natural phenomena.

One important aspect of analyzing experimental data, especially quantitative data, is determining whether a finding is significant or due to some random error. Often, scientists describe sets of data statistically and perform statistical (i.e., mathematical) tests on the data to determine its significance. Let's examine various ways of examining data statistically in the context of scientific investigations.

Understand and Apply Scientific Models, Theories, and Processes

Theories and models are ways that scientists formulate and express ideas to explain the world around them. Models and theories not only explain but also make predictions that can be tested with experiments. Models may be physical or mathematical.

The most common mathematical model that you will encounter will be the equation of a straight line relating a *y*-variable to an *x*-variable. This equation often has the general form of **y = mx + b**, where *m* is the slope of the line and *b* is the *y*-intercept (the *y*-coordinate of a point where the line crosses the *y*-axis). Here's an example of a linear model:

LINEAR EXAMPLE

Starting 2.0 m away from you, a man walks in a straight line farther from you at a constant velocity. His position with time is shown in the table and the graph. What was the man's velocity?

Time (s)	Position (m)
0	2.00
1	3.50
2	5.00
3	6.50
4	8.00
5	9.50
6	11.00
7	12.50
8	14.00
9	15.50
10	17.00

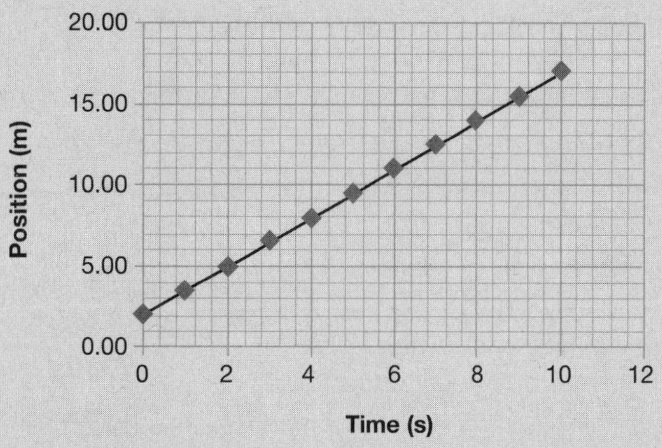

By definition, **velocity** is the rate of change of position with time or the slope of the straight line on a position-time graph. It's a straight line because the man is walking at constant velocity. So, to find the equation of the line, we must first calculate the slope of the line:

1. Pick any two points on the line. We'll use (2,5) and (4,8).
2. Use the slope equation:

   $$m = \frac{(y_2 - y_1)}{(x_2 - y_1)}$$

   $$m = \frac{(8\,m - 5\,m)}{(4\,s - 2\,s)}$$

   $$m = \frac{(3\,m)}{(2\,s)}$$

   $$m = 1.5\frac{m}{s}$$

   So, the man's velocity is 1.5 m/s.
3. Now, let's find the *y*-intercept. At time zero, the man started from 2 m away. Therefore, the *y*-intercept is 2 m. You can see this on the graph as well. It's the point where the line crosses the *y*-axis (vertical axis).
4. So, the equation of the line in the form *y = mx + b* becomes: *y = 1.5x + 2*.

Here are some examples of other mathematical models that you may encounter in science. Don't worry about the math, but just pay attention to the shapes of the curves.

Power Function

$y = ax^n$ where a is a coefficient, x is the base, and n is a whole number exponent. For example, if you had a penny and each day it was doubled, how much would you have on the 30th day? Here are the equation and graph:

$y = ax^n$, where $a = 0.01$, $x = 2$, $n = 30$
$y = (0.01)(2^{30})$
$y = (0.01)(1,073,741,824)$
$y = 10,737,418.24$

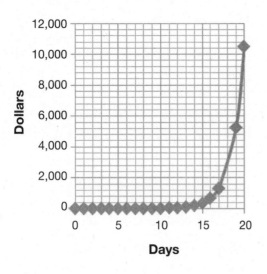

Exponential Function

$y = ce^x$, where c is a constant, e is the base of a natural logarithm, and x is a whole number exponent. Often population growth and decay of radioactive substances follow these functions. For example, radioactive phosphorus-32 has a half-life of 14.26 days. Here is the graph of the decay of 2 g of radioactive phosphorus-32 over time (don't worry about the math; just recognize the shape of the graph):

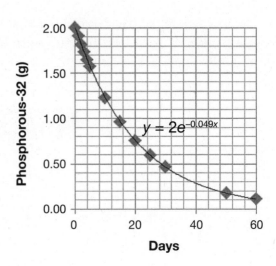

Exponential growth curves have the same shape but increase instead of decrease. Here's one for a population that starts with 10 organisms and grows exponentially:

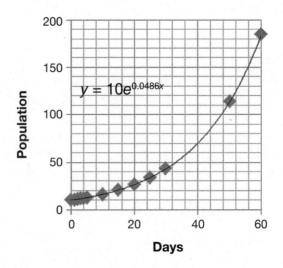

Sigmoidal Curve

Often called an *S-curve*, this function describes the growth of populations where there is a limit to growth or carrying capacity of the environment. (Again, don't worry about the math; just recognize the shape of the curve.) In a population growth curve like this, there is a rapid phase of growth (almost exponential) followed by a slowing phase until the population stabilizes at its limit (carrying capacity). In this graph, the population started at 10 organisms and grew to a limit of 1,000:

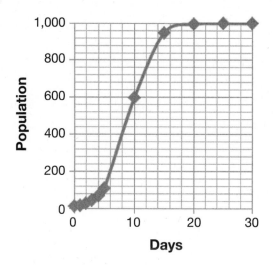

Parabolic Function

This type of curve has the form $y = ax^2 + bx + c$. This equation describes the path of a projectile, like a football kicked at an angle. Here is the graph of a ball thrown with a velocity of 4.47 m/s at an angle of 66°.

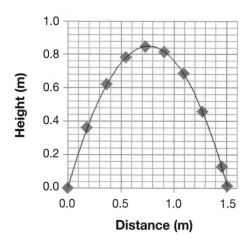

Apply Formulas from Scientific Theories

Equations in science are a guide to thinking. They show how variables relate to each other. For example, Newton's second law of motion relates the net force on an object (F_{net}), the mass of the object (m), and the object's acceleration (a).

$$a = \frac{F_{net}}{m}$$

The law combines two ideas in one equation. First, the greater the force on an object, the greater the acceleration of the object (i.e., acceleration is proportional to the net force). Second, when given the same net force applied to objects, the greater the mass, the slower the acceleration (i.e., acceleration is inversely proportional to mass). So, let's look at how this formula might be addressed in a problem:

> John slides a box horizontally across a frictionless surface with a net force of 10 newtons (10 N). The box has a mass of 2 kg. What is the acceleration of the box? Here's how to solve the problem in a series of steps:

1. **Read the problem.** What do you know? What are you trying to find? Write the information down.
   Given: $F_{net} = 10$ N, $m = 2$ kg
   Unknown: $a = ?$

2. What equation do you need to find the unknown information?
   $a = \frac{F_{net}}{m}$

3. **Is the equation in the form that you need to solve for the unknown?** If not, rearrange the equation algebraically to find the unknown. In this case, the equation is in the correct form to solve for a.

4. **Substitute the known values into the equation and solve for the unknown:**
   $a = \frac{F_{net}}{m}$
   $a = \frac{10 \text{ N}}{2 \text{ kg}}$
   $a = 5$ m/s^2

5. **Check your answer.** Does it make sense? Are the units correct? In this case, yes, m/s^2 is the unit of acceleration.

Use Counting Techniques to Solve Scientific Problems

There are certain types of scientific investigations where the scientist must determine all possible outcomes of some event. Let's look at an example.

KINDS OF DACHSHUNDS

A breeder of dachshunds knows that the dog comes in three coats (long-haired, short-haired, wire-haired), three possible colors (red, brown, black), and two patterns (solid, dappled). How many kinds of dachshunds could there be?

To solve this, we will use the **fundamental rule of counting**, which states:

> In a sequence of n events, in which the first one has k_1 possibilities, the second one has k_2 possibilities, on to the nth one, which has k_n possibilities, the total number of sequences will be: $k_1 \cdot k_2 \cdot k_3 \cdots k_n$

So, for the dachshunds: coat (k_1) = 3, color (k_2) = 3, and pattern (k_3) = 2. Therefore, by the fundamental rule of counting, the total number of outcomes = $3 \cdot 3 \cdot 2 = 18$.

Practice

CODONS

Inside each cell of your body, ribonucleic acid (RNA) contains information to build proteins. A molecule of ribonucleic acid has four nitrogen bases: adenine (A), guanine (G), cytosine (C), and uracil (U). A sequence of three nitrogen bases makes up a *codon*, which is a unit that codes for one amino acid.

33. How many distinct codons can be made from the nitrogen bases of RNA? _____

Now, suppose a molecular biologist wants to make an artificial RNA codon of three nitrogen bases without repeating any single base. How many possibilities are there? In this type of problem, the scientist is using a permutation. A **permutation** is an ordered arrangement of r objects, which are chosen from n different objects, and the order is important. So, let's look at it this way:

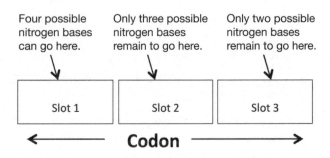

The number of possible permutations is 4 × 3 × 2 = 24.

Permutations are denoted in this manner: $_nP_r$. So, for this example, the permutation can be denoted as $_4P_3$.

We can calculate any permutation according to this formula: $_nP_r = \frac{n!}{(n-4)!}$, where $n!$ means n factorial, which is $n! = n \cdot (n-1) \cdot (n-2) \cdot (n-3) \ldots 1$. (Many calculators with statistical functions have factorial keys on them.) Now let's see how we use the formula for our scientist's example from the previous practice:

$$_nP_r = \frac{n!}{(n-r)!}$$
$$_4P_3 = \frac{4!}{(4-3)!}$$
$$_4P_3 = \frac{4 \cdot 3 \cdot 2 \cdot 1}{1!} = \frac{24}{1} = 24$$

There are 24 possible permutations of nitrogen bases.

Determine the Probability of Events

Sometimes in science, we must make predictions on the outcomes of events. These predictions are called probabilities. The **probability** of an event is the likelihood that that event will occur. Probability is a number between 0 and 1. It can be expressed as a fraction, decimal, or percent. For example, a school organization sells 100 raffle tickets for a prize. Only one ticket will get drawn to win the prize (outcome A). So, the theoretical probability of the event happening is represented by $P(A)$, which can be calculated as follows:

$$P(A) = \frac{\text{number of outcomes of } A}{\text{total number of possible outcomes}}$$

If you buy one ticket, what is the probability that you have the winning ticket?

$$P(A) = \frac{\text{number of outcomes of } A}{\text{total number of possible outcomes}}$$
$$P(A) = \frac{1}{100} = 0.01 = 1\%$$

The probability of having the winning ticket is 1%.

Sometimes, it is not possible to measure all the possible outcomes. So, you must find the **experimental probability**. To do so, you must conduct multiple trials and measure the number of trials where the outcome A occurs.

$$P(A) = \frac{\text{number of trials where } A \text{ occurs}}{\text{total number of trials}}$$

When tall pea plants are mated or crossed, there is a chance that some of the offspring will be short. A scientist conducts 100 crosses. Of these 100 crosses, six produce short pea plants. What is the experimental probability of producing a short pea plant in any one cross?

$$P(A) = \frac{\text{number of trials where } A \text{ occurs}}{\text{total number of trials}}$$
$$P(A) = \frac{6}{100} = 0.06 = 6\%$$

If the height of the pea plant and whether it produces round or wrinkled seeds are independent events, then what will the probability be of producing a plant that is short and has wrinkled seeds? For independent events (A, B), the probability of both of them occurring $[P(A \text{ and } B)]$ is the product of the probabilities of each individual event: $P(A \text{ and } B) = P(A) \cdot P(B)$. So, if we know the probability of wrinkled seeds is 2.5%, we can calculate the probability of producing an offspring that is short and will produce wrinkled seeds:

$$P(A \text{ and } B) = P(A) \cdot P(B)$$
$$P(A \text{ and } B) = 0.06 \cdot 0.025$$
$$P(A \text{ and } B) = 0.0015 \cdot 0.15\%$$

Practice

34. An agricultural scientist conducts 800 trials in crossing pea plants that produce seeds with round seed coats. In these trials, 20 produce seeds with wrinkled seed coats. What is the probability of producing a plant that will yield wrinkled seeds? _____

Summary

This chapter has given you a solid foundation of how to approach scientific information with an analytic and critical eye. The ability to understand science data, passages, and experiments is the main skill you need to score well on the GED® Science test. Remember, all the information you need to answer science questions is presented to you on the test. What the GED® test asks you to do is analyze this information with a scientific mind. The skills in this chapter will help you approach science questions with confidence on test day.

Now, let's apply what was reviewed here to the science knowledge itself in the next three chapters, starting with life science.

Science Practices Review

Use the following information to answer question 1.

REDUCING OBESITY IN CHILDREN

Today, about 30% of the children in the United States are overweight or obese. This puts them at increased risk for diseases such as diabetes (measured by fasting glucose levels) and heart disease (due to high cholesterol levels). The local county health department wants to improve the health of the young children in the community. Most research indicates that changing diet and exercise is the best way to reduce obesity in children, but the health department suspects that children may not be willing to change both diet and exercise.

The county health department undertakes a new program to encourage children to eat better and exercise. They enroll 200 children in a six-month program and plan to set up three groups:

- Group 1: diet and exercise
- Group 2: diet only
- Group 3: exercise only

The county health department hypothesizes that the children in the diet and exercise group will have the best outcomes.

1. Design a controlled experiment that the county health department can use to determine the effectiveness of the program. Include descriptions of data collection and how the health department will determine if their hypothesis is correct. Write your experiment plan on the lines.

_____

_____

_____

_____

_____

_____

_____

_____

_____

_____

_____

_____

_____

_____

_____

Use the following information to answer questions 2–6.

ARE PRESERVATIVES EFFECTIVE?

Katy always buys bread with preservatives so that it will last longer. She wants to know if the preservatives really do make a difference in slowing the growth of mold on bread. She conducts the following experiment:

1. obtains one slice of bread containing preservatives and one slice of bread without any preservatives
2. dampens two paper towels
3. places each paper towel inside a separate zip-top plastic bag
4. places one slice of bread in each bag, seals the bags, and labels the bags
5. puts the bags in a dark, temperature-controlled environment for one week
6. records the mold growth once a day for one week

3. Which is the dependent variable in Katy's experiment?
   a. time
   b. moisture
   c. mold growth
   d. bread with preservatives

4. Which is the independent variable in Katy's experiment?
   a. time
   b. moisture
   c. mold growth
   d. bread with preservatives

5. Which is a controlled variable in Katy's experiment?
   a. bread without preservatives
   b. moisture
   c. mold growth
   d. bread with preservatives

6. Which is a weakness in Katy's experiment?
   a. the use of damp paper towels
   b. the use of plastic bags
   c. not specifying how mold growth is measured
   d. placing one slice of bread in each bag

2. What is the most likely hypothesis for Katy's experiment?
   a. If bread is damp, then it will grow mold faster than dry bread.
   b. If bread is placed in a cool, dark environment, then it will stay preserved longer.
   c. If bread with preservatives is placed in plastic, then it will resist mold for more than one week.
   d. If bread has preservatives, it will grow mold more slowly than bread without preservatives.

Use the following information to answer questions 7–9.

When the brakes are applied in a moving car, the force of friction between the road surface and the vehicle's tires is what stops the car. The force of friction depends on the coefficient of friction, which varies with the road conditions (dry, wet, icy) and seasons (summer, winter). In a collision, a police officer can measure the braking distance by the skid marks, note the road conditions, and determine the initial velocity of the car. The data are shown in the graph.

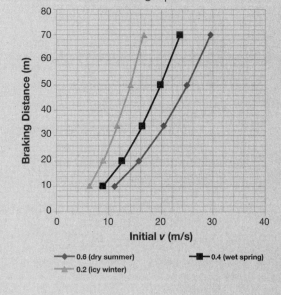

7. On a road under icy winter conditions, a car is traveling at 10 m/s initially when it brakes. The car will travel _____ m before it stops.

8. On a road under wet summer conditions, a car has a braking distance of 60 m. How fast was the car going initially?
   a. less than 15 m/s
   b. 15 to 22 m/s
   c. 22 to 27 m/s
   d. greater than 27 m/s

9. On a road under wet spring conditions, a car has a braking distance of 40 m. The initial speed of the car was _____ m/s.

10. Jenny does an experiment with her friend to test her friend's ability to hear loud (indicated by positives) or soft (indicated by negatives) sounds relative to a reference sound. The data are shown in the table.

SOUND	RELATIVE INTENSITY
A	+ +
B	– –
C	–
D	+ + +
E	– – –

Which sound was closest to the reference sound?
   a. Sound C
   b. Sound B
   c. Sound A
   d. Sound D

11. A forecast shows the chance of rain on Friday is 10%, 30%, 70%, and 50% for Miami, Los Angeles, Seattle, and Chicago, respectively. What is the probability that it will rain in all four cities on Friday? _____

12. In a physics experiment, a student makes several measurements of the velocity of a sound wave from a tuning fork. The measurements (in m/s) are:
   341, 343, 330, 335, 338, 345, 341
Which is the mean of the data?
   a. 339
   b. 341
   c. 345
   d. 2,373

13. The probability of having a male offspring is 50%, while the probability of having type O+ blood is 37.4%. The two outcomes are independent of each other. What is the probability of having a baby boy with type O+ blood?
a. 18.7%
b. 12.6%
c. 87.4%
d. 50%

14. A student observes a chemical reaction in a series of tubes. After 5 minutes of reaction time, she rates the development of blue color on a scale of 1 to 5 (1 = pale blue, 5 = navy blue). The results are shown in the table:

TUBE NUMBER	RELATIVE COLOR
A	3
B	5
C	1
D	4
E	2

Which represents the series of tubes in order from least color development to most color development?
a. A < B < C < D < E
b. C < E < A < D < B
c. E < D < A < B < C
d. E < D < C < B < A

15. A chemistry student conducts an experiment in which he keeps the temperature and volume of a gas constant. He increases the amount of the gas and measures the pressure. The data are shown in the table. He creates a graph in his lab report and the teacher marks it wrong.

AMOUNT (mol)	P (kPa)
0	0
1	101
2	203
3	304
4	406
5	506

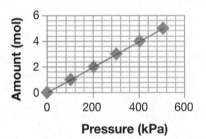

Which error did the student commit in making the graph?
a. The x-axis is not graded in even increments.
b. The y-axis is not graded in even increments.
c. There should be no line through the data points.
d. The variables are plotted on the wrong axes.

Answers and Explanations

Chapter Practice

1. b. The second sentence mentions that bundles contain many *cylindrical* muscle cells.

2. c. The fifth sentence of the passage states, *First, muscle cells have more than one nucleus.*

3.

IRON	OXYGEN	IRON OXIDE
Fe	O_2	Fe_2O_3

4. The pH scale in this chart has values from **0 to 14.**

5. a. Note that each number on the pH scale corresponds to a negative exponent when the hydrogen ion concentration is expressed in scientific notation. pH 2 = 10^{-2} moles per liter, pH 4 = 10^{-4} moles per liter, and pH 6 = 10^{-6} moles per liter. So, pH 9 = 10^{-9} moles per liter.

6. a. acidic. Any pH value below 7.0 indicates an acidic substance.

7. evaporation. The bodies of water in the diagram are the ocean and freshwater. From both you will see an upward arrow labeled "Evaporation." So, evaporation is the process by which water moves from bodies of water into the atmosphere.

8. c. On the left-hand side of the diagram you can see that melting ice and snow on the surface penetrate or infiltrate into the ground.

9. *Answers will vary:*
In this case, the hypothesis predicts that the meat tenderizer will break down proteins but not starches or fats. However, what is meant exactly by *break down* is not specified.

10. *Answers will vary:*
Yes, the size of the jars, as well as the amount of water added, is not specified. Also, were the jars glass or plastic?

11. *Answers will vary:*
Although the amount of meat tenderizer is specified, no brand or type of meat tenderizer is specified. This might be important.

12. *Answers will vary:*
Although the directions say to place one sample of starch, fat, and protein in each jar, the amounts and types of the samples are not specified. What is the source of the starch: bread flour, cornmeal, or something else? What is the source of the fat: butter, lard, vegetable oil, or something else? What is the source of the protein: ground beef, pork, chicken, fish, soybeans, or something else?

13. *Answers will vary:*
What types of changes should you look for: changes in size, weight, color, and so on? Under what conditions were the jars kept? Temperature, humidity, and the amount of light are critical variables in many experiments.

14. *Answers will vary. The following are examples of high-scoring responses.*
Hypothesis:
If Jim places one dog on the new dog food, then that dog should lose weight compared to the other.
Suggested experiment:
Feed both dogs at the same time with the same amount of dog food. Substitute the new reduced-calorie dog food for the normal dog food for one of the dogs. Separate the dogs when they are eating so that one dog does not eat the other's food. Measure the weight of both dogs weekly over the course of six weeks.
Predicted result:
The dog on the reduced-calorie dog food should lose weight compared to the dog on the regular dog food.

15. *Answers will vary:*

If Brand X is more durable than Brand Y under outside conditions, then the paint coatings on boards painted with Brand X will be thicker than Brand Y.

16. **Yes.** The hypothesis is testable.

17.

CONTROLLED	UNCONTROLLED
The boards were painted with the same number of coats to the same paint thickness.	Weather conditions varied.
The boards were matched in size.	The boards were made of different woods.
The boards were exposed to the same weather conditions for the same amount of time.	

18. *Answers may vary:*

No. After 1995, the moose population crashed and remained low due to the severe winter and disease, but the wolf population increased.

19. *Answers may vary:*

The increase in the moose population (1964–1972) induced increased predation by wolves and a subsequent increase in the wolf population. Once the wolf population crashed from disease (1981–1990), the moose population recovered and increased through 1995.

20. The mean height of the plants is **9.98 cm.** First arrange the heights in ascending order:

9.8, 9.9, 10.0, 10.1, 10.1

$$\text{mean} = \frac{9.8 + 9.9 + 10.0 + 10.1 + 10.1}{5}$$

$$\text{mean} = \frac{49.9}{5}$$

$$\text{mean} = 9.98$$

21. The median height of the plants is **10.0 cm.** First arrange the heights in ascending order:

9.8, 9.9, 10.0, 10.1, 10.1.

The median is the middle value, which is 10.0 cm.

22. The mode height of the plants is **10.1 cm.** The mode is the most frequent value, which is 10.1 cm: 9.8, 9.9, 10.0, 10.1, 10.1.

23. a. Yes. The fertilizer-treated plants produced almost twice as many tomatoes as the control plants.

24. b. No. The plants treated with Brand X produced slightly fewer tomatoes than those treated with Brand Y.

25. *Answers will vary:*

The results of this study show that while the company's claim that plants treated with Brand X grow faster is true, their claim that the plants will produce more fruit is not true.

26. **400 atm** at **350°C.** The best conditions to produce the greatest percent yield of ammonia would be 400 atm at 350°C. These conditions have the highest yield of ammonia (68%).

27. b. Achieving a 200-atm pressure is the highest that can be done without the cost significantly increasing.

28. d. Temperatures up to 550°C can be achieved with only a 6% increase in cost (not significant by definition).

29. **pink.** After looking at the table and the timing, you would probably determine that the solution is almost pink.

30. **red.** The solution develops a red, perhaps a slightly dark red color, as indicated by 6 being slightly above the middle of the scale.

31. a. The biochemist would want to show the rate versus temperature data, as that is what is changing.

32. *Answers may vary:*

The pH of the reaction does not significantly change with temperature and could be easily stated verbally as *The pH of the reaction mixture was constant at approximately 7.20.*

33. **64.** There are three nitrogen bases in each codon. Each position can be filled with one of four nitrogen bases. So, using the fundamental rule of counting, we get:

$$k_1 \cdot k_2 \cdot k_3 = 4 \cdot 4 \cdot 4 = 64.$$

34. $\frac{1}{40}$ **or 0.025 or 2.5%.**

$$P(A) = \frac{\text{number of trials where } A \text{ occurs}}{\text{total number of trials}}$$

$$P(A) = \frac{20}{800} = \frac{1}{40} = 0.025 = 2.5\%$$

Science Practices Review

1. *Answers will vary:*

The county health department should randomly assign the 200 children to one of three experimental groups, as well as a control group, as follows:

- Group 1: diet and exercise (50 children)
- Group 2: diet only (50 children)
- Group 3: exercise only (50 children)
- Control group: no change in daily routine (50 children)

The health department employees would have to take measurements on all of the children before the intervention begins, at two months, and at six months to measure the change over time. They would take height, weight, cholesterol level, and fasting blood glucose level. They would also need to ask questions about the diet of the children and the amount of exercise they do on a daily basis.

The children in Group 1 (diet and exercise) would be on a diet lower in fat and sugar (weekly menus provided by the health department) and would be asked to double the amount of exercise they do in a week (e.g., if they normally exercise 20 minutes per week, then they will be asked to exercise 40 minutes per week). Parents would be asked to keep a food log and record the exercise on a daily basis.

The children in Group 2 (diet change only) would be on the same reduced-fat and lower-sugar diet as the children in Group 1 but would not change their exercise routines. Parents would be asked to keep a food log and record the exercise on a daily basis.

The children in Group 3 (exercise change only) would not be asked to change their diets, but would be asked to double the amount of exercise they do on a weekly basis, as in Group 1. Parents would be asked to keep a food log and record the exercise on a daily basis.

The children in the control group would not be asked to change anything, but parents would be asked to keep a food log and record the exercise on a daily basis.

After the conclusion of the experiment, the health department can compare the weights, cholesterol levels, and fasting blood glucose levels of each group and draw conclusions about the effectiveness of the interventions.

2. d. Katy's experiment involves two types of bread—with preservatives and preservative-free. The experiment uses temperature, moisture, and time as controls in order to discover if the preservative is the true variable in resisting mold growth.

3. c. Mold growth is the responding variable to the presence or absence of preservatives in bread.

4. d. Bread with preservatives is the independent variable.

5. b. Moisture is kept constant, so it is one of the controlled variables.

6. c. By not specifying how she intended to measure mold growth, Katy could prevent others from replicating her findings.

7. The car will travel **26 m** before it stops. First, trace the vertical line from 10 m/s on the *x*-axis until it meets the curve for icy winter conditions. From that point, trace the horizontal line to the *y*-axis and read the braking distance, which is 26 meters.

8. c. There is no curve for wet summer conditions, but these conditions must fall between the curves for wet spring and dry summer. Trace the horizontal line from 60 m on the y-axis until it meets the curve for wet spring conditions. This is the minimum speed. From that point, trace the perpendicular line to the x-axis and read the initial speed, which is 22 m/s. Repeat the process, but continue the horizontal line until it reaches the dry summer curve. This is the maximum speed. From that point, trace a perpendicular line to the x-axis and read the initial speed, which is 27 m/s. The car had to be traveling between 22 m/s and 27 m/s.

9. The initial speed of the car was **18 m/s**. First, trace the horizontal line from 40 m on the y-axis until it meets the curve for wet spring conditions. From that point, trace a perpendicular line to the x-axis and read the initial speed, which is 18 m/s.

10. a. Sound C had only one negative and was the closest to the reference sound.

11. 0.0105 or 1.05%.

   $P(\text{Miami}) = 10\% = 0.1$
   $P(\text{Los Angeles}) = 30\% = 0.3$
   $P(\text{Seattle}) = 70\% = 0.7$
   $P(\text{Chicago}) = 50\% = 0.5$
   $P(\text{all 4 cities}) = P(\text{Miami}) \cdot P(\text{Los Angeles})$
       $\cdot P(\text{Seattle}) \cdot P(\text{Chicago})$
   $P(\text{all 4 cities}) = 0.1 \cdot 0.3 \cdot 0.7 \cdot 0.5$
   $P(\text{all 4 cities}) = 0.0105 = 1.05\%$

12. a. Calculate the mean:

   $$\text{mean} = \frac{330 + 335 + 338 + 341 + 341 + 343 + 345}{7}$$
   $$\text{mean} = \frac{2{,}373}{7}$$

   mean = 339

   Choice **b** is both the median and the mode of the data set.

13. a. Let A represent the outcome of having a male child and B represent the outcome of type O+ blood:

   $P(A \text{ and } B) = P(A) \times P(B)$
   $P(A \text{ and } B) = 0.5 \times 0.374$
   $P(A \text{ and } B) = 0.1870 = 18.7\%$

   Choice **b** is the difference between the two probabilities. Choice **c** is the sum of the two probabilities. Choice **d** is the probability of having a baby boy.

14. b. The tubes are in the correct order from least color development (Tube C = 1) to most color development (Tube B = 5).

15. d. *Amount* is the independent variable and should be plotted on the x-axis. In contrast, *pressure* is the dependent variable and should be plotted on the y-axis. Choices **a** and **b** are not student errors because these scales do have even increments. Choice **c** is not an error because a line drawn through the data points is fine.

4 ▶ LIFE SCIENCE REVIEW

This chapter begins our study of the science topics that are presented on the GED® Science test. Remember, the focus of the exam isn't to assess your science content knowledge; it's to test your science reasoning skills. On the test, you will never encounter a question that asks you to provide your own definition of a specific science term or concept. However, according to the GED® Testing Service, you should be "broadly and generally familiar" with each of the basic science concepts covered in the next three chapters. In other words, to do your best, you should strive to generally understand and recognize all the concepts and terms you'll encounter. Answers and explanations for all practice questions are at the end of this chapter.

What Is Life Science?

Life science explores the nature of living things, from the smallest building blocks of life to the larger principles that unify all living beings. Fundamental questions of life science include:

- What constitutes life?
- What are its building blocks and requirements?

- How are the characteristics of life passed on from generation to generation?
- How did life and different forms of life evolve?
- How do organisms depend on their environment and on one another?
- What kinds of behavior are common to living organisms?

Before Antoni van Leeuwenhoek looked through his homemade microscope more than 300 years ago, people were not aware that there were cells in our bodies and that microorganisms existed. People even believed that fleas, ants, and other insects came from dust or wheat. Leeuwenhoek looked through his microscope and saw blood cells in blood, studied microorganisms in ponds, and showed that pests come from eggs laid by adult pests. It took more than 200 years for Leeuwenhoek's observations to gain wide acceptance and find application in medicine, and yet the questions he asked have led us to learn all that we know now about life science.

Life science questions on the GED® Science test will cover many topics studied in high school biology classes. Reviewing some of the basics of biology will help you to understand passages and find the answers to questions on the GED® Science test.

Cell Theory

Let's start with the cell, which we know today is the building block of life. Every living organism is composed of one or more cells, and all cells come from other cells. Cells are alive—if blood cells, for example, are removed from the body, given the right conditions, they can continue to live independently of the body.

Cells are made up of organized parts, perform chemical reactions, obtain energy from their surroundings, respond to their environments, change over time, reproduce, and share an evolutionary his-

tory. All cells contain a membrane, cytoplasm, and genetic material. More complex cells also contain cell organelles.

The following is a description of cell components and some of the functions they serve, as well as a figure showing the parts of animal and plant cells.

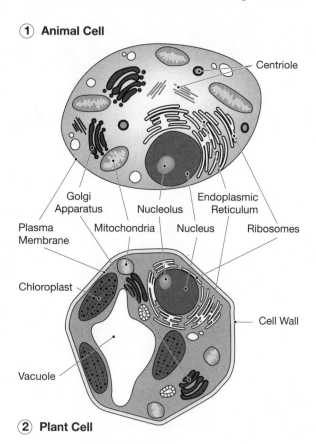

① **Animal Cell**

Centriole

Golgi Apparatus · Nucleolus · Endoplasmic Reticulum

Plasma Membrane · Mitochondria · Nucleus · Ribosomes

Chloroplast

Cell Wall

Vacuole

② **Plant Cell**

Cell Membranes

The **cell**, or **plasma**, **membrane** is the outer membrane of the cell. It carefully regulates the transport of materials in and out of the cell and defines the cell's boundaries. Membranes have selective permeability—meaning that they allow the passage of certain molecules, but not others. A membrane is like a border crossing. Molecules need the molecular equivalent of a valid passport and a visa to get through.

The movement of water and other types of molecules across membranes (including cell membranes) is important to many life functions in living organisms. Movement of these molecules occurs by **diffusion** through semipermeable membranes, which means that the membranes allow small molecules, like water, to pass but block larger molecules, like sugar or glucose. The processes of diffusion and **osmosis** are sometimes called **passive transport** since they do not require any active role for the membrane. The molecules move across the membrane because of osmotic pressure. **Osmotic pressure** forces highly concentrated molecules to move across a membrane into areas of lower concentration until a balance is reached. This balance is called **equilibrium**.

Conversely, sometimes molecules are moved from areas of low concentration to areas of higher concentration. This is the opposite of passive transport, so what do you think it is called?

This process is called **facilitated** or **active transport**. Active transport requires the cell to use energy. You will read more about osmosis and diffusion in the Physical Science Review chapter.

The **cell wall** is the layer outside of the membrane on plant cells. It is made of cellulose, which surrounds, protects, and supports plant cells. Animal cells do not have a cell wall.

Interior Parts of a Cell

These are parts of a cell that will be useful to review:

- The **nucleus** is a spherical structure, often found near the center of a cell. It is surrounded by a nuclear membrane, and it contains genetic information inscribed along one or more molecules of DNA. The DNA acts as a library of information and a set of instructions for making new cells and cell components. In order to reproduce, every cell must be able to copy its genes to future generations. This is done by exact duplication of the DNA. The **nucleolus** is located inside the nucleus. It is involved in the synthesis of ribosomes, which manufacture proteins.
- **Cytoplasm** is a fluid found within the cell membrane but outside of the nucleus.

- **Ribosomes** are the sites of protein synthesis. They are essential in cell maintenance and cell reproduction.
- **Mitochondria** are the powerhouses of the cell. They are the sites of **cellular respiration** (breakdown of chemical fuels to obtain energy) and production of adenosine triphosphate (ATP), a molecule that provides energy for many essential processes in all organisms. Cells that use a lot of energy, such as the cells of a human heart, have a large number of mitochondria. Mitochondria are unusual because, unlike other cell organelles, they contain their own DNA and make some of their own proteins.
- The **endoplasmic reticulum** is a series of interconnecting membranes associated with the storage, synthesis, and transport of proteins and other materials within the cell.
- The **Golgi apparatus** is a series of small sacs that synthesizes, packages, and secretes cellular products to the plasma membrane. Its function is directing the transport of material within the cell and exporting material out of the cell.
- **Lysosomes** contain enzymes that help with intracellular digestion. Lysosomes have a large presence in cells that actively engage in phagocytosis—the process by which cells consume large particles of food. White blood cells that often engulf and digest bacteria and cellular debris are abundant in lysosomes.
- **Vacuoles** are found mainly in plants. They participate in digestion and the maintenance of water balance in the cell.
- **Centrioles** are cylindrical structures found in the cytoplasm of animal cells. They participate in cell division.
- **Chloroplasts** exist in the cells of plant leaves and in algae. They contain the green pigment chlorophyll and are the site of photosynthesis—the process of using sunlight to make high-energy sugar molecules. Ultimately, the food supply of most

organisms depends on photosynthesis carried out by plants in the chloroplasts.

Organization of Cells

In a multicellular organism, individual cells specialize in different tasks. For example, red blood cells carry oxygen, white blood cells fight pathogens, and cells in plant leaves collect the energy from sunlight.

This cellular organization enables an organism to lose and replace individual cells and consequently outlive the cells of which it is composed. For example, you can lose dead skin cells and give blood and still go on living. This differentiation or division of labor in multicellular organisms is accomplished by expression of different genes within the cells.

Types of Biomolecules

There are four basic classes of biomolecules that occur in the cell: lipids, proteins, carbohydrates, and nucleic acids.

Lipids are generally composed of long chains of hydrocarbons (-CH$_2$-) and are effective energy storage molecules. The hydrocarbon portions of lipids are generally hydrophobic, or "water-fearing," but some lipids have hydrophilic, or "water-loving," polar head groups. In a lipid bilayer, the hydrophilic parts of the lipids form the outer portion of the bilayer because this is the region that interacts with water and solutions, while the hydrophobic portions of the bilayer interact with one another. Within the cell, lipids are the major components of cell membranes, in the form of a lipid bilayer. Cholesterol is not part of the bilayer, but it occurs in cell membranes as a means of regulating rigidity.

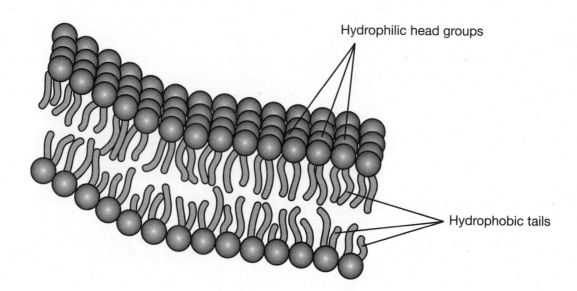

Hydrophilic head groups

Hydrophobic tails

Proteins make up most of the biomolecules within a cell. Almost all enzymes found in the cell are proteins. Additionally, proteins are found in the plasma membrane and in the cytosol. Proteins are composed of subunits called amino acids. There are 20 standard amino acids, which are made up of a central atom bonded to four groups: a carboxyl group, an amino group, a hydrogen atom, and a variable R group that gives unique properties to the amino acid and allows for proteins to perform different functions. Polypeptides are long chains of amino acids that are connected via peptide bonds. Examples of proteins found in cells include DNA polymerase and hemoglobin.

Proteins have four levels of structure: **primary**, **secondary**, **tertiary**, and **quaternary**. The primary structure of a protein refers to its unique amino acid sequence; with 20 available amino acids that can be arranged in any number of ways, the primary structure of the protein is often considered the structural level that provides the most diversity among proteins. The secondary structure of a protein refers to features formed by hydrogen bonding between amino acids, most importantly the alpha helix and beta sheet.

Carbohydrates, as their name suggests, are technically hydrates of carbon, having the chemical formula $C_m(H_2O)_n$. This class of biomolecules includes starch, cellulose, and sugars. A saccharide is a carbohydrate monomer, a disaccharide is a carbohydrate dimer, and a polysaccharide is a carbohydrate polymer. Saccharides within disaccharides and polysaccharides are bonded through glycosidic linkages. The names of monosaccharides and disaccharides generally end in the suffix –*ose*. Examples of monosaccharide carbohydrates are glucose and galactose. Examples of disaccharide carbohydrates are sucrose and lactose. Examples of polysaccharide carbohydrates include glycogen and starch. In the cell, the carbohydrate glucose is a common input molecule for respiration and output molecule for photosynthesis.

Nucleic acids are the key biomolecules responsible for genetic information. Nucleic acids are composed of subunits called nucleotides, which consist of a nitrogenous base, a five-carbon sugar, and a phosphate group. There are five nucleotides, named by the base they contain: adenine (A), cytosine (C), guanine (G), thymine (T), and uracil (U). The linkages that form between nucleotides in nucleic acids are called *phosphodiester bonds*. Nucleotide subunits are prevalent outside of nucleic acids; for example, the high-energy molecule adenosine triphosphate (ATP) is a nucleotide, but it is not a component of any nucleic acid. The two kinds of nucleic acid are deoxyribonucleic acid (DNA) and ribonucleic acid (RNA). DNA, which forms a double helix in its double-stranded form, only uses the nucleotides A, C, G, and T, while RNA, which is usually single-stranded, only uses the nucleotides A, C, G, and U.

Respiration and Photosynthesis

Cellular respiration is the process by which glucose and other food molecules are oxidized to form carbon dioxide and water. Respiration releases trapped energy in the form of ATP that can be used in other cellular activities.

The complete balanced chemical equation for cellular respiration, using glucose since it is the most commonly discussed input chemical, is: $C_6H_{12}O_6 + 6O_2 \rightarrow 6CO_2 + 6H_2O$. In eukaryotes, the process of respiration begins in the cytosol and ends in the mitochondrion.

Mitochondria are organelles that are enclosed by an inner and outer membrane. The outer membrane contains a number of integral membrane proteins that facilitate molecule transport into and out of the mitochondrion. The inner membrane also contains a number of complexes of integral membrane proteins, which will become important in the discussion of the electron transport chain. The inner membrane is characterized by a number of folded projections called *cristae* that extend into the matrix. The region between the inner and outer membranes is called the *intermembrane space*. Within the inner membrane is the matrix, which is filled with fluid and contains a number of soluble enzymes involved in pyruvate respiration. Mitochondria also have several circular DNA molecules. A typical eukaryotic cell has anywhere from several hundred to several thousand mitochondria.

The first step of cellular respiration is **glycolysis**, the process by which a single glucose molecule is broken down into two molecules of pyruvate. Glycolysis is oxygen-independent. In addition to producing pyruvate, ATP is formed along with NADH, a reduced molecule that will later be used in the electron transport chain. Glycolysis generally occurs in the cytosol of the cell, and it occurs in essentially all organisms, both aerobic and anaerobic. After pyruvate forms, it is oxidized by NAD^+ in the mitochondrial matrix, producing NADH, a molecule of CO_2, and acetyl-CoA. Acetyl-CoA then combines with oxaloacetate to form citric acid, which begins the citric acid cycle. During the citric acid cycle, NADH and $FADH_2$ are formed, along with two molecules of CO_2. Between pyruvate oxidation and the citric acid cycle, each of the three carbon atoms that had been present in pyruvate upon entry into the mitochondria has now been released in the form of carbon dioxide.

The aforementioned integral membrane proteins in the inner membrane now come into play during the activities of the electron transport chain. The electron transport chain transfers electrons from NADH and $FADH_2$ to oxygen to form water, H_2O. In the meantime, protons (H^+) are pumped into the intermembrane space from the matrix against their concentration gradient, and then the protons can reenter the matrix, down their concentration gradient, through ATP synthase via chemiosmosis. The energy released during this process is harnessed for ATP synthesis. From start to finish, aerobic respiration can produce 36 to 38 ATP molecules per glucose molecule. In contrast, anaerobic respiration only uses glycolysis and produces 2 ATP molecules per glucose molecule.

Photosynthesis is the process by which plants, algae, and some bacteria use the energy from sunlight to produce carbohydrates, namely glucose. This glucose can later be used to generate ATP via cellular respiration to free up useable energy for the cell. The green pigment chlorophyll is largely responsible for the conversion of sunlight energy into useful chemical energy. Chlorophyll is found in cyanobacteria and eukaryotic chloroplasts and allows the absorption of energy from light. Photosynthesis uses water and releases oxygen, so its complete balanced chemical equation is $6CO_2 + 6H_2O \rightarrow C_6H_{12}O_6 + 6O_2$.

Photosynthesis occurs in the **chloroplast** in eukaryotes. Like the mitochondrion, a chloroplast has an inner membrane and an outer membrane, with an intermembrane space between them. Within the chloroplast are disc-like structures called thylakoids, which are the basic structural units of photosynthe-sis. Stacks of thylakoids are called *grana*, and the areas between the grana are called the *stroma*.

There are two basic stages of photosynthesis: the light-dependent reactions and the light-independent reactions. As their names suggest, the light-dependent reactions require light while the light-independent reactions do not. The light-dependent reactions use direct sunlight for production of energy-carrying molecules that are then used in the light-independent reactions to form carbohydrates. The light-dependent reactions take place in the grana, while the light-independent reactions take place in the stroma.

During the light-dependent reactions, light strikes chlorophyll a, exciting electrons to a higher energy state. This energy, through a series of reactions, is used to generate ATP and NADPH in a process known as *photophosphorylation*. Water is split, and oxygen is consequently released as a byproduct. Noncyclic photophosphorylation involves electron transfers through, in order, Photosystem II, a redox chain, and then Photosystem I. Photophosphorylation is linked with chemiosmotic synthesis of ATP. During the light-independent reactions, or carbon fixation reactions, which occur in the stroma of chloroplasts, carbon dioxide enters the Calvin cycle and combines with ribulose bisphosphate (RuBP), a 5-carbon molecule. The entry of six carbon dioxide molecules ultimately leads to the production of one glucose molecule upon completion of the Calvin cycle.

Typical photosynthesis is called *C3 photosynthesis*, but two other variations exist to help plants in conditions that are less amenable to photosynthesis. In C4 photosynthesis, carbon fixation and the Calvin cycle are spatially separated. In C4 plants, carbon dioxide incorporation occurs in mesophyll cells, while the Calvin cycle occurs in bundle-sheath cells. C4 photosynthesis accordingly requires a few more steps and extra energy, but this allows plants to more efficiently fix carbon in drought, high temperatures, and under N_2- or CO_2-limiting conditions. In CAM photosynthesis, carbon fixation and the Calvin cycle are temporally separated; that is, carbon dioxide incorporation occurs during the night and the Calvin cycle occurs during the day. CAM photosynthesis has evolved as a means for plants to adapt to arid conditions. The stomata in the leaves of CAM plants remain closed during the day, avoiding the loss of water through evapotranspiration, and then open at night for carbon dioxide collection.

Considering the foregoing passages, let's see if you can pull information from what was presented to answer the following questions.

Practice

1. Match the interior parts of a cell with the correct descriptions. Write the letter next to each statement in the appropriate place in the table.

INTERIOR PARTS OF A CELL	DESCRIPTION
nucleus	
mitochondria	
ribosomes	
plasma membrane	

a. the element that controls the transfer of material into and out of the cell

b. where the DNA of a cell is found

c. the site in the cell where substances are broken down to obtain energy

d. the part of the cell where the synthesis of protein takes place

2. Name the parts of a cell found only in animal cells and those found only in plant cells.
Animal cells _____
Plant cells _____

3. *Facilitated transport* and *passive transport* refer to what? _____

4.

To which class of biomolecules does the molecule above belong? _____

5. With regard to ATP production, aerobic respiration is approximately _____ times more efficient than anaerobic respiration.
a. 2–3
b. 9–10
c. 18–19
d. 23–24

Reproduction and Heredity

Once you've gotten a handle on how to think about cells, let's go a bit deeper into a specific set of cell processes—reproduction and heredity. **Reproduction** is simply the process of an organism creating a new organism and passing along its genetic material. **Heredity** involves what an organism looks like and how it functions, and this is determined by its genetic material. Obviously, these two things are intrinsically related.

Here's a fun fact: The basic principles of heredity were developed by Gregor Mendel, who experimented with pea plants in the nineteenth century. He mathematically analyzed the inherited traits (such as color and size) of a large number of plants over many generations in order to understand how heredity works. The units of heredity are **genes** carried on **chromosomes**. Genetics, which is the study of genes, can usually explain why children look like their parents and why they are, at the same time, not identical to the parents.

Let's look at some of the key terms that will help you to understand questions about reproduction and heredity.

Phenotype and Genotype

The collection of physical and behavioral characteristics of an organism is called a **phenotype**. For example, your eye color, foot size, and ear shape are components of your phenotype. If a puppy is born with brown eyes, what is this an example of? Phenotype!

The genetic makeup of a cell or organism is called the **genotype**. Phenotype (what an organism looks like or how it acts) is determined by the genotype (its genes) and its environment. By environment we don't mean the earth, but the environment surrounding the cell. For example, the hormones in a human mother's body can influence the gene expression in a baby. Essentially, you can think of the genotype as being like a cookbook for the recipe of the phenotype and the environment as being like the kitchen.

Cellular Reproduction

You may have heard the terms *mitosis* and *meiosis*. These are forms of **cellular reproduction**.

Asexual reproduction on the cellular level is called **mitosis**. Because it is asexual, that means it requires only one parent cell, which, after exactly multiplying its genetic material, splits in two. The resulting cells are genetically identical to each other and are clones of the original cell.

Since asexual reproduction requires only one parent cell, **sexual reproduction** requires how many parent cells? Two! Most cells in an organism that reproduces sexually have two copies of each chromosome, called **homologous pairs**—one from each parent. Even though an organism reproduces sexually, these cells reproduce through mitosis to keep all the genetic material.

However, there must be an exception to this rule, right?

Gamete cells (sperm and egg cells) are exceptions to the mitosis rule! They carry only one copy of each chromosome, so there are only half as many chromosomes as in the other cells. For example, human cells normally contain 46 chromosomes, but human sperm and egg cells have 23 chromosomes.

Why would these cells do this? Well, at fertilization, male and female gametes (sperm and egg) come together to form a zygote, the offspring, and the two sets of chromosomes join together to make sure the cell has the normal 46 chromosomes. This is how the genetic information of a zygote is a mixture of genetic information from both parents.

Gamete cells are manufactured through a process called **meiosis** whereby a cell multiplies its genetic material once but divides twice, producing four new cells, each of which contains half the number of chromosomes that were present in the original cell before division. In humans, gametes are produced in testes and ovaries. **Meiosis**, and how it is used in sexual reproduction, is necessary for **genetic diversity** within a species by generating combinations of genes that are different from those present in the parents. Genetic diversity is important for healthy populations of any specific species. This is why purebred animals have very well documented genetic lines—to avoid inbreeding and unhealthy animals.

During **mitosis**, a cell divides to form two identical cells. During the S phase of interphase, the DNA replicates. This is followed by the second gap phase, G2, which then leads into the first stage of mitosis, prophase. During prophase, chromatin condenses into chromosomes, gene transcription temporarily stops, and the nucleolus disappears. Each pair of chromosomes is connected at its centromere. During metaphase, the chromosomes are aligned at the central metaphase plate, an imaginary line located at the midline of the cell. During anaphase, the microtubules attached to the chromosomes start to pull them apart. During telophase, the nucleolus reappears. With mitosis complete, cytokinesis occurs such that the cell splits into two daughter cells. Plant and animal cells undergo cell division in different ways due to differences in structure. Animal cells pinch apart, forming a cleavage furrow. In plant cells, on the other hand, a cell plate forms to initiate cell wall formation in the daughter cells.

During **meiosis**, the chromosome number of the dividing cell is divided by half. Each round of meiosis involves two rounds of cell division, meiosis I and meiosis II. Prior to meiosis, all DNA has been replicated during the S phase of the cell cycle, followed by meiotic prophase. During prophase I, the nucleolus and nuclear envelope disappear, and homologous chromosomes pair with one another and undergo genetic recombination, with some genetic exchange taking place in the process. This is called *chromosomal crossover*. During the next phase, metaphase I, homologous chromosome pairs move together along the central metaphase plate. During anaphase I, the microtubules linked to the chromosomes shorten, pulling apart the homologous chromosomes to opposite poles. Even though the homologous chromosomes have separated, the sister chromatids remain together because the centromere remains intact. During telophase I, the microtubules disintegrate, and the cell physically splits during cytokinesis. This completes meiosis I. There may be a period of rest called *interkinesis*, but no additional DNA replication occurs here.

The second meiotic division, meiosis II, then begins with prophase II, during which the nucleolus and nuclear envelope again disappear. During metaphase II, the sister chromatids align at the center plate, and in anaphase II, the sister chromatids are pulled apart toward opposite poles. In telophase II, as in telophase I, the microtubules disintegrate and the nuclear envelopes reform. The second cell split results in a total of four daughter cells from the original parent cell. If the parent cell had *2n* chromosomes, or a diploid number of chromosomes, each daughter cell will have *n* chromosomes, or a haploid number of chromosomes. This completes meiosis.

Alleles are alternative versions of the same gene, such as the gene that determines whether a human has blue or brown eyes. An organism with two copies of the same allele is **homozygous**, and one with two different alleles is **heterozygous**. For example, a human with one gene for blue eyes and one gene for brown eyes is heterozygous, while a human with two genes for blue eyes or two genes for brown eyes is homozygous. In a heterozygous organism, whichever of the two genes is expressed (e.g., whether the human is brown-eyed or blue-eyed) is determined by the dominance of the gene. An allele is dominant if it alone determines the phenotype, or expression, of a heterozygote.

If a plant has a gene for making yellow flowers and a gene for making red flowers, and the red flower gene is dominant, what color will the flowers be?

If you said red, you're correct. A plant that has both the dominant gene for red and the gene for yellow will still look red. The gene for yellow flowers in this case is called **recessive**, as it doesn't contribute to the phenotype (appearance) of a heterozygote (a plant containing two different alleles).

What way would this plant make yellow flowers?

The only way this plant would make yellow flowers is if it had two recessive genes—two genes both coding for yellow flowers.

Punnett Squares

A **Punnett square** is the visual representation of this type of heredity. It can be used to represent the possible phenotypes that offspring of parents with known genotypes could have. Here's how it works:

- The genes of one parent are listed along the left side of a grid.
- The genes of the other parent are listed on top of the grid.
- The genes are then combined to show offspring in the grid.

Let's look at the example with the yellow and red flowers. Let's label the allele for the dominant red gene as **R** and the allele for yellow flowers as **r**. Cross a plant with yellow flowers (genotype must be **rr**) with a plant with red flowers and genotype **Rr**. A genotype of **RR** or **rr** is considered homozygous. A genotype of **Rr** is considered heterozygous.

What possible genotypes and phenotypes can the offspring have? Remember, in a Punnett square, the genes of one parent are listed along one side of the square and the genes of the other parent on top of the square. They are then combined in the offspring as illustrated here:

Plant (rr)

		r	r
Plant (Rr)	R	Rr	Rr
	r	rr	rr

Homozygous Yellow Plant Crossed with Heterozygous Red Plant

The possible genotypes of the offspring are listed inside the square. Their genotype will be either **Rr** or **rr**, causing them to be either red or yellow, respectively.

> 50% of the offspring would be homozygous yellow (**rr**)
>
> 50% of the offspring would be heterozygous red (**Rr**)

What happens if we breed two of the offspring (heterozygous red—**Rr**)? *What would the percentages be then?*

Then the Punnett square would look like this:

Plant (Rr)

		R	r
Plant (Rr)	R	RR	Rr
	r	Rr	rr

Heterozygous Red Plant Crossed with Another Heterozygous Red Plant

> 25% would be homozygous yellow (**rr**)
>
> 50% would be heterozygous red (**Rr**)
>
> 25% would be homozygous red (**RR**)

Punnett squares can also be used for two or more genes. Consider the example below, in which B and b represent the alleles for brown hair (B) and blonde hair (b), and W and w represent widow's peak (W) and absence of a widow's peak (w). One parent is heterozygous for hair color and widow's peak; the other parent is homozygous for blond hair and heterozygous for widow's peak. To begin, match each allele for each gene with each allele for the other gene per parent, as done in the Punnett square below. The Punnett square is then filled out exactly like a simpler Punnett square, so it is important to pay attention to which letters appear in each allele duo.

	bW	bw	bW	bw
BW	BbWW	BbWw	BbWW	BbWw
Bw	BbWw	Bbww	BbWw	Bbww
bW	bbWW	bbWw	bbWW	bbWw
bw	bbWw	bbww	bbWw	bbww

Based on this Punnett square, 75% of the offspring of this cross will have a widow's peak (WW or Ww) and 50% will have brown hair (Bb).

There are also several alternative types of inheritance: incomplete dominance, codominance, sex linkage, multiple-gene contribution, and epistasis:

- **Incomplete dominance** occurs when an allele for a certain trait is not completely expressed over its paired allele. For example, if *R* is the allele for a red flower and *r* is the allele for a white flower, an organism with the genotype *Rr* would be pink if color inheritance follows incomplete dominance because pink is an intermediate between red and white.
- **Codominance** occurs when the contributions of both dominant alleles in a genotype are visible in the phenotype. For example, if *B* represents brown fur and *O* represents orange fur on a cat, an organism with the genotype *BO* might be brown with orange spots or orange with brown spots. Another example of codominance occurs with blood types. Individuals with $I^A I^A$ or $I^A i$ genotypes have type A blood, individuals with IBIB or IBi genotypes have type B blood, and individuals with the ii genotype have type O blood. I^A and I^B both represent dominant alleles that code for proteins on red blood cells. Codominance comes into play for individuals with the genotype $I^A I^B$, as they have type AB blood with both A and B proteins present.
- **Sex linkage** refers to the location of alleles on either the *X* or *Y* chromosome, the sex chromosomes. Humans have far more genes on the X chromosome than on the Y chromosome, so *X*-linked traits are more common than *Y*-linked traits. An example of a sex-linked trait is color blindness, which predominantly affects males.
- Some traits, or phenotypes, may receive contributions from multiple genes. This concept is called the **multiple-gene hypothesis** and can explain why there is such wide variation in particular traits such as skin color or aspects of personality.
- **Epistasis** occurs when the phenotypic expression of one gene depends on the presence of at least one other modifier gene. For example, if a person has the dominant allele for widow's peak at one gene but has a gene that leads to baldness, the widow's peak phenotype will not be expressed.

Practice

Answer the following questions. Consider using a Punnett square to help you.

6. Angelfish come in a number of different colorations. Black angelfish have the genotype (DD), indicating that the black gene is dominant. If you breed a black angelfish (DD) with a recessive gold (gg) genotype, what will result?
   Note: A Dg genotype will produce a hybrid black angelfish that is a milky black coloration.
   black _____%
   hybrid black _____%
   gold _____ %

7. You have your mother's brown eyes. The color of your eyes is an example of
   a. genotype.
   b. allele.
   c. mitosis.
   d. phenotype.

Sex Determination

In many organisms, one of the sexes can have a pair of unmatched chromosomes. In humans, the male has an X chromosome and a much smaller Y chromosome, while the female has two X chromosomes. The combination XX (female) or XY (male) determines the sex of humans. In birds, the males have a matched pair of sex chromosomes (WW), while females have an unmatched pair (WZ). In humans, the sex chromosome supplied by the male determines the sex of the offspring. In birds, the sex chromosome supplied by the female determines the sex. Plants, as well as many animals, lack sex chromosomes. The sex of these organisms is determined by other factors, such as plant hormones or temperature.

Identical twins result when a fertilized egg splits in two. Identical twins have identical chromosomes and can be either two girls or two boys. Two children of different sex born at the same time can't be identical twins and are instead fraternal. Fraternal twins can also be of the same sex. They are genetically not any more alike than siblings born at different times. Fraternal twins result when two different eggs are fertilized by two different sperm cells.

Mutation

Changes in DNA (**mutations**) occur randomly and spontaneously at low rates. Mutations occur more frequently when DNA is exposed to mutagens, including ultraviolet light, X-rays, and certain chemicals. Most mutations either are harmful to or don't affect the organism. In rare cases, however, a mutation can be beneficial to an organism and can help it survive or reproduce, like polar bears having a mutation for white fur. Ultimately, genetic diversity depends on mutations, as mutations are the only source of completely new genetic material. Only mutations in germ cells can create the variation that changes an organism's offspring.

There are several different types of mutations that can occur within a DNA sequence: substitutions, insertions, deletions, and frameshift mutations.

- A **substitution** is a mutation in which one base in a DNA sequence is exchanged for another. Substitutions can drastically affect the produced protein, or they can have no effect at all. There are two main ways in which a substitution can dramatically alter a produced protein. The first is by changing a codon that encodes an amino acid to a codon that encodes a completely different amino acid; if this amino acid is critical for the function of the protein, then that protein may not function correctly. For instance, sickle cell anemia is caused by a substitution mutation in the gene

for β-hemoglobin; even though only one amino acid in the resulting protein is affected, sickle cell anemia results. The second is that a substitution could change a codon to a "stop" codon, namely the DNA sequences TAA, TAG, or TGA. The result of this kind of substitution could be serious because it would result in a truncated, or shortened, protein that is incomplete and might not function. On the other hand, a substitution might have no effect at all. The amino acid code is redundant, which means that several different codons might code for the same amino acid. For example, both AGT and AGC code for serine. So if a substitution changes the T in a codon to a C, serine will still be in the protein, and the protein will not have changed. This is called a **silent mutation**.

- An **insertion** is a mutation in which one or more extra base pairs are added into a DNA sequence. The following is an example of an insertion mutation in a DNA sequence:

Original Sequence
GAC TAG GGA

Mutated Sequence
GAA GCT AGG GA

In this example, the two highlighted bases have been added to the sequence, which alters the codons throughout the sequence.

- A **deletion** is a mutation in which one or more base pairs are removed, or deleted, from a DNA sequence. The following is an example of a deletion mutation in a DNA sequence:

Original Sequence
GAC TAG GGA

Mutated Sequence
GAC GGG A

In this example, the TA from the original sequence have been deleted from the sequence, which again alters the codons throughout the sequence.

- A **frameshift** is a mutation that alters the codons downstream, usually by inserting or deleting a number of base pairs that is not a multiple of three. Both of the provided examples for insertions and deletions are examples of frameshifts because the codons that come after the mutation have changed such that they no longer encode the amino acid they would normally encode. If an insertion or deletion adds or removes three (or a multiple of three) base pairs, this would not be a frameshift mutation because the codons downstream would not have been altered.

Evolution

Evolution is the theory that explains how life developed on earth. It explains the diversity of forms of life, including the vast array of various species across all types of plants and animals.

Through a process of **natural selection**, certain genes or gene combinations give individual members of a species an edge in surviving in the natural world. Such changes, or adaptations, are passed down to future generations and eventually—over very long periods of time—create variations in species or new species altogether.

Evidence for Evolution

Several factors have led scientists to accept the theory of evolution.

Fossil Record

One of the most convincing forms of evidence is the fossil record. **Fossils** are the remains of past life, often in the form of impressions in mud and debris that has since turned into sedimentary rocks, which form during compression of settling mud, debris, and sand. The order of layers of sedimentary rock is consistent with the proposed sequence in which life on Earth evolved. The simplest organisms are located at the bottom layer, while top layers contain increasingly complex and modern organisms; this reflects a pattern that suggests evolution. The process of **carbon dating**, which is the calculation of the consistent rate of carbon decay over time, has been used to confirm how old the fossils are. It also is used to determine that fossils found in the lower layers of sedimentary rock are indeed older than the ones found in the higher layers. This helps scientists to chart evolutionary history based on time. New fossils are turning up all the time; for example, the fossil called *Tiktaalik*, which was found in 2004, is believed to mark the transition from fish to land animals.

Biogeography

Another form of evidence comes from the fact that species tend to resemble nearby species in different habitats more than they resemble species that are in similar habitats but far away. For example, there are marsupials in both North America (opossums) and Australia (possums, koalas, kangaroos, wombats, etc.), but the North American opossums have white and gray fur and look entirely different from the Australian possums and other marsupials.

Comparative Anatomy

Comparative anatomy provides us with another line of evidence. It refers to the fact that the limb bones of different species, for example, are similar. Species that closely resemble one another are considered to be more closely related than species that do not resemble one another. For example, a horse and a donkey are considered to be more closely related than are a horse and a frog. Biological classifications (domain, kingdom, phylum, class, order, family, genus, and species) are based on how organisms are related.

Organisms are classified into a hierarchy of groups and subgroups based on similarities that reflect their evolutionary relationships. The same underlying anatomical structures of groups of bones, nerves, muscles, and organs are found in all animals, even when the functions of these underlying structures differ.

Embryology

Embryology provides another form of evidence for evolution. Embryos go through the developmental stages of their ancestors to some degree. The early embryos of fish, amphibians, reptiles, birds, and mammals all have common features, such as tails.

Comparative Molecular Biology

Comparative molecular biology studies the relatedness of two different species by comparing their DNA. These studies at the molecular level confirm the lines of descent suggested by comparative anatomy and fossil records.

Selection and Adaptation

Darwin proposed that evolution occurs gradually, through mutations and **natural selection**. He argued that some genes or combinations of genes give an individual a survival or reproductive advantage, increasing the chance that these useful combinations of genes will make it to future generations. Whether a given trait is advantageous depends on the environment of the organism.

One example of natural selection can be seen in antibiotic-resistant bacteria. When a drug is used on a species of bacteria, those that cannot resist die and do not produce offspring. Those bacteria that survive pass on the resistance gene to the next generation. Over time, the population of bacteria will become resistant to the antibiotic.

What other possible forms of natural selection can you think of?

Natural selection is only one of several mechanisms by which gene frequency changes in a population. Other factors include mating patterns and breeding between populations. Mating patterns, as an example, may account for why in certain species of birds, such as cardinals and peacocks, the male birds are very brightly colored while the female birds are less so.

A contrast to natural selection is **artificial selection** (or selective breeding)—the process by which farmers or breeders intentionally select for desirable characteristics or traits (e.g., disease resistance, size, etc.). Only individuals with the desired trait are allowed to breed.

Another way in which organisms change is that over time, living organisms adapt to their environments. **Adaptation** is the process of developing specific advantageous features. An adaptation may also be the feature itself. These features may be anatomical (physical features of the body), such as a certain color wing that provides protection from predators by camouflage or fur that allows a predator to get closer to its prey unseen. An adaptation may also be behavioral, such as a certain way of evading predators. For example, some tiger moths confuse their predators, bats, by emitting ultrasonic clicks that jam the bats' echolocation.

In the context of evolution, individuals with certain adaptive traits tend to be more successful reproductively—meaning that they produce more offspring. And what happens to that trait (if you remember back to reproduction and heredity)? Yes, the offspring will inherit the adaptive traits from their parents. Any time a trait results in a reproductive advantage in a population, **selection pressure** is occurring. Think of selection pressure as an evolutionary push or pressure on the population toward the adaptive trait.

A **species** is defined as a group that can interbreed and produce viable offspring. **Speciation** is the evolutionary process by which a new species emerges.

There are a number of other taxonomic levels besides species that are worth knowing, as a species represents the most specific classification for a given organism. From the broadest to the most specific taxonomic level, the eight levels are domain, kingdom, phylum, class, order, family, genus, and species. A widely used mnemonic device that can be used for remembering the order of taxonomic levels is "Determined King Phillip Came Over From Great Spain." The first letters of the words in this sentence represent the corresponding taxonomic levels. For almost any organism, you can find each taxonomic level to see how it relates to other organisms. The following chart shows the taxonomic levels for a red fox and for a human.

TAXONOMIC LEVEL	RED FOX	HUMAN
Domain	Eukarya	Eukarya
Kingdom	Animalia	Animalia
Phylum	Chordata	Chordata
Class	Mammalia	Mammalia
Order	Carnivora	Primates
Family	Canidae	Hominidae
Genus	*Vulpes*	*Homo*
Species	*vulpes*	*sapiens*

You can see that these two organisms have the same broad taxonomic levels, but they diverge at the level of order. That means that the red fox and human share the same domain, kingdom, phylum, and class, but all other taxonomic levels are different.

It is also worth noting for genus and species that the name of a genus is usually capitalized and italicized, while the name of the species is usually lowercase and italicized. When specifying the most specific classification of an organism, we often refer to the genus and species in succession. Humans, for instance, would be *Homo sapiens*.

Practice

8. The fossil record provides evidence for the process of evolution. Another form of evidence for evolution comes from the field of biogeography. Species in different but nearby habitats tend to resemble each other more closely than they resemble species in similar habitats farther away. Which statement explains how this is evidence for evolution?
   a. Neighboring species in different habitats often can share a common ancestor.
   b. Species are less likely to interbreed with their neighbors, and over time they will resemble species farther away.
   c. Species are more likely to interbreed with species farther away, and over time they will resemble species farther away.
   d. Species are not likely to interbreed at all.

9. The peppered moth lives in the United Kingdom and has both light and dark variations. During the Industrial Revolution (1760–1840), many of the trees on which the moths lived became covered with dark soot. Over a period of just 50 years, the population of peppered moths in Manchester, England, changed so that almost the entire local population was made up of dark moths. After the Clean Air Act of 1956, the air quality changed and so did the population of peppered moths: Dark moths became rare.

   This information is an example of
   a. speciation.
   b. meiosis.
   c. extinction.
   d. natural selection.

10. Speciation, or cladogenesis, is the formation of new species over time. During allopatric speciation, a species is split geographically into two (or more) isolated populations. Over time new species emerge. This process provides evidence for the theory of _____.

11. A particular gram negative bacterium is taxonomically named *Escherichia coli*. Its genus is _____.

The Human Body and Health

Since we've reviewed some of the basic elements of life, let's take a look close to home at the human body. The human body is made up of cells, as are all living things. These cells take different characteristics, depending on their purpose, and are organized into systems that govern the functions of the human body, such as the skeletal or nervous system.

Organization and Function

The organization of the body is good to keep in mind, and of course goes from smallest part to larger part. In this case cells, the smallest part of the body, are organized into tissues. Muscle tissue, for example, is made up of muscle cells. Tissues then make up organs, and finally organs (e.g., liver, heart, brain, kidneys) make up body systems.

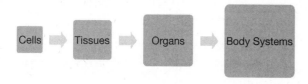

Levels of Body Organization

The body systems interact with each other to make sure the human body functions properly.

The Nervous System

The nervous system allows us to monitor and interact with the environment around us. It is made up of the central nervous system (the brain and spinal cord) and the peripheral nervous system (the nerves that transport signals to and from the brain). Messages are sent from our sense organs via nerves to other body systems. Our sense organs include the eyes, nose, ears, skin, and tongue.

The nervous system is the boss of the body systems and coordinates all of the systems working with one another to maintain a state of balance or **homeostasis** (function within a normal range). For example, shivering, goose bumps, and sweating are your body's response to being too cold or too hot. If your skin senses cold and sends that signal through the spinal cord, signals come back to the muscles to contract, causing shivering. In contrast, as your temperature rises, the blood vessels in your skin get larger. This process, called *vasodilation*, allows for cooling of the blood. Sweat glands are also activated when you are hot in an attempt to cool the body and return to homeostasis.

The peripheral nervous system can be further divided into the somatic and autonomic nervous systems. The **somatic nervous system** includes the sensory neurons that relay information about the environment from the organs and muscles to the central nervous system, as well as the motor neurons that relay information from the brain and spinal cord to the muscles. In short, the somatic nervous system is associated with perception of the environment and voluntary control of bodily movement. On the other hand, the autonomic nervous system controls bodily functions that are not consciously regulated. This includes breathing and digestion.

The **autonomic nervous system** can be broken down into the sympathetic and parasympathetic nervous systems. Stimulation of the sympathetic nervous system activates the fight-or-flight response, while stimulation of the parasympathetic system returns the body to normal and regulates various typical bodily functions. For example, the sympathetic nervous system controls such functions as pupil dilation, increased heart rate and blood pressure, and goose bump production, while the **parasympathetic nervous system** controls such functions as pupil constriction, decreased heart rate and blood pressure, and increased salivary secretion.

KEY ORGANS IN THE CENTRAL NERVOUS SYSTEM	FUNCTIONS
Brain	Command center of the nervous system; monitors all conscious and unconscious body processes; coordinates body organs; controls voluntary actions and senses
Spinal Cord	Nerve bundle that runs down the back from the brain; relays internal and external information from the body to the brain

The cerebral cortex consists of four lobes, each of which has a unique set of functions:

- The **frontal lobe** is found at the front of the brain, as its name indicates. This region of the brain is responsible for voluntary motor skills, higher-level cognition and reasoning, and integration of longer non–task based memories.
- The **parietal lobe** is found in the middle region of the brain and is involved in the processing of tactile sensory information, which includes pain and pressure. Essential to the ability of the body to process its sensory information is the somato-sensory cortex, which is found in this lobe of the brain.
- The **temporal lobe** is found toward the bottom of the brain and is responsible for interpretation of speech and other sounds that are heard. The temporal lobe is also involved with the formation of memories, largely due to the presence of the hippocampus in this lobe.
- The **occipital lobe,** found in the back portion of the brain, is associated with the interpretation of visual stimuli and information. The occipital lobe includes the primary visual cortex, which receives and integrates information sent from the retinas of the eyes.

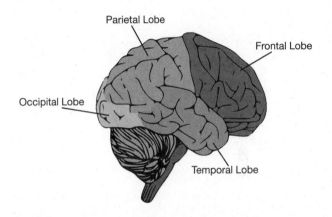

Parietal Lobe
Frontal Lobe
Occipital Lobe
Temporal Lobe

The Musculoskeletal System

The musculoskeletal system includes your bones—all 206 of them—as well as your ligaments, muscles, tendons, and cartilage. The bones meet at joints and are held together by ligaments. Bones are connected to the muscles through the tendons. Cartilage is flexible connective tissue (in the tip of your nose and ears, for instance) and is found in some of your joints, like the knee.

The skeletal system includes a number of different types of joints:

- **Gliding joints,** like the intercarpal and intertarsal joints in the hands and feet
- **Hinge joints,** like the elbow and knee joints
- **Pivot joints,** like the proximal radio-ulnar joints
- **Ball-and-socket joints,** like the hip and shoulder joints
- **Saddle joints,** like the first carpometacarpal joints
- **Ellipsoid joints,** like the radiocarpal joints

There are three main types of muscle tissue:

- **Cardiac** muscle can be found in the walls of the heart. These muscles are under involuntary control and their fibers appear striated due to the presence of repeating functional units called *sarcomeres*.
- **Skeletal** muscle fibers are present in muscles that are attached to the skeleton. They also appear striated, but these muscles are under voluntary control.
- **Smooth muscles** are located within the walls of hollow internal organs, excluding the heart. Their fibers are spindle-shaped rather than striated in appearance, and these muscles are under involuntary control.

The Circulatory System

The circulatory system moves blood through the body. It includes the heart, blood, and blood vessels. The function of blood is to carry nutrients and oxygen to the cells and to transport waste products from cells. Arteries carry oxygen-rich blood from the heart. Veins carry blood back to the heart. The lymphatic system is also part of the circulatory system. It collects excess tissue fluids. Have you ever had swollen glands? If so, you have felt your lymphatic system at work.

A helpful way to keep track of the functions of arteries and veins is to remember that the letter *A* begins "arteries" and "away"; therefore, arteries carry blood away from the heart. Veins, in turn, have the opposite function, bringing blood toward the heart.

The **heart** is the driving force of the circulatory system. It is found in the chest between the lungs, though not exactly central; in humans, the heart can be found just to the left of the central axis. The four chambers of the heart are the **right atrium**, the **right ventricle**, the **left atrium**, and the **left ventricle**. Blood is transported from the rest of the body to the heart through the superior and inferior vena cavae. The blood enters the heart through the right atrium. It is then pumped into the right ventricle through the tricuspid valve. The right ventricle then pumps the blood through the pulmonary valve into the pulmonary artery, and then into the lungs to be oxygenated. After oxygenation, the blood passes through the pulmonary veins into the left atrium. From here, the blood passes through the mitral valve and enters the left ventricle. Finally, the oxygenated blood exits the heart through the **aortic valve**, at which point it enters the aorta and can then be transported throughout the body.

The Respiratory System

The respiratory system helps in bringing oxygen into and removing waste products from our bodies. Some important parts of the respiratory system are the lungs, the larynx, and the diaphragm, which is a thick muscle that is just beneath the lungs. The diaphragm controls the mechanism of breathing by contracting during inhalation and relaxing during exhalation. Oxygen moves into the blood and carbon dioxide is taken out of the lungs at the alveoli.

The following table summarizes the functions of the main organs in the respiratory system:

ORGAN	FUNCTION
Nasal Cavity	Air entry and exit; foreign particle entrapment by cilia and mucus
Pharynx	Tube that connects the mouth to the larynx for air passage
Larynx	Tube that connects the pharynx to the trachea for air passage and houses the vocal cords
Trachea	Tube that connects the larynx to the bronchi; often called the *windpipe*
Bronchi	Airways that conduct air into the lungs; not responsible for gas exchange
Lungs	Organs responsible for respiration, that is, the transfer of inhaled oxygen into the bloodstream, and the removal and release of carbon dioxide; capable of expanding and contracting to accommodate air
Alveoli	Tiny sacs through which oxygen and carbon dioxide gases are exchanged
Diaphragm	Muscular organ that contracts to expand and relaxes to contract the thoracic cavity

The Digestive System

Your digestive system is made up of organs that break down the food you eat into usable molecules that can be absorbed by the blood. These molecules are necessary for life. The breakdown of food starts in the mouth with the enzymes found in saliva. Food then passes through the esophagus to the stomach. Enzymes in the stomach further break down food. The term **chyme** describes the mixture of digested food and digesting enzymes formed in the stomach that enters the small intestine. The liver produces bile (stored in the gallbladder), which breaks down fat into small droplets. When chyme enters the small intestine, the gallbladder releases bile into the intestine to help further break down food. The three regions of the small intestine, in order, are the **duodenum**, the **jejunum**, and the **ileum**. Most of the chemical digestion in the small intestine occurs in the duodenum, as this is the portion of the small intestine that receives digestive fluids from the pancreas to help break down starches, fats, and proteins.

The lining of the small intestine has many tiny folds called *microvilli*, which absorb the products of digestion and transfer them to the circulatory system. The large intestine or colon is the last part of the digestive system. The function of the large intestine is to collect waste products. The waste products of digestion, or feces, are removed through the rectum and anus.

Most of the structures that make up living organisms are made from amino acids, carbohydrates, and lipids (often called *fats*). **Metabolism** is the process of building amino acids and other molecules needed for life (as during the construction of cells and tissues) or breaking them down and using them as a source of energy, as in the digestion and use of food. Within cells, the **mitochondria** perform this latter process.

The body needs nutrients to function properly. We get nutrients from the foods we eat. The nutrients that a body needs vary depending on the **calories** that a person burns in a day. A calorie is the way we measure energy in food. For example, a moderately active 30-year-old male of average height and weight needs about 2,600 calories daily to maintain weight. A 30-year-old moderately active female needs approximately 2,200 calories daily to maintain weight.

A **calorie** is a unit of energy. Technically, a calorie is the energy needed to raise the temperature of 1 gram of water 1°C (usually defined as 4.184 joules). Most of us think of calories in relation to food, as in "This apple has 100 calories." It turns out that the calories stated on a food package are actually **kilocalories** (1,000 calories = 1 kilocalorie). A food calorie contains 4,184 joules. A can of soda containing 200 food calories contains 200,000 regular calories, or 200 kilocalories. A gallon of gasoline contains 31,000 kilocalories.

When you consider this information, how many regular calories does a moderately active 30-year-old male of average height and weight need to maintain weight? The answer is 2,600,000 calories!

The Endocrine System

The endocrine system is made up of glands in different parts of the body. The thyroid, parathyroid, pineal, adrenal, pancreas, and pituitary are all glands of the endocrine system. These glands send out chemical messages via hormones to the rest of the body. Hormones are carried in the blood. Just as the nervous system works to maintain homeostasis in the body, the glands in the endocrine system regulate themselves with a type of feedback system that works to keep things in homeostasis.

An example of how the endocrine system regulates itself, and what happens in a disease state, can be seen in glucose (sugar) regulation in the blood.

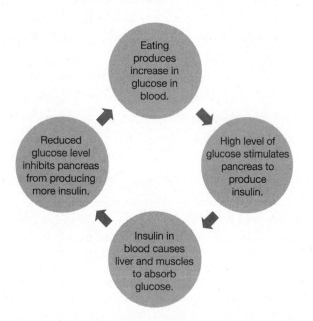

Feedback Mechanism in Glucose Regulation

In diabetes, a metabolic disorder, parts of this system are impaired or do not function. In type 1 diabetes, the body does not produce insulin at all. People with this kind of diabetes have to take insulin throughout their lives. People with type 2 diabetes have difficulty using the insulin that is produced by the pancreas. It often builds up in their blood, which means their cells are not getting the sugar they need. Treatment is necessary for the body to function properly since the endocrine system is unable to create homeostasis itself.

The Reproductive System

All living organisms reproduce. Some very simple organisms just divide into two. Other organisms, including humans, have developed complex sexual reproduction systems. Sexual reproduction for humans involves the joining of two gametes, an egg (female gamete) and a sperm (male gamete). Each of the gametes carries part of that parent's genetic code (DNA), so the offspring will contain genetic information from each of the parents.

Males and females have very different reproductive systems. The following table lists a number of key organs in the male reproductive system, along with their functions.

ORGAN	FUNCTION
Penis	Allows for urine and semen passage, though never simultaneously; male organ used for sexual intercourse
Scrotum	Sac that contains and regulates the temperature of the testes
Testes	Produce sperm and testosterone, the primary male sex hormone
Epididymis	Long, coiled tube that stores and transports sperm cells from the testes
Vas deferens	Transports mature sperm to the urethra
Urethra	Transports urine from the bladder to the outside of the body and ejaculates semen, though never simultaneously
Prostate gland	Nourishes sperm cells
Cowper's glands	Lubricate the urethra and neutralize sperm acidity
Seminal vesicles	Produce fructose to provide sperm with the energy to move

The following table lists some of the key organs in the female reproductive system and their functions.

ORGAN	FUNCTION
Vagina	The birth canal; connects the cervix with the external environment outside of the body
Uterus	Site of fetal development; the main chamber is called the *corpus,* and the section that leads to the vagina is called the *cervix,* through which a channel runs that allows for sperm entry and menstrual blood exit
Clitoris	Sensitive protrusion that is sensitive to stimulation
Ovaries	Produce hormones and eggs
Fallopian tubes	Site of fertilization; tubes through which eggs travel to the uterus from the ovaries
Urethra	Transports urine from the bladder to the outside of the body
Bartholin's glands	Produce mucus secretions

The Integumentary System

The **integumentary system** protects the body from various kinds of damage, serves as a sensory receptor, excretes waste through perspiration, heals minor wounds, and maintains the structure of the human body. This system includes the skin and skin-based structures, such as hair and nails. The two major layers of the skin are the **dermis** and the **epidermis**. The outermost layer of the skin is the epidermis, composed of epithelial cells. It serves as an initial barrier between the body and the outside world. Keratinocyte cells dominate the epidermis and produce keratin, which protects and waterproofs the body. The next layer internally is the dermis, which consists of the papillary and reticular layers. The papillary layer is composed of areolar connective tissue, while the reticular layer consists of dense irregular connective tissue. Present in the dermis are such structures as hair roots, follicles, and sensory nerve endings. In addition to housing these features, the dermis also provides elasticity to the skin. The subcutaneous layer is composed of adipose tissue and is found beneath the dermis. This layer, also called the *hypodermis*, is not technically considered part of the skin and is involved in thermoregulation and fat storage.

Practice

12. Match the functions in **a** through **g** with the body systems listed by filling in the blanks.

  a. movement _____

  b. breathing _____

  c. metabolism _____

  d. homeostasis _____

  e. blood flow _____

  f. hormone regulation _____

  g. reproduction _____

    ▪ digestive system
    ▪ endocrine system
    ▪ circulatory system
    ▪ musculoskeletal system
    ▪ reproductive system
    ▪ nervous system
    ▪ respiratory system

13. Which answer best represents the levels of organization from simple to complex?

  a. cell, tissue, organ, body system

  b. tissue, cell, organ, body system

  c. organ, tissue, cell, body system

  d. body system, organ, tissue, cell

14. Which is an example of your body trying to maintain homeostasis?

  a. bleeding

  b. urination

  c. sweating

  d. digestion

15. Complete the table with checkmarks to describe the three types of muscle tissue:

MUSCLE TYPE	STRIATED APPEARANCE?	VOLUNTARY CONTROL?
Cardiac		
Skeletal		
Smooth		

16. True or false: The olfactory and optic nerves are part of the peripheral nervous system.

  _____

17. The lobe of the brain most responsible for processing touch stimuli is the

  a. frontal lobe.

  b. parietal lobe.

  c. temporal lobe.

  d. occipital lobe.

18. Gas exchange in the respiratory system occurs through the

  a. alveoli.

  b. bronchi.

  c. diaphragm.

  d. larynx.

19. Bile is produced in the _____ and is responsible for breaking down _____.

20. What is the difference between type 1 and type 2 diabetes? _____

_____

_____

21. How do the functions of the urethra differ between males and females? _____

_____

_____

22. Label the layers of the integumentary system using the words in the box.

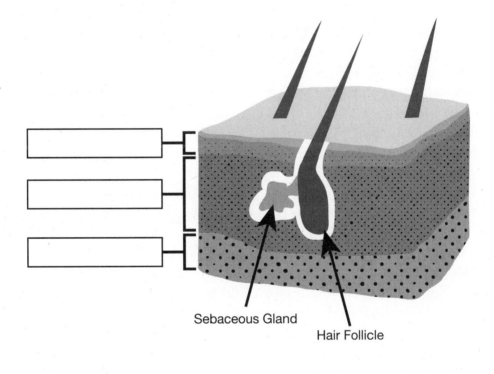

Sebaceous Gland

Hair Follicle

| dermis | epidermis | subcutaneous layer |

Disease and Illness

All living things are subject to disease and illness. Disease can be classified as either infectious or noninfectious. However, the symptoms involved in both can be similar.

Infectious Disease

Many diseases are caused by **pathogens** that invade a host body. Pathogens need a host in order to survive and multiply. Some examples of pathogens are bacteria, viruses, and fungi. These pathogens can spread through **direct body contact**, body fluids, and contact with an object that an infected person has touched (some viruses, like the common cold virus, can exist outside the body for a brief period before they get passed on to another host). One way individuals can protect themselves from infection from these pathogens is by hand washing.

Other diseases are transmitted through the air. This kind of disease is called an **airborne** disease. In this case, viruses, bacteria, or fungi can be spread through coughing, sneezing, dust, spraying of liquids, or other activities that create aerosol particles or droplets. Tuberculosis is an example of an airborne disease. Tuberculosis is also an infectious disease. Treatment and vaccines for tuberculosis exist, and this disease has been almost eliminated in some parts of the world. However, the total number of people in the world infected with tuberculosis keeps growing. Individuals can prevent infection from airborne diseases by avoiding close contact with infected persons.

Blood-borne viruses are transmitted through the blood or bodily fluids. HIV is an example of a blood-borne virus; there is no chance of contracting the virus unless one comes in contact with the blood or bodily fluids of an infected person.

Sexually transmitted diseases (STDs) are diseases that are frequently transmitted through sexual contact. HIV is also an example of an STD, as are gonorrhea, chlamydia, syphilis, human papillomavirus (HPV), and herpes. Many STDs, including HIV and herpes, are incurable. There is a vaccine for HPV.

Noninfectious Disease

If a disease cannot spread from person to person, then it is considered **noninfectious**. Two examples of noninfectious diseases are cancer and heart disease.

Noninfectious diseases can be classified as follows:

- **Hereditary diseases.** Hereditary diseases are caused by genetic disorders that are passed down from previous generations. Since they are inherited, they are more difficult to treat because they are a part of a person's **genetic makeup**.
- **Age-related diseases.** Some diseases start to develop as the body gets older and does not work as efficiently to battle routine diseases and **degenerative diseases** such as Alzheimer's disease. Alzheimer's disease causes mild to severe memory loss or distortion, forgetfulness, anxiety, and sometimes aggressive behavior.

- **Environmentally induced diseases.** An environment that has been polluted with toxins and hazardous waste can affect the population living in or around it. Toxic chemicals in polluted groundwater can cause cancer. Exposure to asbestos can lead to serious lung problems.

Staying healthy by taking care of the body is important in fighting and preventing disease. Diet and lifestyle are major factors that can influence susceptibility to many diseases. Drug abuse, smoking, drinking alcohol, and poor diet, as well as a lack of exercise may increase the risk of developing certain diseases, including type 2 diabetes, heart disease, and some cancers. Recently, scientists and physicians have reported that the numbers of younger people developing diseases (such as type 2 diabetes) are increasing. This is likely related to the increasing rate of obesity among young people. Since 1980, the number of overweight children has doubled and the number of overweight adolescents has tripled.

Looking for Symptoms

Before diagnosing a patient with a disease, a doctor looks for telltale symptoms. Most diseases have specific symptoms caused by processes in the body. Some common symptoms present in many illnesses are fever, nausea, and pain. A doctor is trained to look for signs and symptoms to give a correct diagnosis and issue proper treatment. Specific blood tests and X-rays are special methods that are used to diagnose some diseases.

Epidemics

An **epidemic** is a disease outbreak that has infected a considerable portion of the population and that continues to spread rapidly. Epidemics can occur when there is no medicine for the disease, when diseases develop a resistance to medicine and drugs, or when environmental conditions are favorable for a specific type of disease. For example, cancer is rampant in areas with toxic chemicals and high levels of radiation. Acquired immune deficiency syndrome (AIDS), which is caused by the human immunodeficiency virus (HIV), is an epidemic that has killed millions of people worldwide.

Natural and Medical Defenses

Humans and most other living beings have a natural built-in disease-fighting mechanism known as the **immune system**. The immune system is composed of cells, molecules, and organs that defend the body against pathogens. The immune system is responsible for finding the pathogen in the body and killing it, rendering it harmless, or expelling it from the body.

The development and use of vaccines and antibiotics have added to our defenses against diseases. Not only have advances in medicine found ways to fight disease from inside the body, but methods have also been developed to prevent the onset of disease.

Vaccines

Vaccines are usually made from either a dead version of an actual organism known to cause an immune response (such as a virus) or from a weakened or inactive form of the organism. By presenting the body with a weaker or deactivated form of an organism that would normally make a person very ill, the body will produce an immune response without causing any illness. Then if the body ever comes in contact with the strong form of a virus, the **antibodies** that were formed during the immune response to the weaker version will be able to fight off this strong version.

Some people are concerned about the safety of vaccines, but scientists have not found any significant safety concerns related to vaccinations. In the United States, all vaccines must be approved by the U.S. Food and Drug Administration (FDA) and go through extensive testing and trials before they can be used. Some very serious diseases, including smallpox, measles, and polio, have been almost eradicated through vaccination.

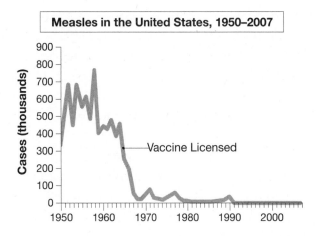

Measles in the United States, 1950–2007

According to the United Nations Children's Fund (UNICEF), vaccines save approximately nine million lives annually around the world.

Antibiotics and Resistance

Antibiotics are chemical compounds that kill bacteria without harming our own cells. Some antibiotics, such as penicillin, kill bacteria by preventing it from synthesizing a cell wall. Other antibiotics interfere with bacterial growth by disrupting their genes or protein production. Bacteria can become resistant to antibiotics—there are strains of bacteria that are resistant to every known antibiotic.

In every population, a small number of bacteria naturally have genes that make them resistant to antibiotics. With increased exposure to antibiotics, a normal population of bacteria, a few of which are resistant, becomes resistant on average. This is a result of natural selection. The bacteria that survive are the ones that are resistant. Their offspring are also resistant, and as a result, the whole population becomes resistant.

Some resistance enables bacteria to survive in the presence of an antibiotic. Another kind of resistance enables the bacteria to actually destroy the antibiotic. This kind of resistance is most dangerous. For example, someone who took antibiotics for treating acne could accumulate bacteria that are capable of destroying the antibiotic. If that same person became infected with a serious disease that is treated with the same antibiotic, the resistant bacteria could destroy the antibiotic before it was able to act on the disease.

Ecological Networks

Just as the human body has systems, an ecological community also has a network. The many species in a community interact in many ways, competing for space and resources, sometimes as predator and prey, or as host and parasite.

Flow of Energy in Ecosystems

The energy in an ecosystem always flows in a specific direction. Starting with plants and other photosynthesizing organisms, they harness and convert solar energy and supply the rest of the food chain. They are considered **producers**. Herbivores (plant eaters) are next on the energy flow, as they obtain energy directly from plants and are considered **primary consumers**. **Secondary consumers** eat primary consumers, and include carnivores, who obtain energy only by eating other animals, and omnivores, who eat both meat and plants. Animals that eat the secondary consumers are called **tertiary consumers**, while **decomposers** feed on dead organisms. The flow of energy can then be represented as follows:

Producers → Primary Consumers → Secondary Consumers → Tertiary Consumers → Decomposers

Flow of Energy in Ecosystem Food Chain

Producers are greater in number in most ecosystems than primary, secondary, and tertiary consumers, as shown in the following diagram. Think about the number of insects versus the number of foxes in one forest ecosystem, for example. If the foxes were to outnumber the insects or the plants, they would soon starve.

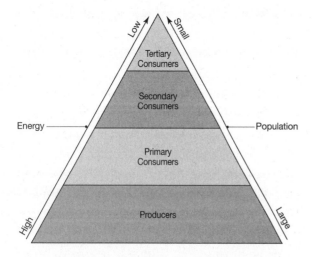

Energy Flow and Population Size in Ecosystems

The food chain is not the only example of the interdependence of organisms. Species often have to compete for food and space, so the increase in population of one can cause the decrease in population of the other. Organisms also may have a **symbiotic** relationship (live in close association), which could be classified as parasitism, commensalism, or mutualism.

- In a **parasitic** relationship, one organism benefits at the expense of the other.
- **Commensalism** is symbiosis in which one organism benefits and the other is neither harmed nor rewarded.
- In **mutualism**, both organisms benefit.

Under ideal conditions, with ample food and space and no predators, all living organisms have the capacity to reproduce infinitely. However, resources are limited, limiting the population of a species. This is called the **carrying capacity** of the population. The carrying capacity of a population is the maximum population size that the environment can sustain given the necessary resources (food, habitat, water) available in the environment. Expanding beyond that will usually result in the organisms self-limiting by moving away or not procreating, or by the organisms overwhelming that environment.

Practice

Select from the following three terms to fill in the blanks in questions 23–25:

- parasitism
- commensalism
- mutualism

23. African oxpeckers feed on the insects that are on the backs of zebras and other large African animals. This is an example of _____, a type of symbiotic relationship.

24. Lice feed on the skin and blood of the host. This is an example of _____, a type of symbiotic relationship.

25. Some spiders build their webs on blades of grass. This is an example of _____, a type of symbiotic relationship.

Humans' Influence on the Environment

Humans may be the exception to the carrying capacity rule, as our species probably comes closest to having a seemingly infinite reproductive capacity. The population keeps increasing. When we need more food, we grow more, and when we need more space, we clear some and end up damaging or even destroying other ecosystems. Humans modify ecosystems and destroy habitats through direct harvesting, pollution, atmospheric changes, and other factors. These actions are threatening current global stability and have the potential to cause irreparable damage.

Climate change is one example of the impact humans have on their environment. Scientists now agree that the climate is changing as a result of human activities. Warming of the atmosphere results from increased levels of carbon dioxide and other gases (greenhouse gases), which produce a **greenhouse effect**. The greenhouse effect occurs when the sun's rays, after hitting the earth's crust and bouncing back into space, get trapped in the atmosphere because of the greenhouse gases. What happens when the rays cannot escape the earth's atmosphere? The trapped heat causes a rise in global temperature.

There are other visible examples of how human behavior can disrupt ecosystems.

Invasive species are animal or plant species that are non-native and invade or take over the niche of a native species of an ecosystem. They can have a substantial negative impact on an ecosystem because they use resources such as nutrients, light, physical space, water, or food that the native species need to survive. The relationship to human behavior is that invasive species are sometimes purposely or accidentally introduced by humans into an ecosystem.

An example of an invasive species that you may be familiar with is the kudzu vine, now very common in the southeastern United States.

Desertification is another area of human influence on the environment. This particular situation occurs when an already dry land area becomes increasingly arid and is less able to support plants and animals. Humans contribute to desertification of ecosystems through deforestation (often for fuel or for construction materials), overgrazing, and poor farming practices.

The impact of humans on an environment is often catastrophic. Awareness of the human influence is important for understanding the breaks in some ecological networks.

Life Science Review

1. Answer the question based on the information and graph.

WHAT CAUSES COLONY COLLAPSE DISORDER?

Out of some 100 crop species that provide 90% of food worldwide, 71 of these are pollinated by bees. Over the past six years, colony collapse disorder (CCD) has wiped out an estimated 10 million beehives, worth $2 billion. Scientists have suspected that pesticides, disease-bearing parasites, and poor nutrition may be to blame.

This graph shows the number of honey-producing colonies in the United States since 1940.

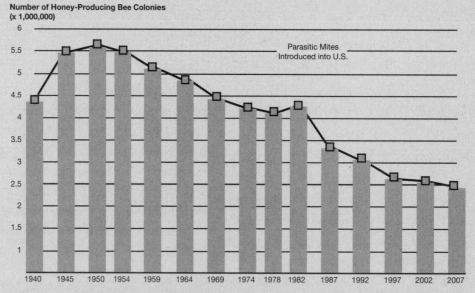

Number of Honey-Producing Bee Colonies (x 1,000,000)

Parasitic Mites Introduced into U.S.

Data source: U.S. Department of Agriculture (USDA)'s National Agricultural Statistics Service (NASS). NB: Data collected for producers with five or more colonies. Honey-producing colonies are the maximum number of colonies from which honey was taken during the year. It is possible to take honey from colonies that did not survive the entire year.

What can you conclude from the information on the graph?

a. Parasitic mites may have contributed to a decline in bee populations.

b. Parasitic mites have caused the decline in bee populations.

c. Bee populations are going to go extinct because of parasitic mites.

d. There was a steady increase in bee populations until the introduction of the parasitic mite.

2. Tapeworms are segmented flatworms that attach themselves to the insides of the intestines of host animals such as cows, pigs, and humans. They survive by eating the host's partly digested food, depriving the host of nutrients. This is an example of which kind of relationship?

a. mutualism

b. commensalism

c. speciation

d. parasitism

Use the following information to answer questions 3–5.

Radiocarbon decays at a measurable rate, called its half-life. The unstable carbon-14 (^{14}C) atom has a half-life of 5,730 years. In 5,730 years, half of the ^{14}C atoms will have decayed into a stable nitrogen atom. Scientists measure the amount of radiocarbon (^{14}C) in the fossil to determine its age.

This graph shows the percentage of radiocarbon remaining over time:

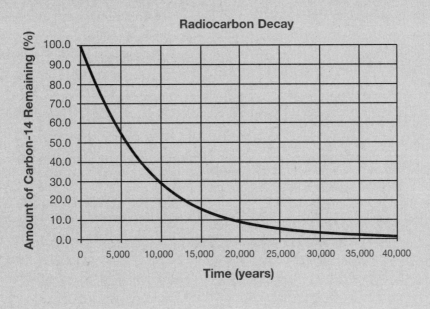

Radiocarbon Decay

3. After 10,000 years, _____% of the carbon-14 remains.

4. After 25,000 years, _____% of the carbon-14 remains.

5. A scientist finds a fossilized bone that has about 25% of the natural amount of the ^{14}C remaining. Using the chart, what is the approximate age of the bone?
   The bone is roughly _____ years old.

6. Which of the following statements explain(s) how biogeography is evidence for evolution? Check all that apply.
   ❑ Offspring carry the traits of both parents.
   ❑ Different species are not likely to interbreed.
   ❑ The fossil record shows the sequence of evolution in layers of sediment.
   ❑ Species in different habitats often can share a common ancestor.

7. Cells are the building blocks of life. Which of the following is NOT true about cells?
   a. Only some cells contain genetic material.
   b. Given the right conditions, cells will remain alive outside of the body.
   c. Cells respond to their environments.
   d. All cells contain a membrane that controls which molecules enter the cell.

8. The genotype of an organism affects the phenotype of that same organism. Label each of the following as either *genotype* or *phenotype*.

Recessive eye color genes _____

Blue eyes _____

Sex determination _____

Female _____

Curling tongue _____

Dominant hair color genes _____

9. Mitosis and meiosis are both forms of cellular reproduction. Mitosis is the splitting of a cell into two cells, with all the same genetic information being reproduced in both new cells. Meiosis involves splitting of a cell, with the genetic information being split in half. Label each of the following parts of cellular reproduction as either *mitosis* or *meiosis*.

Skin regeneration _____

Blood production _____

Pollen production _____

Growth of a multicellular organism _____

Egg cell production _____

10. What is one of the current dangers of using antibiotics for problems like acne?

a. The acne is not cured.

b. Antibiotics are being used for something they aren't meant to be used for.

c. Bacteria become resistant to that antibiotic.

d. Bacteria end up on the person's face.

11. Place each of the organisms listed under the appropriate heading to show its place in the food chain:

PRODUCERS	PRIMARY CONSUMERS	SECONDARY CONSUMERS	TERTIARY CONSUMERS	DECOMPOSERS

- mouse
- cow
- snake
- ant
- grasshopper
- hawk
- mushroom
- fern
- human
- bacteria
- grass
- cougar

Answers and Explanations

Chapter Practice

1.

INTERIOR PARTS OF A CELL	DESCRIPTION
nucleus	**b.** where the DNA of a cell is found
mitochondria	**c.** the site in the cell where substances are broken down to obtain energy
ribosomes	**d.** the part of the cell where the synthesis of protein takes place
plasma membrane	**a.** the element that controls the transfer of material into and out of the cell

2. Animal cells: **centrioles**
   Plant cells: **cell walls; vacuoles** (found mostly in plant cells)

3. *Facilitated transport* and *passive transport* refer to **the movement of molecules across a cell membrane**.

4. **carbohydrate.** The molecule consists of two saccharides linked by a glycosidic linkage, and it fits the $C_m(H_2O)_n$ formula. This molecule is sucrose.

5. **c.** Aerobic respiration produces 36-38 molecules of ATP, while anaerobic respiration produces 2 molecules of ATP. Therefore, aerobic respiration is approximately 18–19 ($36 \div 2$, $38 \div 2$) times more efficient than anaerobic respiration specifically with regard to the production of ATP.

6. Black: **0%**; hybrid black: **100%**; gold: **0%**

Parent (DD)

	D	D
g	Dg	Dg
g	Dg	Dg

Parent (gg)

As you can see from the Punnett square, when you cross a black angelfish (DD) with a recessive gold angelfish (gg), all of the offspring (100%) will be hybrid (Dg).

7. **d.** Phenotype is the physical or behavioral expression of a gene (e.g., eye color, hair color). Choice **a** is incorrect because a genotype is the genetic coding. Choice **b** is incorrect because an allele is an alternative version of the same gene. Choice **c** is also incorrect because mitosis is a process of cell division.

8. **a.** Choice **a** explains how one species can diverge into two species over time when divided into two separate habitats. A classic example of this is the case of Darwin's finches on the Galapagos Islands, where finch species diverged from a common ancestor to adapt to the unique habitats of each island. Answer choices **b**, **c**, and **d** do not explain how biogeography is evidence for evolution.

9. **d.** According to natural selection, whether a given trait is advantageous depends on the environment of the organism. In this case the moths that were better camouflaged (those that were the color of the soot-covered trees) survived and reproduced. No new species developed, and therefore this is not an example of speciation (choice **a**). Meiosis (choice **b**) is cell division. This is not an example of extinction (when there are no more individuals of a species left alive); therefore, choice **c** is not correct.

10. This process provides evidence for the theory of evolution. Evolution is the gradual change of inherited characteristics in a population over time.

11. *Escherichia.* In a taxonomic name like *Escherichia coli*, the first word, capitalized, is the genus, while the second word, lowercase, is the species.

12. **a.** movement: **musculoskeletal system**, which provides structure and allows for movement.

   b. breathing: **respiratory system**, consisting of the organs that help with inhaling and exhaling.

   c. metabolism: **digestive system**, consisting of the organs that aid in breaking down food.

   d. homeostasis: **nervous system**, which is primarily responsible for maintaining functioning within a normal range.

   e. blood flow: **circulatory system**, which controls blood flow through the body.

   f. hormone regulation: **endocrine system**, made up of glands that regulate hormones in the body.

   g. reproduction: **reproductive system**, consisting of the organs involved in producing offspring.

13. **a.** Cells are the smallest and simplest unit in an organism. Tissues are made up of cells (e.g., muscle tissue is made of muscle cells). Organs are made of tissues (a heart is made of muscle and fibrous tissues), and finally, organs are organized into body systems (e.g., the nervous system, the digestive system, etc.).

14. **c.** Sweating is an example of the body trying to maintain homeostasis through evaporative cooling. Choice **a** is incorrect because bleeding is a result of an injury to the body and does not result in homeostasis. Urination is the excretion of waste products, not the body trying to maintain homeostasis, so choice **b** is incorrect. Choice **d** is incorrect because digestion is the process of breaking down the food we eat so it can be used by our body for fuel. It in itself is not a process for maintaining homeostasis.

15.

MUSCLE TYPE	STRIATED APPEARANCE?	VOLUNTARY CONTROL?
Cardiac	✔	
Skeletal	✔	✔
Smooth		

16. **True.** The brain and spinal cord constitute the central nervous system. The rest of the nerves, including sensory nerves, are part of the peripheral nervous system. Olfactory and optic nerves are sensory nerves related to smelling and vision, respectively.

17. **b.** The parietal lobe contains the somatosensory cortex, which is important for processing of sensory information like touch stimuli.

18. **a.** Oxygen and carbon dioxide are exchanged through the alveoli. The other three indicated organs are not in any way involved in the physical exchange of gases.

19. **liver; fat.** Bile aids the digestive process by breaking fat down into small droplets.

20. People with type 1 diabetes are incapable of insulin production. In contrast, those with type 2 diabetes are incapable of using the insulin made by the pancreas, resulting in high blood sugar as it builds up in the blood.

21. In males, the urethra serves as a passageway for both urine and semen, while in females, the urethra only serves as a passageway for urine.

22.

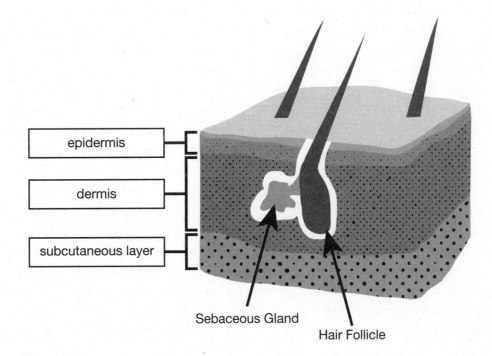

Sebaceous Gland

Hair Follicle

The epidermis is the outer layer of the skin. The dermis is the layer of the skin in which hair follicles can be found. The innermost layer of this surface is the subcutaneous layer; an easy way to remember this is by looking at its name, as the prefix "sub-" means "below" and "cutaneous" refers to an outer covering (i.e., the skin).

23. mutualism. In this case, both the oxpeckers and zebras are benefiting, which describes a mutualistic relationship. Oxpeckers get food, and the host animals are relieved of the bothersome insects.

24. parasitism. The lice are benefiting, and the hosts are being deprived of blood and skin, which is clearly a parasitic relationship.

25. commensalism. Spiders are using the grass as a place to build their nest, but there is no impact on the grass, positive or negative.

Life Science Review

1. a. The only conclusion you can draw based on the information in the graph is that the parasitic mites *may have contributed* to the decline in bee populations; therefore, choice **a** is the correct answer. The graph does not support a causal relationship. The bee population was generally in decline prior to the introduction in 1983, so we cannot conclude definitively that the mites caused the decline, so choice **b** is incorrect. Although there is a downward trend in the population, there is no way to conclude that the population will go extinct, so choice **c** is incorrect. Choice **d** is incorrect because there was a general decline (not an increase) in the population prior to the introduction of the mite.

2. d. The question states that tapeworms are benefiting and the hosts (cows, pigs, humans) are being deprived of nutrition, which is a parasitic relationship. Parasitism describes a relationship between two organisms where one benefits at the expense of the other. Choice **a** is incorrect because mutualism is a relationship in which both organisms benefit, and the host animals do not benefit from the tapeworms. Commensalism describes a benefit for one organism and no harm or benefit to the other; therefore, choice **b** is incorrect because the hosts are being deprived of food by the tapeworm. Speciation is the development of a new species and is not related to types of symbiotic relationships, so choice **c** is incorrect.

3. After 10,000 years, **30%** of the sample remains.

4. After 11,500 years, **5%** of the sample remains.

5. The bone is roughly **12,500** years old.

6. Only *Species in different habitats often can share a common ancestor* is evidence of evolution. It explains how one species can diverge into two species over time when divided into two separate habitats. A classic example of this is the case of finches on the Galapagos Islands, where finch species diverged from a common ancestor to adapt to the unique habitats of each island.

7. a. *All* cells contain genetic material, so choice **a** is not true. Choice **b**, choice **c**, and choice **d** are all true statements.

8. Recessive eye color genes: **genotype**
Blue eyes: **phenotype**
Sex determination: **genotype**
Female: **phenotype**
Curling tongue: **phenotype**
Dominant hair color genes: **genotype**

9. Skin regeneration: **mitosis**
Blood production: **mitosis**
Pollen production: **meiosis**
Growth of a multicellular organism: **mitosis**
Egg cell production: **meiosis**

10. c. Someone who takes antibiotics for treating acne could accumulate bacteria that are capable of destroying the antibiotic. If that same person becomes infected with a serious disease that is treated with the same antibiotic, the resistant bacteria could destroy the antibiotic before it is able to act on the disease.

11.

PRODUCERS	PRIMARY CONSUMERS	SECONDARY CONSUMERS	TERTIARY CONSUMERS	DECOMPOSERS
grass, fern	grasshopper, ant, cow, mouse	snake, hawk, mouse, cougar	human, hawk, cougar	ant, mushroom, bacteria

5 ▶ PHYSICAL SCIENCE REVIEW

Physical science includes the disciplines of physics (the study of energy and how energy affects matter) and chemistry (the study of matter). In this chapter, we review the basic concepts of physical science:

- the structure and properties of matter, including atoms
- chemical properties and reactions
- energy, including conservation of energy, increase in disorder, and interactions of energy and matter
- work, motion, and force

In reviewing these concepts, you'll be better prepared to solve problems and answer questions on the GED® Science test. There are practice questions throughout. Use them to test your ability to work through solutions. Answers and explanations for all practice questions are at the end of the chapter.

Matter

Matter describes everything that exists. Matter has mass and takes up space. It can interact with other matter and with energy, and these interactions form the basis of physical and chemical reactions. But what actually is matter?

Atoms

You and everything around you are composed of tiny particles called **atoms**. The book you are reading, the neurons in your brain, and the air that you are breathing are all collections of various atoms. Atoms make up matter. Atoms are also the smallest known complete particle. Let's look at the history of knowledge of the atom.

The term **atom**, which means *indivisible*, was coined by Greek philosopher Democritus (460–370 B.C.). He disagreed with Plato and Aristotle—who believed that matter could be infinitely divided into smaller and smaller pieces—and postulated that matter is composed of tiny indivisible particles.

In spite of Democritus, the belief that matter could be infinitely divided lingered until the early 1800s, when John Dalton formulated a meaningful atomic theory. It stated:

- Matter is composed of atoms.
- All atoms of a given element are identical.
- Atoms of different elements are different and have different properties.
- Atoms are neither created nor destroyed in a chemical reaction.
- Compounds are formed when atoms of more than one element combine.
- A given compound always has the same relative number and kinds of atoms.

These theories are still used today, but there's more to know about atoms.

Protons, Neutrons, and Electrons

An atom is composed of a nucleus surrounded by electrons. The **nucleus** contains positively charged particles called **protons** and uncharged (neutral) particles called **neutrons**. **Electrons** are the negatively charged particles orbiting the nucleus.

Remember that atoms, as the most basic component of matter, have mass. To define that mass, scientists have determined that neutrons and protons have a mass of about 1 atomic mass unit, abbreviated **amu**. An amu is equivalent to about 1.66×10^{-24} g. That is a very small mass.

Electrons, in comparison, have a mass that is approximately $\frac{1}{1,836}$ that of a proton.

Electrons are not just the orbitals around the nucleus. The ones orbiting in the outermost **electron shell** (the orbit of the electrons) are called **valence electrons**. Valence electrons are most responsible for the properties and reaction patterns of an element to other elements and atoms. In a neutral atom, the number of protons and electrons is equal. A negatively charged atom has more electrons than protons, and a positively charged atom has more protons than electrons. The reason the atom stays together at all is that the negatively charged electrons are attracted to the positively charged nucleus. While this attractive force holds an atom together, the nucleus itself is held together by strong nuclear force.

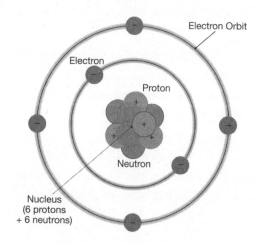

Structure of a Carbon Atom

Periodic Table of Elements

Scientists have been trying to understand the elements of matter through the use of organizational tables since the 1700s. We call the current organizational structure the **Periodic Table of Elements**. As of 2016, the periodic table contains 118 confirmed chemical elements.

The table organizes elements by their properties and helps scientists predict the discovery of new elements. It is a critical tool for understanding how elements react with each other. Each block in the table describes a different element.

1																	18
1 H 1.0079	2											13	14	15	16	17	2 He 4.0026
3 Li 6.941	4 Be 9.0122											5 B 10.811	6 C 12.011	7 N 14.007	8 O 15.999	9 F 18.998	10 Ne 20.180
11 Na 22.990	12 Mg 24.305	3	4	5	6	7	8	9	10	11	12	13 Al 26.982	14 Si 28.086	15 P 30.974	16 S 32.065	17 Cl 35.453	18 Ar 39.948
19 K 39.098	20 Ca 40.078	21 Sc 44.956	22 Ti 47.867	23 V 50.942	24 Cr 51.996	25 Mn 54.938	26 Fe 55.845	27 Co 58.933	28 Ni 58.693	29 Cu 63.546	30 Zn 65.409	31 Ga 69.723	32 Ge 72.64	33 As 74.922	34 Se 78.96	35 Br 79.904	36 Kr 83.798
37 Rb 85.468	38 Sr 87.62	39 Y 88.906	40 Zr 91.224	41 Nb 92.906	42 Mo 95.94	43 Tc (98)	44 Ru 101.07	45 Rh 102.91	46 Pd 106.42	47 Ag 107.87	48 Cd 112.41	49 In 114.82	50 Sn 118.71	51 Sb 121.76	52 Te 127.60	53 I 126.90	54 Xe 131.29
55 Cs 132.91	56 Ba 137.33	57-71 *	72 Hf 178.49	73 Ta 180.95	74 W 183.84	75 Re 186.21	76 Os 190.23	77 Ir 192.22	78 Pt 195.08	79 Au 196.97	80 Hg 200.59	81 Tl 204.38	82 Pb 207.2	83 Bi 208.98	84 Po (209)	85 At (210)	86 Rn (222)
87 Fr (223)	88 Ra (226)	89-103 #	104 Rf (261)	105 Db (262)	106 Sg (266)	107 Bh (264)	108 Hs (270)	109 Mt (268)	110 Ds (281)	111 Rg (272)	112 Uub (285)	113 Uut (284)	114 Uuq (289)	115 Uup (288)	116 Uuh (291)		118 Uuo (294)

* Lanthanide series	57 La 138.91	58 Ce 140.12	59 Pr 140.91	60 Nd 144.24	61 Pm (145)	62 Sm 150.36	63 Eu 151.96	64 Gd 157.25	65 Tb 158.93	66 Dy 162.50	67 Ho 164.93	68 Er 167.26	69 Tm 168.93	70 Yb 173.04	71 Lu 174.97
# Actinide series	89 Ac (227)	90 Th 232.04	91 Pa 231.04	92 U 238.03	93 Np (237)	94 Pu (244)	95 Am (243)	96 Cm (247)	97 Bk (247)	98 Cf (251)	99 Es (252)	100 Fm (257)	101 Md (258)	102 No (259)	103 Lr (262)

Understanding how to read the periodic table is critical to understanding how elements will react with each other. Being able to read a block of the table is useful for the GED® Science test. Look at this example, the block for carbon:

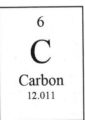

Carbon Entry in the Periodic Table of Elements

- The numeral 6 refers to the atomic number, which is the number of protons in the nucleus.
- C refers to the abbreviation for carbon.
- Carbon is the common name of the element written out under the abbreviation.
- 12.011 is the weighted average of the atomic masses of the element's isotopes.
- Because the electron has such a small mass, only protons and neutrons significantly contribute to the atomic mass of an element. Therefore, you can estimate the atomic mass of an element based on the number of protons and neutrons it has. Carbon, for example, has six protons and six neutrons, so its atomic mass is approximately $12(6 + 6)$.

Isotopes occur when a particular element varies in the number of neutrons it has. For example, carbon-14 is an isotope of carbon that is commonly used in carbon dating. The name *carbon-14* indicates that this isotope has a mass of 14. Since the atomic number (and therefore the number of protons) of a given element never changes, carbon-14 has 6 protons. The atomic mass is equal to the sum of the number of protons and neutrons, so since carbon-14 has 6 protons and an atomic mass of 14, this isotope must have 8 neutrons (14 – 6).

Ions occur when a particular element varies in the number of electrons it has. Since electrons are negatively charged, ions formed by the acquisition of electrons will be negatively charged. On the other hand, ions formed by the loss of electrons will be positively charged. Negatively charged ions are called **anions**. Positively charged ions are called **cations**. Elements tend to gain or lose electrons to obtain a stable octet (8) of **valence** (outer) electrons, or a noble gas configuration. For example, phosphorus forms the stable P^{3-} ion by gaining three electrons. Likewise, magnesium forms the stable Mg^{2+} ion by losing two electrons.

Molecules

Molecules are the next step up in terms of parts of matter. They are composed of two or more atoms held together by **chemical bonds**. These chemical bonds can be ionic or covalent bonds, which are related to how the valence electrons interact between atoms. Specifically, **ionic bonds** form when one atom donates one or more electrons to another. **Covalent bonds** form when the electrons are shared between atoms. With the atoms bonded together to create a molecule, the **mass** of that molecule can be calculated by adding the masses of its component atoms. **Ionic bonds** form between metals and nonmetals, while **covalent bonds** form between nonmetals. A third type of bond that is not as often discussed in depth is the **metallic bond**, which occurs between metals. Metallic bonding places metals in a sea of delocalized electrons that move all around them.

In general, metals appear on the left side of the periodic table while nonmetals appear on the right side of the periodic table. Forming a staircase-shaped border between the metals and nonmetals are the metalloids, which include boron (B), silicon (Si), germanium (Ge), and arsenic (As). The rows, or **periods**, in the periodic table are numbered from top to bottom, starting with 1. The columns, or **groups**, in the periodic table are numbered from left to right, starting with 1. The table below provides the names of the different groups of the elements in the periodic table. All metal groups have the word "metal" in their name, so they should be easy to pick out!

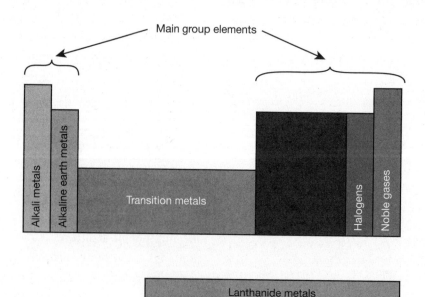

Something that you will most likely see in questions on the GED® Science test is the symbol of an element with a number in a subscript after it. This is shown in a **chemical formula** and is the number of atoms of a given element in a molecule. For example, the glucose (sugar) molecule is represented as $C_6H_{12}O_6$. This formula tells you that the glucose molecule contains 6 carbon atoms (C), 12 hydrogen atoms (H), and 6 oxygen atoms (O). In some cases, you may end up with two chemical formulas interacting and will have to solve what the new formula could be.

States of Matter

Molecules relate to matter, which we've discussed briefly, in that matter itself is held together by **intermolecular forces**—forces *between* different molecules.

A **solid** has a fixed shape and volume. The molecules in a solid have a regular, ordered arrangement and vibrate in place but are unable to move far.

Examples of matter in solid form include

- diamonds (carbon atoms)
- ice (water molecules)
- metal alloys (mixtures of different metals)

Liquids flow, and their **density** (mass per unit volume) is usually lower than the density of solids. Liquids have a fixed volume but take the shape of the container they are in. The molecules in a liquid are not ordered and can move from one region to another through a process called **diffusion.**

Examples of matter in liquid form include

- mercury (mercury atoms)
- vinegar (molecules of acetic acid and water)
- perfume (a mixture of liquids made up of different molecules)

Gases take the shape and volume of the container they are in and can be compressed when pressure is applied. The molecules in gases are disordered and move quickly. The density of gas is much lower than the density of a liquid.

Examples of matter in gaseous form include

- helium gas (helium atoms)
- water vapor (molecules of water)
- air (mixture of different molecules, including nitrogen, oxygen, carbon dioxide, and water vapor)

> Density is calculated by dividing mass by volume:
>
> **Density = mass/volume**

The size and mass of a substance can change, but its density (at a particular temperature) will always remain constant regardless of the size. For example, at 20°C, a very small piece of aluminum will have the same density (2.70 g/cm^3) as a large piece of aluminum.

These may seem like fixed rules regarding states of matter, but matter can change its state depending on various factors.

Changes of State

Changes of state, or **phase changes**, involve the transition from one state of matter into another. Freezing water to make ice, condensation of water vapor as morning dew, and sublimation (going directly from a solid to a gas) of dry ice (CO_2) are examples of phase changes.

A phase change is a physical process. No chemical bonds are formed or broken. Only the intermolecular (physical) forces are affected.

- **Freezing** is the process of changing a liquid into a solid by removing heat.

- **Melting** is the opposite process of freezing, whereby heat energy is added to the solid until it changes into a liquid.
- **Vaporization** is the change of phase from a liquid to a gas and also requires the input of heat energy.
- **Condensation** is the change from gas to liquid, which often involves removing heat.

Some substances **sublimate**, which means that they change directly from the solid phase to the gas phase, without forming a liquid first. Carbon dioxide is such a substance. Solid carbon dioxide, called dry ice, sublimates into the gas phase when heated. When gas changes directly into a solid, the process is called **deposition**. One example of this is snow formation, which is water vapor in the air turning directly into a solid as ice, also known as snowflakes.

All of these transitions of matter generally involve the addition or removal of heat. This helps with understanding the physical and chemical properties of matter.

Physical and Chemical Properties

The **physical properties** of matter include properties that are observable and measurable without having to alter the chemical structure of a substance. We've already discussed a few of these previously, like mass and density, but there are many more. Some physical properties of matter include

- **Mass:** a measure of how much matter is in an object, often measured in grams or kilograms
- **Density:** mass per unit of volume (how tightly packed the molecules are)
- **Volume:** how much space is occupied by a substance, often measured in liters, milliliters, or cubic centimeters
- **Elasticity:** the ability of a substance to return to its original shape after a deforming (e.g., stretching) force is applied

- **Solubility:** the amount of a substance that will dissolve in another substance (often described in terms of *solubility in water*); measured in grams per liter or moles per liter
- **Boiling point:** the temperature at which a substance will boil
- **Hardness:** the measure of how resistant a substance is to shape change when a force is applied (e.g., resistance to stretching)
- **Viscosity:** the measure of a substance's resistance to flow (e.g., honey is highly viscous, which is why it is difficult to get out of a jar, while olive oil has low viscosity and is easy to pour)

Chemical properties of matter include properties that cannot be observed; the substance's internal chemical structure must be affected for its chemical properties to be investigated. Some examples of chemical properties of matter include

- **Heat of combustion:** the energy released when a compound undergoes combustion with oxygen; may be expressed as energy/mole of fuel (kJ/mol)
- **Reactivity:** the tendency of a chemical substance to undergo a chemical reaction
- **Flammability:** the measure of how easily a substance burns or combusts

With all of these bits and pieces about matter and the various descriptions of matter, let's look at some sample questions that focus on matter.

Practice
1. Which of the following would NOT be considered a physical property?
   a. flammability
   b. hardness
   c. solubility
   d. density

2. The smallest unit of matter is the
   a. compound.
   b. atom.
   c. molecule.
   d. proton.

3. Which is an example of a phase change?
   a. oil floating on water
   b. oxygen diffusing in water
   c. paper burning
   d. water freezing

4. A chemical species has 11 protons, 12 neutrons, and 13 electrons.
   a. Identify the chemical element.

   _____

   b. What is the atomic number of the species?

   _____

   c. What is the atomic mass of the species?

   _____

   d. What is the charge of the species?

   _____

5. What kind of bond forms between Ca and Cl in $CaCl_2$? _____

6. Consider the ion Br^-.
   a. Is this an ion or an isotope of Br?

   _____

   b. Were electrons gained or lost by Br to form Br^-? _____
   c. How many electrons were gained or lost by Br to form Br^-? _____
   d. How many valence electrons does Br^- have?

   _____

7. An unknown solid sample has a mass of 100 g and a volume of 20 L. The density of this sample is _____.

8. In the walls of a chimney, soot molecules rise from the fire as hot gas and then become solid, with no liquid transition, immediately upon contacting the cool walls. This phase change is an example of
   a. vaporization.
   b. condensation.
   c. deposition.
   d. sublimation.

9. A **phase diagram** for a particular chemical describes the various pressures and temperatures at which the chemical exists in the solid, liquid, and gas phases. The temperature and pressure at which all three phases can coexist is called the **triple point**. Usually, solids predominate at low temperatures and high pressures, gases predominate at high temperatures and low pressures, and liquids fall in between solids and gases. The lines between the various sections of the diagram describe the pressures and temperatures at which phase changes occur between the three different phases. The following is an example of a phase diagram for water.

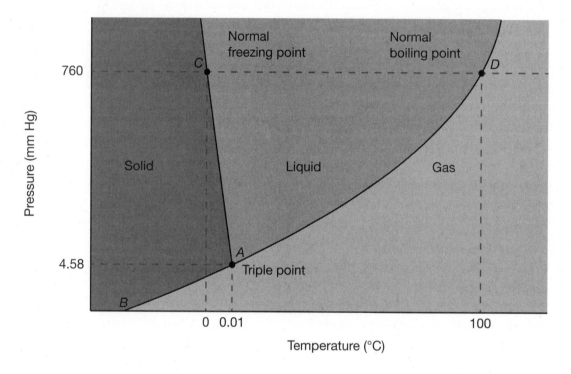

Based on the phase diagram, what kind of phase change is taking place if the temperature of H_2O at 4.50 mm Hg is increased from −10°C to 10°C? _____

Chemical Reactions

Chemical reactions happen around you (and inside you) every day. Removing stains from clothes, digesting food, and burning wood in a fireplace are all examples of chemical reactions. These types of reactions involve changes in the chemical arrangement of the atoms of a molecule and often show or involve the chemical properties of an element. In a chemical reaction, the atoms of reactants combine, recombine, or dissociate to form new products.

Some of the rules of matter do remain the same. Even as the atoms interact, the number of them in a particular element remains the same after a chemical reaction as before. The total mass is also preserved. Similarly, energy is never created or destroyed by a chemical reaction. If chemical bonds are broken, energy from those bonds can be liberated into the surroundings as heat. However, this liberation of energy does not constitute creation, since the energy only changes form—from chemical energy to heat energy.

Knowing these things about chemical reactions will help with answering questions regarding chemical equations, which is how these reactions are often described.

Chemical Equations

A chemical reaction can be represented by a **chemical equation**, where the reactants are written on the left side and the products on the right side of an arrow, which indicates the direction in which the reaction proceeds.

Let's look at an example. The following chemical equation represents the reaction of glucose ($C_6H_{12}O_6$) with oxygen (O_2) to form carbon dioxide (CO_2) and water (H_2O). This reaction occurs constantly in your body as glucose and oxygen in cells recombine to obtain energy.

$$C_6H_{12}O_6 + 6O_2 \rightarrow 6CO_2 + 6H_2O$$

The numbers in front of the molecular formulas indicate the proportion in which the molecules react. No number in front of the chemical formula means that one molecule of that substance is reacting. In the previous reaction, one molecule of glucose is reacting with six molecules of oxygen to form six molecules of carbon dioxide and six molecules of water.

The number of molecules of each of the substances in the reaction tells you in what proportion the molecules react. So if ten molecules of glucose react with 60 molecules of oxygen, you would obtain 60 molecules of carbon dioxide and 60 molecules of water.

$$10C_6H_{12}O_6 + 60O_2 \rightarrow 60CO_2 + 60H_2O$$

In many ways, chemical equations are like food recipes.

2 bread + 1 cheese + 2 tomato = sandwich

With two slices of bread, one slice of cheese, and two slices of tomato, you can make one sandwich. If you had six slices of bread, three slices of cheese, and six slices of tomato, you could make three sandwiches. The same principles of proportion apply in chemical reactions.

You'll be able to answer many chemical reaction questions if you think about the proportions of the chemical formulas.

Types of Chemical Reactions

Similar reactions can be classified and categorized into specific types of reactions. For example, chemical reactions can be classified as **synthesis reactions**, **decomposition reactions**, **single-replacement reactions**, **double-replacement reactions**, and **combustion reactions**. Each of these reactions proceeds as you may expect by its name.

Synthesis reaction: two elements or compounds merging together to become a new product:

$A + B \rightarrow AB$

Decomposition reaction: a single compound splitting into its component parts:

$AB \rightarrow A + B$

Single-replacement reaction: one element is substituted for another in a compound:

$C + AB \rightarrow CB + A$

Double-replacement reaction: two compounds exchange parts, making two new compounds:

$AB + CD \rightarrow AD + CB$

Combustion reaction: a compound containing C, H, and sometimes O reacting with O_2 to form H_2O and CO_2 as products:

$C_xH_y + O_2 \rightarrow H_2O + CO_2$

You may encounter some of these reactions, but just keep in mind that the description fits what is happening in the reaction. What you're more likely to run into are chemical equations that need to be balanced.

Balancing Chemical Equations

Just as in the sandwich equation previously described, the reactants will always combine in specific ratios to form the product. If two slices of bread are on the left side of the equation, then the sandwich formed on the right side will always have two slices, never one or three. If four slices are on the left side, then you will end up with four slices on the right.

Look at the following synthesis reaction:

$$N_2 + 3H_2 \rightarrow 2NH_3 \; (+ \; \textbf{heat})$$

There are two nitrogen atoms on each side of the equation. Also, there are six hydrogen atoms on each side of the equation. Matter is conserved. Now look at this synthesis reaction involving ions:

$$2F^- + Ca^{2+} \rightarrow CaF_2$$

In addition to showing the conservation of matter, this example shows the conservation of charge. The two fluoride ions, each with a charge of −1, combine with a calcium ion, which has a charge of +2. The product formed is neutral; the two −1 charges and the one +2 charge cancel each other out, so charge is conserved.

In fact, all chemical reactions must conserve

- matter (mass)
- energy
- electric charge

With this in mind, you'll be able to see if an equation balances on both sides or if something is wrong in a question.

Heat of Reaction (Enthalpy)

The heat of reaction (**enthalpy**) is absolutely related to the type of chemical reaction happening. As chemical reactions involve the breaking of molecular bonds, they require the input of energy to break those bonds. Similarly, the formation of new bonds releases energy. The stronger the bonds, the more energy is released when they are formed, and the more energy is required to break them. Therefore, a chemical reaction will either absorb or give off heat, depending on how many and what kind of bonds are broken and made as a result of that reaction.

These two types of reactions have names. A reaction that absorbs energy is called **endothermic**. A container in which an endothermic reaction takes place gets cold because the heat of the container is absorbed by the reaction. A reaction that gives off energy is called **exothermic**. Burning glucose ($C_6H_{12}O_6$) is a reaction that is exothermic—it gives off energy. Combustion of glucose is exothermic because the energy released by forming the C–O and O–H bonds in CO_2 and H_2O is greater than the energy required to break the chemical bonds in glucose. It's useful to remember that *exo-* means giving off heat, while *endo-* means absorbing.

Calorimetry

The enthalpy of a chemical reaction (or physical change) can be determined using **calorimetry**. There are a wide array of different types of calorimeters, but two of the most basic and widely used types are the constant-pressure and constant-volume calorimeters.

A **constant-pressure calorimeter** (e.g., a coffee-cup calorimeter) measures the enthalpy of a reaction at constant atmospheric pressure. The coffee cup is a good insulator, and the reaction occurs in water, such that any heat released or absorbed by the reaction is effectively absorbed or released by the water and stays in the cup. By measuring the change in temperature of the water during the chemical reaction, the enthalpy of the reaction can be calculated. A **constant-volume** calorimeter, also known as a **bomb calorimeter**, is different because the reaction occurs in a steel tank of fixed volume, called a *bomb*, that can withstand high pressure. Conceptually, the same idea applies to the bomb calorimeter, in which the measurement of the temperature change of the water surrounding the bomb allows for the calculation of the enthalpy of the reaction taking place. The enthalpies of combustion reactions are often determined using bomb calorimeters.

Catalysts

Often, a reaction needs help getting started. Such help can come from a catalyst. A **catalyst** is a substance that accelerates a reaction, without itself being changed or used up in the reaction. It acts by lowering what is called the **activation energy** of a reaction. This activation energy is often illustrated as a hill separating two valleys, as in the following figure. This hill needs to be crossed in order to get from one valley to the other (one valley representing the reactants, and the other the products). The catalyst acts by making the hill lower and easier to cross.

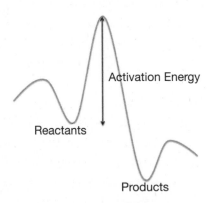

Activation Energy Diagram

Being able to read a diagram like this one will be useful to you in answering questions. The line that is drawn between the level of the reactants and the top of the activation energy shows how much energy is needed to create the products that appear on the right side.

Compounds and Mixtures

There are more ways to look at elements and how they interact. When two or more elements combine chemically, the result is a **compound**. Examples of compounds include carbon dioxide (a product of respiration), sucrose (table sugar), serotonin (a human brain chemical), and acetic acid (a component of vinegar). In each of these compounds, there is more than one type of atom chemically bonded to other atoms in a definite proportion. The combination of these atoms also results in a fixed, definite structure. Compounds are chemically bonded.

When two or more elements combine physically, the result is a **mixture**. In a homogeneous mixture, the components can't be visually separated. Homogeneous mixtures also have the same composition (ratio of components) throughout their volume. An example is a mixture of a small amount of salt mixed in water. A uniform mixture is often called a **solution**.

In a heterogeneous mixture, the components can often be visually identified, and the composition may vary from one point of the mixture to another. A collection of dimes and pennies is a heterogeneous mixture. A mixture of sugar and flour is also heterogeneous since sugar has a very different texture than flour.

Solutions

A solution is a homogeneous mixture in which the different components cannot be visually separated. In a solution, one substance, the **solute**, is dissolved in another, the **solvent**. In a mixture of salt and water, the salt is the solute and the water is the solvent. The solvent is usually present in excess of the solute. A solution reaches **saturation** when it can hold no additional solute; any additional solute added to a saturated solution will float or sink to the bottom rather than dissolve. A solution that does not yet hold enough solute to reach saturation is **unsaturated**, while a solution that has extra solute added beyond the saturation point is **supersaturated**. A substance that is unable to dissolve in a given solvent is **insoluble**.

In general, a greater amount of solute can dissolve in a solvent as temperature increases. A solubility curve can provide information about the solubility of a particular solute in a particular solvent at various temperatures. Consider the example below:

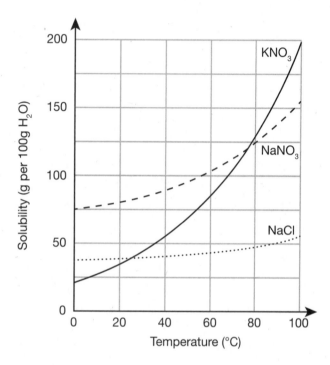

This solubility curve shows that in water, the solubility of KNO_3 increases more rapidly than that of $NaNO_3$ or $NaCl$ as temperature increases because its curve is steeper in its increase. As a result, the solubility of KNO_3 is lower than those of $NaNO_3$ and $NaCl$ at a temperature of 10°C, but it is higher than those of $NaNO_3$ and $NaCl$ at 90°C. Solubility curves can help you determine if a solute is unsaturated, saturated, or supersaturated. For example, if you add 50 g of $NaCl$ to 100 g of water at 90°C, the solution will be saturated because the solubility of $NaCl$ is 50 g/100 g water at 90°C. If you add 20 g of $NaCl$ to 100 g of water at this same temperature, the solution will be unsaturated because the mass of solute added is *lower* than the solubility. On the other hand, if you add 50 g

of $NaCl$ to 100 g of water at 90°C and then cool the saturated solution, it will be supersaturated because the mass of solute is *higher* than the solubility.

The relative amounts of solute and solvent in a solution can be represented using a number of different concentration units. Three of the more common concentration units are percent by mass, molarity, and molality. A percent by mass is simply the fraction of solution mass occupied by the solute, so to calculate the **percent by mass**, you just have to divide the mass of solute by the total mass of the solution. For example, if you have 25 g of solute in a 50-g solution, the percent by mass is equal to $\frac{25 \text{ g solute}}{50 \text{ g solution}} = 50\%$.

Molarity is a very commonly used concentration unit that is equal to the number of moles in a solute divided by the volume of the solution. A **mole** is a measure of the quantity of a particular substance. The units of molarity, mol/L, are represented by the symbol M. If you have 15 moles of solute and 3 liters of solution, the molarity of the solution is equal to $\frac{15 \text{ moles solute}}{3 \text{ L solution}} = 5M$.

Molality gives the particular amounts of solute and solvent, as it is equal to the moles of solute divided by the mass (in kg) of solvent. The units of molality, mol/kg, are represented by the symbol m. For example, if you have 20 moles of solute and 4 kg of solvent, the molality of the solution is equal to $\frac{20 \text{ moles solute}}{4 \text{ kg solvent}} = 5 \, m$.

For most solutions, adding more solute can change the physical properties of the solution. These properties are called **colligative** properties and do not depend on the type of solute, just on the number of solute and solvent particles. Two well-studied colligative properties are boiling point elevation and freezing point depression. *Boiling point elevation* refers to the fact that increasing the amount of solute relative to solvent in a solution will increase the boiling temperature of the solution. On the other hand, *freezing point depression* refers to the fact that increasing the amount of solute relative to solvent in a solution will lower the freezing temperature of that solution.

The Mole

In describing the concentration units of solutions, the concept of the mole was introduced. The **mole** is widely used in calculations in chemistry, but only a basic understanding is required here. A mole describes the amount of a substance that contains 6.022×10^{23} particles of that substance. This number is called **Avogadro's number**. Different chemical compounds have different atoms and therefore different masses, so the mass that makes up a mole of a substance is specific to each individual substance. For example, one mole of oxygen gas (O_2) is 32.0 g, while one mole of iron metal (Fe) is 55.8 g. This means that 32.0 g of O_2 contains 6.022×10^{23} O_2 molecules, and that 55.8 g of Fe contains 6.022×10^{23} Fe atoms.

In a balanced chemical reaction, the numbers present in front of chemical formulas (**coefficients**) represent relative numbers of moles of each chemical, so a balanced chemical reaction can tell you how many particles are reacting. For example, consider the chemical reaction $2CO + O_2 \rightarrow 2CO_2$. This is a synthesis reaction. What the coefficients tell us about this reaction is that 2 moles of CO react with 1 mole of O_2 to form 2 moles of CO_2, or that 2 particles of CO react with 1 particle of O_2 to form 2 particles of CO_2.

Practice

10. This chemical equation represents the combustion (burning) of methane (CH_4). The equation states that 1 mol of methane and 2 mol of oxygen react to produce 1 mol of carbon dioxide and 2 mol of water.

$$CH_4(g) + 2O_2(g) \rightarrow CO_2(g) + 2H_2O(l)$$
$$\Delta H = -890 \text{ kJ}$$

If 890 kJ of heat are released ($\Delta H = -890$ kJ), then this reaction is considered
   a. endothermic.
   b. exothermic.
   c. equivalent.
   d. evaporative.

11.

Solubility of Oxygen with Temperature

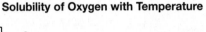

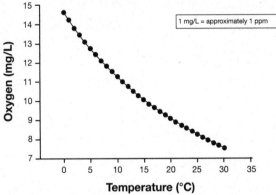

Temperature (°C)

Fish require 5 to 6 ppm of dissolved oxygen and cannot live at levels below 2 ppm.

Which conclusion can you draw based on the data shown in the chart?
   a. As temperature increases, oxygen dissolves more quickly.
   b. Fish cannot survive in water at 25°C.
   c. Warmer water holds less oxygen.
   d. If you double the temperature of the water, the amount of dissolved oxygen is decreased by half.

12. The following chemical equation is completely balanced for all chemicals except for Fe_2O_3:

$$4FE_2 + 3O_2 \rightarrow \underline{\quad} FE_2O_3$$

What coefficient should be placed in front of Fe_2O_3 to complete the balanced equation?

_____

13. Match each of the following reactions to the type of chemical reaction it represents:

_____ $C_2H_4 + 3O_2 \rightarrow 2CO_2 + 2H_2O$ **a.** combustion

_____ $2CA + O_2 \rightarrow 2CaO$ **b.** decomposition

_____ $MG + CuSO_4 \rightarrow Cu + MgSO_4$ **c.** double-displacement

_____ $AgNO_3 + KBr \rightarrow AgBr + KNO_3$ **d.** single-displacement

_____ $2H_2O_2 \rightarrow 2H_2O + O_2$ **e.** synthesis

14. A bowl of cereal and milk would be considered a(n)

a. compound.

b. element.

c. heterogeneous mixture.

d. homogeneous mixture.

15. A solution consists of 20 kg of solvent and 10 moles of solute. What is its molality?

a. 0.5 m

b. 2 m

c. 30 m

d. 200 m

16. Arrange the following solutions in order of increasing freezing temperature:

2 m NaCl in water   10 m NaCl in water   pure water

_____ < _____ < _____

Energy

In science, **energy** is defined as the ability to do work. As with matter in chemical reactions, energy can't be created or destroyed. This is a property called **conservation of energy**. Energy can only change form, which is a property called **transformation of energy**. This property is important in considering the forms of energy.

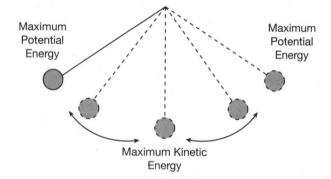

Forms of Energy

Forms of energy include potential energy and kinetic energy. **Potential energy** is energy that is stored. **Kinetic energy** is the energy associated with motion. To understand the difference, look at the following illustration.

As the pendulum swings, the energy is converted from potential to kinetic and back to potential. When the hanging weight is at one of the high points, the gravitational potential energy is at a maximum and kinetic energy is at the minimum. At the low point, the kinetic energy is maximized and gravitational potential energy is minimized.

Examples of potential energy include nuclear energy and chemical energy, where energy is stored in the bonds that hold atoms and molecules together.

Heat, hydrodynamic energy, and electromagnetic waves are examples of kinetic energy, where energy is associated with the movement of molecules, water, and electrons or photons (particles of light).

Heat Energy

Heat as energy moves through various forms of matter. It's transferred three ways: by conduction, convection, and radiation.

Conduction is the transfer of heat from one molecule to another through a substance. Not all substances conduct heat at the same speed. Metals are good conductors. Think of how quickly a metal spoon heats up in a cup of coffee or a pot of boiling water. One end starts out cold, the other end is in heat, and the metal spoon eventually warms consistently throughout. Wood, paper, and air are poor heat conductors and are considered **insulators**. You can stir a pot of boiling soup with a wooden spoon, and the spoon will not get hot.

Another way that heat moves through matter is through **convection**, which is the transfer of heat from one place to another by the movement of fluids. When fluids are heated, density is reduced. This causes the movement of the fluids (e.g., liquids or gases). For example, when a solution is heated on a stove, the heated water rises (as it becomes less dense) and the cooler, denser surface water sinks to the bottom. That movement of heat is the process of convection.

The third way that heat moves is through **radiation**, which is the transfer of energy via one form of electromagnetic waves. This includes the feeling of heat on your face from the sun or from a fire. Electromagnetic waves are one part of energy waves.

Energy Waves

Energy in all its forms can interact with matter. For example, when heat energy interacts with molecules of water, it makes them move faster and boil. Waves—including sound and seismic waves, waves on water, and light waves—have energy and can transfer that energy when they interact with matter. Consider what happens if you are standing by the ocean and a big wave rolls in. Sometimes the energy carried by the wave is large enough to knock you down.

Energy is also carried by electromagnetic waves. The energy of **electromagnetic waves** is related to their wavelengths. These electromagnetic waves include

- radio waves (the longest wavelength)
- microwaves
- infrared radiation (radiant heat)
- visible light
- ultraviolet radiation
- X-rays
- gamma rays

The wavelength of the energy waves depends on the amount of energy the wave is carrying. Shorter wavelengths carry more energy than longer wavelengths. When a wave hits a smooth surface, such as a mirror, it is reflected. In the case of sound waves, those reflections come across as echoes.

Matter not only can reflect waves; it can also **refract** or bend waves. This is what happens when a ray of light traveling through air hits a water surface. A part of the wave is reflected, and a part is refracted into the water.

Wavelengths can be used to identify elements as well. Each kind of atom or molecule can gain or lose energy only in particular discrete amounts. When an atom gains energy, light at the wavelength associated with that energy is absorbed. When an atom loses energy, light at the wavelength associated with that energy is emitted. Measuring whether these wavelengths are there or not describes what element is involved.

Parts of Waves

While considering waves and energy, let's look at the four parts that make up a wave:

1. wavelength
2. amplitude
3. crest
4. trough

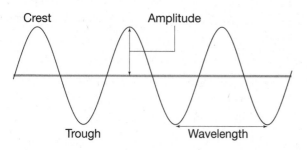

Parts of a Wave

The **crest** is the highest part of the wave, while the **trough** is the lowest part. The **wavelength** is the total distance from trough to trough or crest to crest, and **amplitude** is measured as the height of the wave above neutral. This applies to all types of waves (sound waves as well as ocean waves). In sound waves, the amplitude is equal to the loudness of the sound.

Frequency as it relates to waves is defined as the number of wave cycles that pass in a certain period of time. In sound waves, higher-pitched sounds have a higher frequency. This means that more cycles of waves are compressed into the same period of time. Lower-pitched sounds have lower frequency.

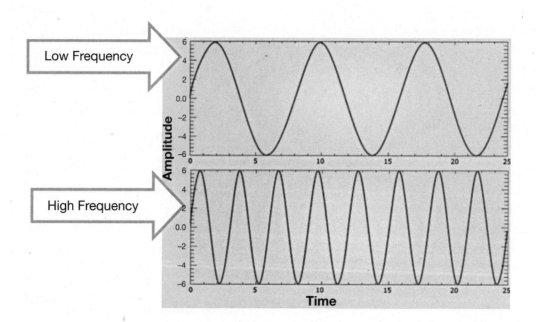

Practice

17. The frequency of the sounds produced by a bottlenose dolphin ranges from 20 Hz to 150 kHz. The lower-frequency vocalizations are likely used in social communication. Higher-frequency clicks (40 kHz to 150 kHz) are primarily used for echolocation. The sound waves travel through water at speeds of approximately 1,400 m/s.

Determine the wavelengths of the waves at the lower end of the frequency range used for echolocation. Speed = wavelength × frequency.

a. 35 mm
b. 1,365 m
c. 0.029 m
d. 56 km

18. When a spring is stretched out as far as possible and held in place, which of the following statements is true?

a. Both its kinetic and potential energies are very high.
b. Both its kinetic and potential energies are very low.
c. Its kinetic energy is very high and its potential energy is very low.
d. Its kinetic energy is very low and its potential energy is very high.

19. On a cold night, you use a heating blanket to keep warm. Which type of heat transfer is represented in this example? _____

20. Consider the two waves below:

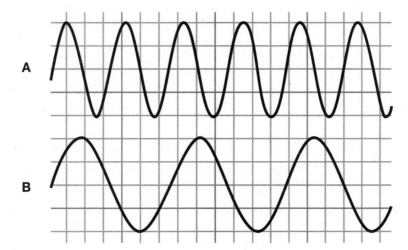

Choose the word or phrase that correctly completes each sentence.
a. The amplitude of wave A is (greater than / less than / equal to) that of wave B.
b. The frequency of wave A is (greater than / less than / equal to) that of wave B.
c. The wavelength of wave A is (greater than / less than / equal to) that of wave B.

Force, Motion, and Work

Energy, which is associated with chemical reactions, also appears in the physical world in familiar ways. A **force** is a push or a pull. Objects move in response to forces acting on them. When you kick a ball, it rolls. A force is also required to stop motion, and in all this, energy is needed to make force happen. It's useful to think about sequential details involved in this action.

1. First your body breaks the chemical bonds in the food you have eaten.
2. This supplies your body with energy.
3. You use up some of that energy to kick the ball.
4. You apply a force, and as a result the ball moves, carrying the energy your foot supplied it with.
5. Some of the energy is transferred from the ball to the ground in the form of heat, due to the frictional force the ball encounters on the surface of the ground.
6. As energy is lost this way, the ball slows down.
7. When all of the energy is used up through friction, the ball stops moving.

This example illustrates the concept of conservation of energy, as well as **Newton's first law—the Law of Inertia**—which is the tendency of an object to remain either at rest or in motion with constant velocity unless acted on by a force. If you were to hit a ball and there was no force working against it (in this case it would be friction), it would continue to move forever.

Measuring Force

Speed, velocity, acceleration, and momentum are all important to an understanding of force. These concepts are used frequently in daily life, but it's a good idea to understand the exact scientific meanings for the GED® Science test.

For example, what is the difference between speed and velocity?

- A **speed**, such as 30 miles per hour, has **magnitude**.
- A **velocity** has **magnitude** *and* **direction** (e.g., 30 miles per hour north).

A similar distinction can be made between the terms **distance** and **displacement**. If you walk 20 feet to your mailbox and 20 feet back, the *distance* you traveled is 40 feet. Your *displacement* is zero, because displacement compares your ending point to your starting point.

While **velocity** has magnitude and direction, it can also be defined as displacement divided by elapsed time. In contrast, **acceleration** is velocity divided by elapsed time. Additionally, an acceleration that is negative (due to an ending velocity that is less than the starting velocity) is called a **deceleration**. But, for velocity to change, the speed and/or the direction must change and a net or unbalanced force must be applied.

All of these aspects are related to force, and these ideas are all important to understanding how force may work in a particular situation, experiment, or question. Often questions on the GED® Science test will be specifically associated with these ideas, so being able to figure out what the question is asking may require you to understand these terms.

When looking at all of these concepts in relation to an object, let's summarize a bit: An object at rest (whose speed is zero) remains at rest unless some force acts on it (e.g., a person pushes it, the wind blows it away, or gravity pulls it down). An object that is moving continues to move at the same speed in the same direction, unless some force is applied to it to slow it down, to speed it up, or to change its direction. The amount of acceleration or deceleration is directly proportional to the force applied. The harder you kick the ball, the faster it will move. The mass of the ball will also determine how much it will accelerate. Kick a soccer ball and then a ball made of lead with the same force (watch your foot!). Which ball moves faster as a result of an equal kick? These observations constitute **Newton's second law—the Law of Acceleration**:

Force = mass × acceleration

A related concept is momentum. If an object is in motion, it has **momentum**. The amount of momentum an object has depends on its mass and velocity. Think of a heavy cart rolling downhill fast; it has a lot of momentum (large mass and high velocity). Now think of a textbook sliding down an incline (relatively small mass and low velocity); it has much less momentum than the cart.

Momentum = mass × velocity

Momentum, acceleration, velocity, distance, and speed are impotant for understanding aspects of force.

Types of Forces

Newton's laws specifically relate to the study of how the motion of objects is affected by force. Types of forces include gravitational, electromagnetic, and contact forces, which are discussed next.

Gravitational Force

Gravitation is an attractive force that each object with mass exerts on any other object with mass. The strength of the gravitational force depends on the masses of the objects and on the distance between them.

When we think of gravity, we usually think of Earth's gravity, which prevents us from jumping infinitely high, keeps objects stuck to the ground, and makes things thrown upward fall down. We, too, exert a gravitational force on the earth, and we exert forces on one another, but these are not very noticeable because our masses are very small in comparison with the mass of our planet.

The greater the masses involved, the greater the gravitational force between them. The sun exerts a force on the earth, and the earth exerts a force on the sun. The moon exerts a force on the earth, and the earth on the moon. The gravitational force of the moon is the reason there are tides. The moon's gravity pulls the water on Earth. The sun also exerts a force on our water, but this is not as apparent because the sun, although more massive than the moon, is very far away. As the distance between two objects increases, the gravitational force between them decreases by the square of the distance (e.g., doubling the distance decreases the force four times, and tripling the distance decreases it nine times).

What is the difference between weight and mass? On Earth, the **acceleration due to gravity** (g) is -9.8 m/s^2 (meters per second squared). Your weight (w) is really a force. The formula *Force = mass × acceleration* becomes *Weight = mass × gravitational acceleration*. Since the acceleration, g, is -9.8 m/s^2, the overall force (w) is negative, which just means that its pull is in the downward direction: the earth is pulling you toward its center.

A fun way to think about this is that you have probably heard somebody say, "You'd weigh less on the moon!" This is true because the gravitational force on the moon is less than the earth's gravitational force. Your mass, however, would still be the same, because mass is just a measure of your density and the volume you take up.

Weight is commonly measured in newtons (N), so when you see an N, you'll be dealing with weight and force. Fun fact: 1 N = 0.222 pounds on Earth.

Electromagnetic Force

Electricity and magnetism are two aspects of a single **electromagnetic force**, another type of force that you may run into. It is exactly what it sounds like, electricity and magnetism. Moving electric charges produce magnetic forces, and moving magnets produce electric forces. The electromagnetic force exists between any two charged or magnetic objects: for example, a proton and an electron or two electrons. Opposite charges attract (an electron and a proton), whereas like charges repel (two protons or two electrons). The strength of the force depends on the charges and on the distance between them. The greater the charges, the greater the force. The closer the charges are to each other, the greater the force between them.

Contact Forces

Contact forces, yet another type of force, are those that exist as a result of an interaction between objects physically in contact with one another. They include frictional forces, tensional forces, and normal forces.

The **frictional force** opposes the motion of an object across a surface. For example, if a glass slides across the surface of the dinner table, there exists a friction force in the direction opposite to the motion of the glass. Friction is the result of attractive intermolecular forces between the molecules of the surface of the glass and the surface of the table. Friction depends on the nature of the two surfaces. There would be less friction between the table and the glass if the table was highly polished. The glass would glide across the table more easily. Friction also depends on the degree to which the glass and the table are pressed together. Also, air resistance is a type of frictional force. An example of air resistance is how it affects something like a ball that has been thrown. Both gravitational and frictional force slow it and lead it to land back on the ground.

Tensional force is the force that is transmitted through a rope or wire when it is pulled tight by forces acting at each end. The tensional force is directed along the rope or wire and pulls on the objects on either end. A kite may use air resistance to catch the wind and rise in the air, while the person holding the end of the kite's line is using tensional force to hold on to and guide the kite and pull it back to the ground.

A last type of contact force is **normal force**, which is exerted on an object in contact with another stable object. A normal force is always perpendicular (forming a 90° right angle) to the object upon which it is acting. For example, the dinner table exerts an upward force on a glass at rest on the surface of the table.

All of these forces are used in everyday objects like simple machines, which use energy and force to do various types of work.

Work and Machines

Machines are built to do work, and at their most basic level, this relates to overcoming the effects of force on an object. A **simple machine** is a device that changes the direction or magnitude of a force. A simple machine can be defined as a mechanism that provides **mechanical advantage** or leverage. In other words, simple machines make it easier to do work.

WORK AND POWER

Work is defined as the product of force and distance:

Work = force × distance

The metric unit for work is the joule. One joule equals a force of 1 newton over 1 meter.

Power is the rate at which work is done:

Power = work/time

The metric unit for power is the watt. One watt equals 1 joule/second. So power is sometimes measured in joules per second. When you see this, remember that it's power related.

There are six basic types of simple machines:

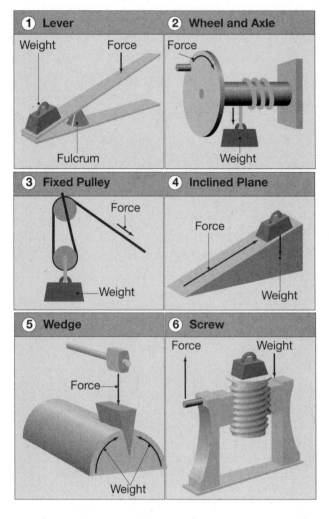

1. **Lever** — Weight, Force, Fulcrum
2. **Wheel and Axle** — Force, Weight
3. **Fixed Pulley** — Force, Weight
4. **Inclined Plane** — Force, Weight
5. **Wedge** — Force, Weight
6. **Screw** — Force, Weight

A **lever** produces a mechanical advantage by transferring an applied force over a distance and exerting an output force on an object (example: think of a crowbar).

A **wheel and axle** assembly is formed by two disks, or cylinders, of different diameters that rotate together around the same axis. Force applied to the edges of the two disks, or cylinders, provides mechanical advantage (example: think of a steering wheel in a car or a doorknob).

A **fixed pulley** can make it easier to lift an object. Although the same amount of force is needed to lift an object with a fixed single pulley as without the pulley, giving it no mechanical advantage, certain types of pulleys do produce a mechanical advantage. The more pulleys that are added to the system, the less force that is needed to move the object. The mechanical advantage is increased because the force is distributed over the length of the pulley ropes. For example,

- Fixed single pulley: if you wanted to lift a 100-kg object 10 cm, you would need to apply 100 N of force.
- Double pulley system: if you wanted to lift a 100-kg object 10 cm, you would need to apply 50 N of force.
- Triple pulley system: if you wanted to lift a 100-kg object 10 cm, you would need to apply 33.3 N of force.
- Four-pulley system: if you wanted to lift a 100-kg object 10 cm, you would need to apply 25 N of force.

An **inclined plane** produces a mechanical advantage by allowing a smaller force to be applied to increase the vertical distance of an object (example: think of pushing a cart up a hill versus lifting it straight up).

A **wedge** produces a mechanical advantage by concentrating force on a small area (example: think of an ax splitting a log).

A **screw**, which is an inclined plane wrapped around a cylinder, produces a mechanical advantage by amplifying the force applied. A small rotational force on the shaft can exert a large force on the load (example: think of a corkscrew).

Understanding how these various simple machines work is useful for both the GED® Science test and daily life. A question you encounter on the test involving pulleys may include determining from a diagram how much force you would need to apply to lift 100 kg. The diagram might show a single-, double-, and triple-pulley system with all the information previously given here, but the four-pulley system would not tell you how much force you would need. Since each additional pulley reduces the amount of force, this would give you a clue as to how much force you would need. When answering physical science questions, take the information presented and work out the solution with that information and any science knowledge you have learned.

Practice

21. If there were no gravity, what would happen if you threw a ball straight up in the air, according to Newton's first law?

_____

_____

_____

_____

22. Over the course of 2 minutes, the velocity of a jogger steadily decreases from 50 m/min to 30 m/min. Which statement best describes her change in velocity?
   a. Her acceleration is 10 m/min^2.
   b. Her acceleration is 20 m/min^2.
   c. Her acceleration is –20 m/min^2.
   d. Her acceleration is –10 m/min^2.

23. A 2.0-kg mass has a momentum of 6.0 $\frac{kg \cdot m}{s}$. What is its velocity?
   a. 3.0$\frac{m}{s}$
   b. 4.0$\frac{m}{s}$
   c. 8.0$\frac{m}{s}$
   d. 12$\frac{m}{s}$

24. You would weigh _____ on the planet Jupiter than on Earth because _____.
   a. more; your mass has changed
   b. more; the gravitational acceleration has changed
   c. less; your mass has changed
   d. less; the gravitational acceleration has changed

25. Consider the image below:

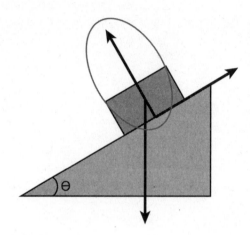

The type of contact force represented by the circled arrow above is
   a. an electromagnetic force.
   b. a frictional force.
   c. a normal force.
   d. tension.

26. The twist lid of a jar represents which kind of simple machine? _____

Physical Science Review

1. A blue whale is 30 m long and has a mass of 40,000 kg (400 metric tons). Determine the weight of a blue whale in newtons. _____
Weight = mass × acceleration due to gravity (g)
$g = 9.8$ m/s^2

2. Newton's second law of motion is the Law of Acceleration. The calculation can be stated as
acceleration = force ÷ mass.
If a force of 10 N is applied to a 2-kg object, the object will accelerate at _____ m/s^2.

3. Balance the following equation by writing the correct numbers in the blanks provided.
____ NH_3 + ____ O_2 → ____ NO + ____ H_2O

4. Calculate the momentum of a 0.25-kg ball that is moving toward home plate at a velocity of 40 m/s. (*Hint:* Refer to the chapter for any formula you need to solve this problem.) _____

5. This is an image of a section of a roller coaster. What kind of energy is represented at the top of the roller coaster (W)?

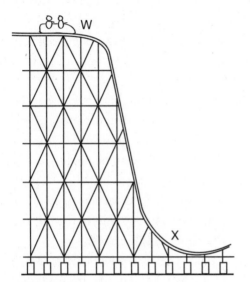

a. kinetic
b. mechanical
c. potential
d. leverage

6. While hiking in a deep canyon, a hiker yells out loud. He hears the echo 0.86 seconds after the yell. The speed of the sound wave in the air is 342 m/s. Calculate the distance to the nearest canyon wall. _____
Hint: Remember that the echo represents sound traveling to the wall and back. Here are two formulas that will help:

Velocity = distance/time
Distance = velocity × time

7. Classify each substance as an **element**, a **compound**, or a **mixture**.
water (H_2O): _____
hydrogen (H): _____
salt (NaCl): _____
glucose ($C_6H_{12}O_6$): _____
oxygen (O): _____
saltwater: _____

8. Which of the below is NOT a change of state?
a. dew forming
b. gold liquefying
c. boiling water
d. blending fruit

9. Assign each of the following terms to its correct definition.

1. Volume
2. Elasticity
3. Solubility
4. Hardness
5. Viscosity

a. The measure of how much of a substance will dissolve in another substance

b. The measure of how resistant a substance is to shape change when a force is applied

c. The ability of a substance to return to its original shape after a deforming force is applied

d. The measure of a substance's resistance to flow

e. How much space is occupied by a substance

10. What is the following reaction an example of?

$$AgNO_3 + NaCl \rightarrow AgCl + NaNO_3$$

a. synthesis

b. decomposition

c. single-replacement reaction

d. double-replacement reaction

11. If a person walks forward one mile in 15 minutes and then back one mile in 15 minutes, what measurement would be described as zero miles: distance or displacement?

_____

Answers and Explanations

Chapter Practice

1. a. A physical property is something that is observable and measurable and does not involve a chemical reaction. Flammability is the correct choice as it involves the ability of a substance to burn, a property that cannot be determined without chemically altering the substance. Choices **b**, **c**, and **d** are each observable and measurable properties of substances; therefore, none of them is the correct choice.

2. b. The smallest unit of matter is the atom. A compound is a substance made up of multiple different elements, so choice **a** is incorrect. A molecule can be made up of multiple atoms, so choice **c** is incorrect. A proton is a positively charged particle in an atom, but it is not considered a unit of matter, and therefore choice **d** is incorrect.

3. d. A phase change is when matter changes from a solid to a liquid or gas, from a liquid to a solid or gas, or from a gas to a solid or liquid. Choice **d** is the correct answer because water freezing is a phase change from liquid to solid. Choice **a** is incorrect because oil floating represents a difference in density, not a phase change. Choice **b** is incorrect because when oxygen diffuses in water, it stays as a gas in the water and does not change phase. Choice **c** is not correct because there is no change in state when paper burns. This is an example of a chemical reaction, not a phase change.

4. a. Sodium. Based on the periodic table, the element with 11 protons is sodium, Na.

   b. 11. The atomic number is the number of protons.

   c. 23. The atomic mass is equal to the sum of the numbers of protons and neutrons: $11 + 12 = 23$.

   d. 2–. Each proton has a charge of 1+ and each electron has a charge of 1–. There are two more electrons than protons. Therefore, the species has an overall charge of 2–.

5. Ionic. Calcium is a metal and chlorine is a non-metal. An ionic bond forms between a metal and a nonmetal.

6. a. Ion. The charge next to the symbol indicates an ion, not an isotope. An isotope would not change in charge because differences in numbers of neutral neutrons would not impact the charge of the atom.

   b. Gained. The charge is negative, which means that the Br atom gained electrons to form Br^-.

   c. 1. The charge is 1–, which means that one electron is gained.

   d. 8. Br^- is a stable ion of Br, so it has an octet of valence electrons, 8.

7. 5 g/L. Density $= \frac{\text{mass}}{\text{volume}} = \frac{100\text{ g}}{20\text{ L}} = 5$ g/L.

8. c. Deposition is the direct conversion of a gas to a solid. Boiling is the change from a liquid to a gas upon addition of energy, which is not the case in this example. Nor is it condensation, the change from a gas to a liquid, or sublimation, the change from a solid to a gas.

9. sublimation. 4.50 mm Hg is below the triple point on the y-axis, so H_2O will never be a liquid at this pressure. At 4.50 mm Hg and –10°C, H_2O is a solid, and at 4.50 mm Hg and 10°C, H_2O is a gas. This transition crosses the line from solid to gas without passing through the liquid portion of the diagram. The transition from solid directly to gas is called *sublimation*.

10. b. Because heat is released during the reaction (and indicated by $\Delta H = -890$ kj), the reaction is considered exothermic. Choice **a** is incorrect because a reaction that absorbs energy is called *endothermic*. Choice **c** is incorrect because it refers to balancing equations, not heat of reaction. Choice **d** is incorrect because it refers to part of the hydrologic cycle, not heat of reaction in chemical reactions.

11. c. The graph shows that the amount of oxygen dissolved in water decreases as water temperature increases. Choice **c** is correct because you can conclude that warmer water holds less oxygen based on the information in the graph. Choice **a** is incorrect because the graph does not show the rate at which oxygen dissolves. Choice **b** is incorrect because the caption states that fish can live at 2 ppm and the graph indicates a level of more than 8 ppm at 25°C. Choice **d** is incorrect because the graph does not show this relationship.

12. 2. There are four Fe atoms on the left side of the reaction, so there need to be four on the right side also. A coefficient of 2 for Fe_2O_3 gives four total Fe atoms on the right side of the reaction. This coefficient also gives us six oxygen atoms on both sides of the equation.

13.

   a. $C_2H_4 + 3O_2 \rightarrow 2CO_2 + 2H_2O$

   e. $2Ca + O_2 \rightarrow 2CaO$

   d. $Mg + CuSO_4 \rightarrow Cu + MgSO_4$

   c. $AgNO_3 + NaCl \rightarrow AgCl + NaNO_3$

   b. $2H_2O_2 \rightarrow 2H_2O + O_2$

14. c. The cereal and milk represent distinct substances within the mixture that can be easily distinguished visually, so this is a heterogeneous mixture.

15. a. Molality is equal to the moles of solute divided by the mass (in kg) of solvent. Therefore, molality $= \frac{10 \text{ moles solute}}{20 \text{ kg solvent}} = 0.5 \, m$.

16. 10 m NaCl in water < 2 m NaCl in water < pure water

Increasing the number of solute particles lowers the freezing temperature. Therefore, a solution with a higher molality will have a lower freezing point than a solution with a lower molality. Arranging the solutions in order of increasing freezing temperature, therefore, requires the arrangement of the solutions in order of decreasing molality.

17. a. The correct answer is 35 mm. You solve this by the following:

1,400 m/s = wavelength × 40 kHz

40 kHz = 40,000 Hz = 40,000 s^{-1}

Divide each side of the equation by 40,000:

1,400/40,000 = W

W = 0.035 m = 35 mm

18. d. The spring is being held in place, so its kinetic energy is zero because it is not moving. The spring is, however, extended as far as possible, which means that its potential energy is very high.

19. conduction. Heat is being transferred directly from the blanket to your body.

20. a. equal to. Both waves have an amplitude of 2, as amplitude is equal to the height of the wave above neutral.

b. greater than. Frequency refers to the number of wave cycles per given time period. Wave A has more cycles compressed into the same period of time as wave B, so its frequency is higher than that of wave B.

c. less than. Wavelength is the distance between two consecutive troughs or two consecutive crests. That distance is shorter for wave A than for wave B.

21. The ball would keep moving upward forever. According to Newton's first law, in the absence of oppositional forces, an object at rest tends to remain at rest, and an object in motion tends to remain in motion. This is also known as the law of inertia.

22. d. The jogger's velocity is decreasing, so it should be negative. Acceleration/deceleration is equal to the change in velocity divided by elapsed time: $\frac{30 \text{ m/min} - 50 \text{ m/min}}{2 \text{ min}} = \frac{-20 \text{ m/min}}{2 \text{ min}} = -10 \text{ m/min}^2$.

23. a. Momentum = mass × velocity, so velocity $= \frac{\text{momentum}}{\text{mass}} = \frac{6.0 \text{ kg·m/s}}{2.0 \text{ kg}} = 3.0 \frac{\text{m}}{\text{s}}$.

24. b. Weight = mass × gravitational acceleration. Your mass doesn't change in this scenario, but the gravitational acceleration does because Jupiter is much bigger than Earth and therefore has a much stronger gravitational pull and a much more highly negative gravitational acceleration. Therefore, your weight will increase on the planet Jupiter.

25. c. This is not an electromagnetic force because electromagnetic forces are not contact forces and rely on electrical charges. This is not a frictional force; the arrow pointing up the inclined plane is actually a frictional force. This is not tension because there are no ropes or wires involved here. This is a normal force because an object is exerting a force perpendicularly to another stable object.

26. a screw. A twist lid must be rotated for removal or tightening around the inclined plane built into the jar.

Physical Science Review

1. **392,000 N.** 40,000 kg × 9.8 m/s² = 392,000 N

2. The object will accelerate at **5 m/s².**
   10 N/2 kg = 5 m/s²

3. $4NH_3 + 5O_2 \rightarrow 4NO + 6H_2O$
   This equation is balanced because there are 4 atoms of nitrogen (N), 12 atoms of hydrogen (H), and 10 atoms of oxygen (O) on each side of the equation.

4. **10 kg · m/s.** The formula for momentum is mass multiplied by velocity. The mass of the ball is 0.25 kg; multiply that by the velocity, 40 m/s, and it's equal to 10 kg · m/s.

5. **c.** The point (W) at the top of the roller coaster represents high potential energy. The other point (X) shows the point at which the coaster has high energy of movement (kinetic energy).

6. **147.06 m.** The velocity of the sound is 342 m/s. The time it takes to hear the sound (the time to travel to the wall and back) is 0.86 s.
   $v = 342$ m/s, $t = 0.86$ s (2-way)
   If it takes 0.86 seconds to travel to the canyon wall and back, then it takes 0.43 seconds to travel the one-way distance to the wall.
   Now use $d = v \cdot t$
   $d = v \cdot t = (342$ m/s$) \cdot (0.43$ s$) = 147.06$ m

7. water (H_2O): **compound**
   hydrogen (H): **element**
   salt (NaCl): **compound**
   glucose ($C_6H_{12}O_6$): **compound**
   oxygen (O): **element**
   saltwater: **mixture**

8. **d.** Blending fruit is not a change of state, as this is the chopping of an object until its solid form becomes something only similar to liquid.

9. 1. Volume: **e.** How much space is occupied by a substance.
   2. Elasticity: **c.** The ability of a substance to return to its original shape after a deforming force is applied.
   3. Solubility: **a.** The measure of how much of a substance will dissolve in another substance.
   4. Hardness: **b.** The measure of how resistant a substance is to shape change when a force is applied.
   5. Viscosity: **d.** The measure of a substance's resistance to flow.

10. **d.** This is an example of a double-replacement reaction.

11. **Displacement** compares the ending point to the starting point. If a person were to walk forward one mile in 15 minutes and then back one mile, the displacement would be zero miles. If a person were to walk one mile forward and one mile back in half an hour, the **distance** traveled would two miles. Final velocity would be zero and speed would be four miles per hour.

EARTH AND SPACE SCIENCE REVIEW

Earth and space science is concerned with the formation of the earth, the solar system, and the universe; the history of Earth (its mountains, continents, and ocean floors); and the weather and seasons. All of these elements combined have made Earth a unique planet. The special conditions on Earth, including the distance from the sun, the makeup of the atmosphere, and the presence of freshwater and oceans, allow life to occur.

This chapter reviews areas of Earth and space science that will likely appear on the GED® Science test as parts of diagrams or passages. Elements of both physical and life sciences will appear within Earth and space science. All of these sciences are interconnected, allowing you to use ideas from one area to interpret questions from another.

Practice exercises are included throughout the chapter. Use them to help with practicing applying the science knowledge presented to solve problems and questions. Answers and explanations are at the end of the chapter.

Let's start close to home, with Earth's systems.

Earth's Systems

Earth is made up of a series of systems involving the planet's atmosphere, land masses, and oceans. The interdependence of these systems is one of the most important principles involved in Earth science and is the basis for how the planet supports life.

Composition of the Earth

Let's start with Earth's composition. It is formed from a series of four main layers:

- inner core
- outer core
- rocky mantle
- crust

The **inner core** is a solid mass of iron with a temperature of about 10,000°F. The high heat at the earth's core is a combination of three factors: (1) residual heat from the formation of the earth, (2) frictional heating caused by denser parts of the core moving toward the center and the frictional force that creates, and (3) the decay of radioactive elements such as uranium in the core. The inner core is approximately 1,500 miles in diameter. To give a comparison, the widest point from the East Coast to the West Coast of the United States is more than twice that at 3,400 miles. This inner core is also, as you may guess from its name, the absolute center of the planet.

The **outer core** is the next layer out from the inner core and is a mass of molten iron and nickel surrounding the inner core. Electrical currents generated from this area produce the earth's magnetic field. The magnetic field assigns the North and South Poles and protects the earth from the charged particles of solar winds and cosmic rays.

The **rocky mantle**, the next layer, is composed of silicon, oxygen, magnesium, iron, aluminum, and calcium and is about 1,750 miles thick. This mantle accounts for most of the earth's mass. When parts of this layer become hot enough, they turn to slow-moving molten rock or magma. This is what comes out of volcanoes when they erupt; however, volcanoes are on the next layer.

The earth's crust is the outermost non-gaseous layer of the planet. It is from 4 to 25 miles thick and consists of sand and rock. This is the part of the planet that we live on and that is most familiar to us. Since it is called *the crust*, you could think of it like a pizza or bread crust—the outermost part of a pizza or a loaf of bread.

The following is a diagram of the layers of the planet. You may encounter a question where the layers are not labeled and you are asked to label these parts. One helpful thing about science is that the naming of things usually follows some form of logic. The name of each part of the planet tells you where it is located.

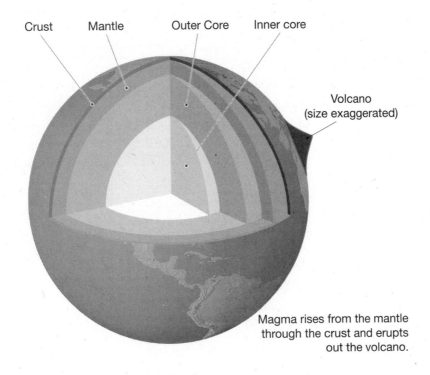

Crust   Mantle   Outer Core   Inner core

Volcano
(size exaggerated)

Magma rises from the mantle
through the crust and erupts
out the volcano.

Geology refers to the scientific study of Earth's physical solid structure, namely the rocks that compose it and the processes that affect it. The three main types of rock on Earth are igneous, metamorphic, and sedimentary.

- **Igneous** rocks form when molten rock buried deep in the earth flows upward toward the surface of the Earth, cools, and solidifies. Examples of igneous rocks include basalt and granite.
- **Metamorphic** rocks form when igneous or sedimentary rocks are exposed to such intense pressure or heat that they become denser and more compact, transforming them structurally. Marble and slate are examples of metamorphic rocks.
- **Sedimentary** rocks form on land or in water at Earth's surface due to the accumulation of sediments. Since temperature and pressure are moderate, these rocks are usually fairly soft and they can fall apart relatively easily. Examples of sedimentary rocks include limestone and shale.

Practice

Next, let's look at the absolute outermost layer of Earth, the atmosphere.

1. Compared to the earth's crust, the inner core is hotter and contains
   a. more molten iron.
   b. more solid iron.
   c. most of Earth's mass.
   d. mostly sand and rock.

2. The majority of Earth's mass is its
   a. crust.
   b. inner core.
   c. outer core.
   d. rocky mantle.

3. The type of rock most likely to form via weathering, erosion, deposition, and compaction is
   a. igneous.
   b. metamorphic.
   c. sedimentary.
   d. any of the three types.

Atmosphere and Water

The atmosphere is a thin layer of gases surrounding the earth. Our atmosphere contains about 78% nitrogen, 21% oxygen, 1% water vapor, and a small amount of other gases. These gases combine to absorb ultraviolet radiation from the sun and warm the planet's surface through heat retention. The atmosphere is divided into four layers:

1. **troposphere**—closest to the earth; up to about 6 miles above. This is the part that we live in and birds fly in.
2. **stratosphere**—second layer, from about 6 to 30 miles above the earth. The lowest part of the stratosphere is as high as planes will fly.
3. **mesosphere**—third layer, from about 30 to 50 miles above the earth.
4. **thermosphere**—fourth layer, from about 50 to 300 miles above Earth.

When you think of atmosphere, it's easy to assume it's mostly water and oxygen; however, our atmosphere is more nitrogen than oxygen, and it can't hold a lot of water. But living beings need water for both the outside and the inside of their cells. In fact, vertebrates (you included) are about 70% water. Water moves through the atmosphere in a cyclical way. At its simplest, sunlight **evaporates** the water from the oceans, rivers, and lakes. The evaporated water then **condenses** to form clouds that produce rain or snow onto the earth's surface (**precipitation**). This cycle is sometimes called the **water** or **hydrologic cycle** and is critical to sustaining life on Earth. The diagram that follows shows elements of this cycle and is an example of the kind of diagram you might see on the GED® test if you were asked a question about the hydrologic cycle.

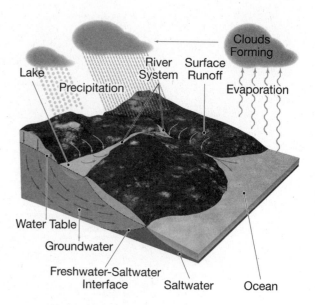

Water or Hydrologic Cycle

Carbon Cycle

Another system of Earth is the **carbon cycle**. These systems are characterized by complex patterns of interconnectedness, which are often cyclical in nature. The carbon cycle is one of the most important examples of this.

Carbon is found in the oceans in the form of bicarbonate ions (HCO_3^-); in the atmosphere, in the form of carbon dioxide; in living organisms; and in fossil fuels (such as coal, oil, and natural gas). The bicarbonate ions in the ocean settle to the bottom and form sedimentary rocks, while plants remove the carbon dioxide in the atmosphere and convert it to sugars through photosynthesis. The sugar in plants enters the food chain, first reaching herbivores, then carnivores and omnivores, and finally scavengers and decomposers. All of these organisms release carbon dioxide back into the atmosphere when they breathe.

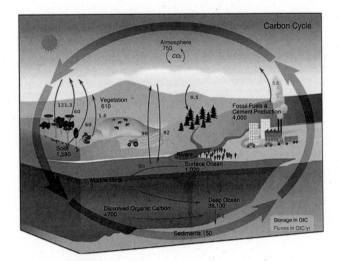

Carbon Cycle
Numbers in black indicate storage of carbon in gigatons (GtC), and numbers in gray alongside arrows indicate annual exchange of carbon (GtC/yr). *Source:* Wikimedia Commons.

Fossil fuels, the last of this list of sources of carbon, represent the largest reserve of carbon on Earth. Fossil fuels come from the carbon of organisms that lived millions of years ago. Burning fossil fuels releases energy, which is why these fuels are used to power machines. When fossil fuels burn, carbon is released into the atmosphere in the form of carbon dioxide (which then is used by the plants, and the cycle continues). However, since the Industrial Revolution, when the consumption of energy began to increase substantially to power machinery, people have increased the concentration of carbon dioxide in the atmosphere by 30% by burning fossil fuels and cutting down forests that would otherwise assist in reducing the higher concentration of carbon dioxide.

Burning fossil fuels and forests also releases nitrogen, and all forms of fixed nitrogen are among the greenhouse gases that cause global warming. In addition, nitric oxide, another gas released when fossil fuels are burned, can convert into nitric acid. This is a main component of acid rain, which destroys habitats. This information is important when considering the health of the planet and the humans and creatures living on it. People are already suffering the consequences of the pollution they have caused. The focus on preventing further damage to the ecosystems and fixing the damage that has been done is another challenge for today's scientists.

With all of these cycles and systems, another part of the earth's composition is the plates in the upper part of the rocky mantle.

Practice

4. What is the role of the ocean in the carbon cycle?
   a. The ocean absorbs carbon from the atmosphere.
   b. The ocean produces carbon dioxide.
   c. The ocean currents transfer heat.
   d. Water evaporates from the ocean surface.

5. The most abundant gas in Earth's atmosphere is
  a. carbon dioxide.
  b. nitrogen.
  c. oxygen.
  d. water vapor.

6. Which physical change of H_2O accompanies precipitation during the water cycle?
  a. condensation
  b. evaporation
  c. freezing
  d. melting

Plate Tectonics

While the earth's upper mantle (or layer) is rigid and is part of the **lithosphere** (together with the crust), the lower mantle flows slowly, at a rate of a few centimeters per year. The crust is divided into plates that drift slowly (only a few centimeters each year) on the less rigid mantle. This motion of the plates is caused by convection (heat) currents, which carry heat from the hot inner mantle to the cooler outer mantle. This process is called **plate tectonics**. This motion also results in earthquakes and volcanic eruptions.

Evidence suggests that about 200 million years ago, all continents were a part of one landmass, named Pangaea. Over the years, the continents slowly separated in a process called **continental drift**. Oceanic crust is thinner than continental crust but still affects continental drift. The theory of plate tectonics says that there are now 15 large plates that fit together like a puzzle and yet continue to slowly move on the mantle.

Tectonic plates can slide past each other, separate from each other (**diverge**), or come together (**converge**). The force needed to move billions of tons of rock is unimaginable, and when plates move, some of that energy is released as earthquakes. Faults, or places where the tectonic plates meet, exist all over the world and are often the sites of strong earth-

quakes. An example of plates sliding past each other is the San Andreas fault in California.

Converging plates often result in the creation of mountains. For example, the Andes Mountains were formed by the Nazca Plate being pushed under the South American Plate. When two oceanic plates meet each other, this often results in the formation of an island arc system. When two plates separate, or diverge, energy is released, earthquakes occur, and magma is released. The Atlantic Ocean was formed by the separation of plates over millions of years.

At some plate boundaries, one plate slides under the other (**subduction**). As the plate slides under the other, the crust melts as it goes deeper into the earth. This creates magma, which rises to the surface and can form volcanoes. Another spot where molten material breaks through to the surface from inside the earth is through the floor of the ocean. It flows from fissures, where it is cooled by the water, resulting in the formation of igneous rocks. As the molten material flows from a fissure, it also forms ridges adjacent to it. One large version of this ridge formation is the Mid-Atlantic Ridge, which is where the Eurasian and North American Plates diverge.

These plates have created the areas where the oceans are contained and also affect the way the oceans behave as a system.

Ocean Currents

Oceanic currents, measured in meters per second or in knots (1 knot = 1.15 miles per hour or 1.85 kilometers per hour), are driven by several factors. One is the rise and fall of the tides, which are affected by the gravitational force of the moon. A second factor that drives ocean currents is wind, which is caused by many things, from high- and low-pressure systems to the rotation of the earth. A third factor that drives currents is density differences in water due to temperature and salinity in different parts of the ocean.

The reason that ocean currents are so important among the systems of Earth is that they can impact weather globally and locally. For example, the Gulf Stream is an ocean current that runs from the tip of Florida, flowing along the eastern coastline of the United States and to Newfoundland before crossing the Atlantic Ocean. Because it carries warm water, it makes northern Europe warmer than it would be otherwise.

Another example you may have heard of is the weather phenomenon called **El Niño**. El Niño is a band of very warm ocean water that develops off the western coast of South America and can cause climatic changes. Typically, El Niño happens every two to seven years and lasts nine months to two years. Because El Niño's warm waters feed thunderstorms, it creates increased rainfall across the eastern Pacific Ocean. Along the west coast of South America, El Niño reduces the upwelling of cold, nutrient-rich water that sustains large fish populations. This reduction in upwelling has led to lower fish populations off the shore of Peru. The impact of El Niño as a weather phenomenon caused by ocean currents can be felt across the globe. With the tropical thunderstorms fueled by the hot, humid air over the oceans, the atmosphere produces patterns of high and low pressure in response. This can result in higher temperatures in western Canada and the upper plains of the United States and colder temperatures in the southern United States. Additionally, in contrast to the flooding rains experienced in South America, the eastern coast of Africa can experience severe drought during an El Niño event. All this is caused by a band of very warm ocean water.

Natural Hazards

While the earth's systems interact in a way that creates an environment most beneficial to sustaining life, these systems also can lead to natural hazards. Floods, earthquakes, hurricanes, tsunamis, and droughts are all examples of natural hazards, and all of these conditions produce stresses on the environment.

Floods can erode the topsoil; destroy trees, grass, and crops; and even tear down homes. Floods can also contribute to the spread of disease by damaging sewage and waste disposal mechanisms. The results of a flood can take years to undo.

Earthquakes can tear up the land and produce rockslides. They can even cause flooding if a river is redirected. The effects of an earthquake in a big city can be devastating.

Hurricanes, also known as typhoons or cyclones in other parts of the world, are tropical cyclones with very high sustained winds. A tropical cyclone is a rapidly rotating storm system with a low-pressure center, strong winds, and a spiral arrangement of thunderstorms that produce heavy rain. They form over large bodies of relatively warm water. Hurricanes can wreak havoc along the coasts, destroying plants, trees, buildings, and even highways.

Tsunamis are very large, destructive water waves that are caused by earthquakes, volcanic eruptions, or landslides (not wind). They used to be called *tidal waves* because they resembled a rising tide, but tsunamis have nothing to do with tides.

Drought occurs when an area receives substantially less precipitation than normal. Drought might be designated after as few as 15 days with reduced rainfall in some places. Significant and sustained droughts can impact crops and livestock and result in widespread food shortage, malnutrition, and famine.

All of these natural hazards are a part of the cycles of Earth, but they aren't pleasant and they cause damage to habitats and ecosystems.

Practice

7. Earthquakes are caused by
   a. tsunamis.
   b. global warming.
   c. plate tectonics.
   d. ocean currents.

8. Which type of plate tectonic movement is represented in the following image?

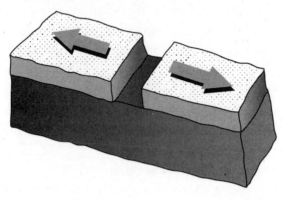

a. continental drift
b. convergence
c. divergence
d. subduction

9. El Niño is
a. a rapidly rotating storm system with a low-pressure center, strong winds, and a spiral thunderstorm arrangement.
b. a band of very warm water that develops off the western coast of South America and can cause changes in the climate.
c. the generation of magma due to subduction of plate tectonics.
d. the rigid shell of the Earth that includes the crust and upper mantle.

Natural Resources and Energy

While nature may have some major hazards, it also is full of resources that humans depend on to sustain life. A good part of the resources we use every day come directly from the environment. These are called **natural resources**—resources provided by nature.

Resources

Air, water, sunlight, topsoil, plants, and animals are examples of Earth's natural resources. This huge variety of plant and animal life is referred to as **biodiversity**. The effects of human activity on biodiversity are a growing concern of environmental activists and scientists, as habitat destruction has reduced the diversity of life forms in many regions throughout the world.

There are two kinds of natural resources: renewable and nonrenewable.

Renewable resources are resources that can be replaced or replenished over a short period of time. Plants and crops are examples of resources that, with proper agriculture, are replenishable.

Nonrenewable resources are resources that cannot be replaced or that take many years to replenish. Fossil fuels such as oil and coal are examples of nonrenewable resources, as they are formed from organisms that lived millions of years ago.

Oceans

Oceans are a major renewable resource, and even if you live hundreds of miles from the shore, you are still dependent on the ocean. We rely on the ocean for food, jobs, energy, and recreation. At the same time, oceans cover 70% of Earth's surface and contain more than 97% of all water on Earth. About half of the world's population lives near the ocean, and ocean-based businesses contribute more than $500 billion to the world's economy. In fact, there are more than 140 million jobs in fishing, aquaculture, and other related activities. The ocean contains important mineral and energy resources such as oil and gas, and shipping accounts for the transport of 90% of the world's international traded goods. In addition to their economic importance, the oceans contain rich biodiversity. Coral reefs and estuaries (salty or brackish freshwater that runs into the ocean) sustain 75% of all commercial fish and shellfish during some point of their life cycles, and one in six people on Earth depend on ocean fish as their primary source of protein.

Even with all of this, global climate change is having significant negative effects on our oceans. The oceans absorb about one-fourth of the CO_2 emitted from human activities. This is called a **carbon sink**. The oceans contain 500 times more carbon than the atmosphere. When CO_2 is absorbed by the ocean, it interacts with saltwater to form carbonic acid. As the levels of CO_2 in the atmosphere continue to increase, the levels of carbonic acid in the ocean also increase. This rising acidification of the ocean ends up causing harm to plankton, adversely affecting shellfish larvae, hindering the ability of corals to build new reefs, and causing serious food chain disruptions.

Another result of warmer global temperatures is that the ice sheets in the Arctic are melting. This melting is having negative consequences for many species of marine mammals that live there. With the usually frigid ocean water warming, the results are increased marine diseases and invasive species, changes in weather systems, and the death of coral reefs. This causes larger and more frequent storms that are accelerating shoreline erosion and affecting how the oceans interact with the land. Along with this, sea levels rising will end up causing habitat loss, and people will need to be relocated as their island and coastal homelands are eliminated.

So while the ocean is a huge resource, climate change is altering our relationship to it and the way it acts as a resource.

Energy

Energy as a resource of the earth comes in many varieties. Heat or thermal energy is transferred between the earth's surface and the atmosphere via conduction, convection, and radiation. Radiation specifically comes from the sun and passes through the atmosphere; some is reflected back into space while some is absorbed by clouds or the earth's surface.

Solar Power

Ultimately our energy comes from the sun. The sun's energy reaches our planet mainly in the form of visible light and infrared (heat) radiation. Plants use this light to synthesize sugar molecules, which are consumed when the plants are eaten by animals or humans. We obtain energy from the sugar molecules, and our bodies use it. The sun also drives the earth's geochemical cycles.

Along with generally heating the planet, the sun heats the earth's surface and drives convection within the atmosphere and oceans, producing winds and ocean currents. The winds cause waves on the surfaces of oceans and lakes and transfer some of their energy to the water through friction between the air molecules and the water molecules.

Solar power also refers to the conversion of solar energy to another, more useful form. Sunlight can be harnessed and collected in special greenhouses, and photovoltaic cells can produce electricity when sunlight hits them. The energy that strikes the earth's surface from the sun in one hour is nearly as much energy as is used by all of humanity in one year. Considering this, many scientists are convinced that this form of energy will one day replace ordinary fossil fuels.

This all sounds pretty great, but solar-powered cars and houses are not that common yet. One reason is because fossil fuels are cheaper to collect and use. But the solar technology is catching up—solar plants are now being constructed, and in 2015, about 0.6% of all electricity generation was from solar power. This may seem like a small percentage of overall energy production, but it represents a 58% increase over 2011. Along with this, many people are finding employment in the solar industry. In 2015, there were more than 209,000 solar workers in the United States, a 20% increase over 2014.

The sun provides energy and jobs to humans. It also helps create wind, which is another big energy resource.

Wind Power

Wind power refers to the conversion of wind energy into a useful form of energy. Large **wind farms** consist of hundreds of individual wind turbines, which are connected to the electric power grid. These farms are established on land and offshore (in the ocean).

Wind power, like solar power, acts as an alternative to fossil fuels. It is plentiful, is renewable, and produces no greenhouse gas emissions. Some countries are far ahead of the United States in harnessing the power of the wind for usable energy. For example, Denmark generates 42% of its electricity from wind. In 2015, wind energy production was 3.7% of total worldwide electricity usage. The cost per unit of energy produced is similar to the cost for new coal and natural gas installations, but in the long term it could be less costly in terms of impact on the environment.

Geothermal Power

Geothermal energy, another energy resource, comes from the heat that is produced in the rocks and fluids beneath Earth's crust. It can be found anywhere from shallow depths to several miles below the surface, and even farther down to the extremely hot molten rock called *magma*. Deep wells are drilled into the underground reservoirs to tap steam and very hot water that drive turbines linked to electricity generators. This particular type of energy is also renewable simply because the heat of the planet is not cooling that quickly.

Energy from Fossil Fuels

Fossil fuels are a major energy resource, but they are a nonrenewable resource. This energy source includes oil, natural gas, and coal and is used for heat, electricity, and gasoline. Since fossil fuels come from the remains of creatures that died millions of years ago, they are decreasing worldwide as we use them up. Additionally, burning them causes various gases to be released into the atmosphere, as stated earlier.

Carbon dioxide and other gases in the atmosphere can trap solar energy—a process known as the **greenhouse effect**. The greenhouse effect is a naturally occurring process that has been accelerated by human production of so-called greenhouse gases such as CO_2. Increased levels of carbon dioxide and other greenhouse gases can cause **global warming**—an increase of temperatures on Earth. In the past 100 years, the average temperature has increased by 0.74°C. This doesn't seem like much, but the temperature increase is already creating noticeable climate changes and problems, such as the melting of polar ice caps and the rising of ocean levels. Reducing carbon dioxide concentrations in the atmosphere, either by finding new energy sources or by actively removing the carbon dioxide that forms, is a challenge for today's scientists.

Practice

10. Which of the following is considered a nonrenewable natural resource?
    a. wind
    b. oil
    c. solar
    d. water

11. The greenhouse effect is
    a. when the sun's rays bounce off the earth's surface and are trapped in the atmosphere by greenhouse gases.
    b. when the sun's rays pass through the atmosphere and warm the surface of the earth.
    c. when the sun's rays bounce off the clouds and get absorbed by the greenhouse gases.
    d. when the sun's rays move through the atmosphere and are absorbed by the ocean.

12. Read the following passage and explain how human behavior has indirectly contributed to the destruction of coral reefs across the globe. Include multiple pieces of evidence from the text to support your answer.

CORAL REEFS IN JEOPARDY

Coral reefs are found around the world. They are built by marine invertebrates called *coral polyps*. The coral polyps that build coral reefs rely on zooxanthellae. Zooxanthellae are a form of photosynthetic algae that live symbiotically in the tissue of corals and provide some of the corals' food supply. For this reason, corals can thrive only in very clear water in a very specific temperature range. They rarely grow deeper than 40 m, and they prefer saltwater. The best temperature for coral reefs is between 25°C and 31°C, and the best salinity is between 34 and 37 parts per 1,000. Also, the pH of ocean water can affect coral growth. Even relatively small increases in ocean acidity can decrease the capacity of corals to build skeletons. Bleaching or whitening of coral reefs occurs when the corals lose their zooxanthellae and can result in the death of the corals.

Coral reefs are important for ecological and economic reasons. They are some of the most diverse ecosystems in the world. They occupy less than 0.1% of the world's ocean surface, yet they provide a home for 25% of all marine species. Coral reefs are often referred to as the *rain forests of the sea*. Economically, they are important to fishing and tourism industries. The annual global economic value of coral reefs was more than US$350 billion in 2002. Yet, they are being destroyed around the world at alarming rates. About 10% of the world's coral reefs have already been completely destroyed. In parts of the world, the Philippines for example, over 70% of the coral reefs have been destroyed.

Humans have contributed to the destruction of coral reefs both directly and indirectly. Certain fishing practices such as the use of poisons and explosives harm or kill reefs directly. Indirectly, humans have damaged the ocean environment of the corals through warming ocean temperatures, sedimentation, and pollution, including increasing the carbon dioxide in the atmosphere. Because the ocean absorbs carbon dioxide from the atmosphere (and changes it to carbonic acid), an increase in CO_2 in the atmosphere has resulted in a decrease in oceanic pH of 0.1. This change may seem small but has had catastrophic consequences for corals and the coral ecosystem.

Write your answer on the lines or on a separate sheet of paper. You should take approximately 10 minutes to complete this task.

_____

_____

_____

_____

_____

_____

_____

_____

_____

Structure of the Universe

Having gone over the earth in detail, let's take a look at the universe at large. Nobody knows for sure how the universe originated, but a major theory is the **Big Bang theory**. This theory states that the universe started off in a hot, dense state under high pressure between 10 billion and 20 billion years ago, then expanded rapidly, and it has been expanding ever since. The universe is still expanding and cooling. Some data suggest that the rate of expansion of the universe is increasing. Whether the universe will continue to expand forever and eventually reach an equilibrium size or shrink back into a small, dense, hot mass is unknown at this point, but it's a mystery that scientists are still looking into.

Stars and Galaxies

Some of the most common objects in the universe are stars. **Stars** are formed by the gravitational attraction of countless hydrogen and helium molecules. The energy of stars stems from nuclear reactions, mainly the fusion of hydrogen atoms to form helium. These nuclear processes in stars lead to the formation of elements, and the stars become gravitationally bound to other stars, forming galaxies, another major part of the universe.

A **galaxy** is a system of stars, stellar dust, and dark matter. It is bound together by gravity, and black holes exist in the center of many of them. There are billions of galaxies in the known universe (some say over 170 billion!). Our solar system is part of the Milky Way galaxy, which in addition to the sun contains about 200 billion other stars.

When considering the universe, we have a particular perspective on what is out there based on what we can see from Earth. Constellations are a big part of that.

Constellations

If you have seen the Big Dipper in the night sky, then you have seen a **constellation**, which is a pattern or grouping of stars. Because of the rotation of the earth, certain constellations are visible only at certain times of the year. The reason we even have constellations at all is that organizing these stars into some kind of configuration that looks like something familiar has helped people to remember which stars are which. Also, for centuries people have looked to skies to navigate the seas, to know when to have religious ceremonies, and to know when to plant and reap their crops. All of these things were aided by humans looking into the sky and using the stars to guide their way.

Planets

Earth is a planet, but not all planets are like Earth. A **planet** is now defined as a celestial body that has enough mass to be spherical, orbits a star, and is not part of a belt (such as an asteroid belt). In our immediate neighborhood, these planets are situated in our solar system.

Solar Systems

Our **solar system** is made up of the sun and all of the objects that orbit around it, including the planets, moons, asteroids, and comets. The sun is very massive, and it has a strong gravitational pull on the objects in the solar system.

There are eight **planets** in our solar system. In order (closest to farthest from the sun), they are Mercury, Venus, Earth, Mars, Jupiter, Saturn, Uranus, and Neptune. The first four planets (Mercury, Venus, Earth, and Mars) are called *terrestrial planets* because they are rocky. The other planets (Jupiter, Saturn, Uranus, and Neptune) are called *gas giants* because they are made up mainly of gas.

You may have learned that Pluto was one of nine planets in our solar system. In the 1990s, astronomers discovered that Pluto was not a planet in its own orbit but part of a belt of asteroids. This asteroid belt also included several other small planet-like bodies that were around the same size as Pluto. Because of this, in 2006 astronomers voted to change Pluto's designation to that of a dwarf planet. We now recognize only eight true planets.

Planets of the Solar System
Compared with each other, the sizes are correct but the distances are not.

A **comet** is a small, icy celestial body that, when passing close to the sun, may display a tail. The tail is caused by solar radiation and the solar wind. Comets range from a few hundred meters to tens of kilometers across and are composed of loose collections of ice, dust, and small, rocky particles. Comets have orbits that range from a few years to several hundred years. Halley's comet, for example, is visible from Earth about every 75 years. Its next appearance should be in 2061. There are over 4,000 known comets, and most are not bright enough to be seen by the naked eye. A very few are extraordinarily bright and are considered *great comets*. The Hale-Bopp comet and Halley's comet are examples of great comets.

Some other objects typical of the solar system are asteroids. **Asteroids** are similar to comets but differ in composition. They're made up of metals and rocky materials and have no tail (because they are not composed of ice). There are millions of asteroids, some of which are as small as particles of dust, while others are as large as half a mile in diameter. Most of the known asteroids orbit in the asteroid belt between the orbits of Mars and Jupiter. Astronomers estimate that this belt contains between 1.1 million and 1.9 million asteroids larger than 1 km (0.6 mi) in diameter and millions of smaller ones.

Our solar system is full of a variety of celestial bodies, some of which are occasionally visible in our night sky, and all of which, through studying them, help us learn more about our universe and our planet.

Development of Stars

Understanding how stars are formed helps us to understand how our own sun and solar system were created. Scientists now know that the formation of stars occurs within what are called "stellar nurseries," which are a type of nebula. A **nebula** is a cloud of dust and gas, composed primarily of hydrogen (97%) and helium (3%). Nebulae may be giant, with 1,000 to 100,000 times the mass of the sun, or smaller, with less than a few hundred times the mass of the sun. Also, there are areas within a nebula where gravity causes the dust and gas to clump together. As the clump gains mass, its gravitational attraction increases, which in turn draws more mass to it. This clump is called a **protostar** at this stage and is the beginning of a star forming.

The protostar keeps drawing in more gas and growing even hotter. Once the protostar gets hot enough, its hydrogen atoms start fusing. If the protostar gathers enough mass, the young star blasts the remaining gas and dust away, stabilizes, and becomes a main sequence star. After a star has formed, it generates thermal energy in its core through the nuclear fusion of hydrogen atoms into helium. This process of stellar (star) development can take millions of years. A star the size of our sun takes about 50 million years to mature to adulthood. Our sun will stay in the mature phase for approximately 10 billion years.

The life span of a star is determined by the type of star it is. In some stars, when the core runs out of hydrogen fuel, it contracts under the weight of gravity and heats up. The core's rising temperature heats the upper layers, causing them to expand. As this happens, the radius of the star increases and it becomes a **red giant**. When the helium fuel runs out entirely, the core expands and cools and the upper layers expand and eject material that collects around the dying star to form a **planetary nebula**. Finally, the core cools into a **white dwarf** and then eventually into a **black dwarf**. This entire process takes a few billion years.

In other (more massive) stars, when the core runs out of hydrogen, the stars fuse helium into carbon just like the sun. However, after the helium is gone, their mass is enough to fuse carbon into heavier elements such as oxygen, neon, silicon, magnesium, sulfur, and iron. Once the core has turned to iron, it can no longer burn and the star collapses by its own gravity. The core becomes so tightly packed that protons and electrons merge to form neutrons. In less than a second, the iron core, which is about the size of Earth, shrinks to a neutron core with a radius of about 6 miles (10 kilometers). The core heats to billions of degrees and explodes (**supernova**), releasing large amounts of energy and material into space. The remains of the core can form a **neutron star** or a **black hole**, depending on the mass of the original star.

These are all things that will occur with our own sun and with stars in nearby star systems. Almost all of these ideas are big picture ideas but still applicable to understanding how our universe functions.

Motion of the Earth and Moon

Coming back closer to home, let's look at the motion of the earth and moon and how they intereact. The earth **rotates** (spins) on its axis once about every 24 hours. This causes day and night and makes most extraterrestrial objects seem to move around the sky in about one day. The earth also moves around the sun in an elliptical (nearly circular) orbit. It is moving about 67,000 miles per hour (107,000 km/hr) in its orbit around the sun.

The earth moves around the center of the earth-moon system once a month. In comparison, Earth's **revolution** around the sun takes much longer than its rotation on its axis. One complete revolution takes 365.24 days, or approximately one year. The earth revolves around the sun because the sun's gravity keeps it in a roughly circular orbit around the sun.

Have you noticed the sun seems to shine a bit differently in the winter sky? It does. The tilt of Earth causes the sun to hit the earth differently at different points in the revolution. Because of this tilt of the earth's axis, we experience spring, summer, fall, and winter. The northern hemisphere experiences summer when Earth is in the part of its orbit where the northern hemisphere is oriented more toward the sun. The sun therefore rises higher in the sky and is above the horizon longer, and the rays of the sun strike the ground more directly. Likewise, during winter in the northern hemisphere, the hemisphere is oriented away from the sun, the sun rises low in the sky and is above the horizon for a shorter period, and the rays of the sun strike the ground more obliquely.

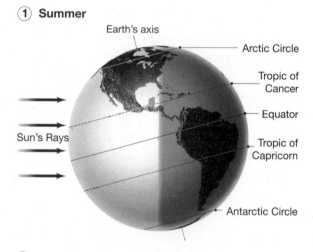

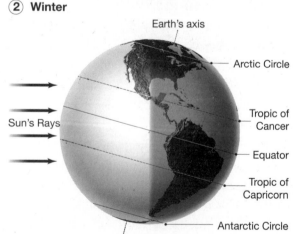

Summer and Winter in the Northern Hemisphere

An interesting occurrence that happens regularly for viewers on Earth and gives us information about the movement of the sun, earth, and moon are eclipses. An **eclipse** occurs when an astronomical object is obscured from view either by passing into the shadow of another object or by having another object pass between it and the viewer. A **solar eclipse** is when the moon crosses between the earth and the sun. A **lunar** eclipse, in contrast, is when the moon moves into the earth's shadow.

The **tides**, which are also a major part of the movement of the earth and moon, are the rise and fall of sea levels caused by the gravitational forces of the moon and the sun and the rotation of the earth. Some regions of the world have two high tides and low tides each day, and some experience only one of each.

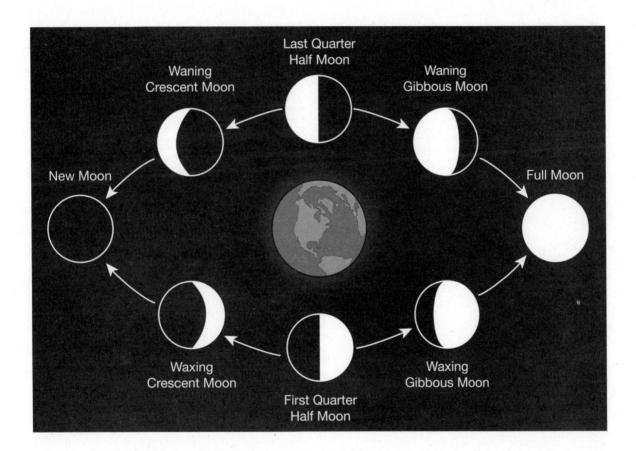

The phases of the moon represent various positions of the earth and moon relative to the sun. The four principal lunar phases are the new moon, first quarter half moon, full moon, and last quarter half moon. The intermediary lunar phases are called *waxing* or *waning*, and *crescent* or *gibbous*, depending on the phases to follow. Waning intermediary phases can be found en route from the full moon to the new moon, so as the brighter portion of the moon decreases in size over time, it's called *waning*. On the other hand, on the way from the new moon to the full moon, the term *waxing* is used as the brighter portion of the moon increases in size. When the size of the brighter portion of the moon exceeds that of the darkened portion of the moon, the term *gibbous* is used. When the size of the darkened portion of the moon exceeds that of the bright portion of the moon, the term *crescent* is used. Remembering these rules will make it easy to remember the names of the eight main phases of the moon. The phases vary in appearance and timing depending on where the viewer is located on Earth.

Practice

13. The length of an Earth day is determined by the time it takes for one
   a. Earth rotation.
   b. Earth revolution.
   c. sun rotation.
   d. sun revolution.

14. Describe the differences between a comet and an asteroid.

_____

_____

_____

_____

15. An exploding star core that expels energy and material into space is called a
   a. black hole.
   b. nebula.
   c. red giant.
   d. supernova.

16. Which moon phase occurs between the last quarter half moon and the new moon?
   a. waning crescent
   b. waning gibbous
   c. waxing crescent
   d. waxing gibbous

Summary

Earth and space science covers the basic concepts of how the universe works, from the composition of the earth to Earth's interacting systems and renewable resources, from the birth and death of stars to the orbits of planets around them. Earth and space are governed by interacting systems, and Earth cycles, such as the hydrologic cycle, are mirrored in cosmic cycles, including the creation of stars and galaxies.

If one of Earth's systems is disrupted, other parts of the system are affected. For example, burning fossil fuels contributes to global warming. It is possible that there are ways in which cosmic systems can also be disrupted, but these ideas are still being discovered.

After we study Earth's systems and the composition of the universe, it is easier to understand how human actions can affect our world and the universe around us. Earth and space science provides a basis for this understanding.

Earth and Space Science Review

1. What occurs when the moon moves between the earth and the sun?
   a. solar eclipse
   b. lunar eclipse
   c. night
   d. solar flares

2. Which of these statements most accurately explains why the northern hemisphere experiences warming in summer?

   a. The northern hemisphere is closer to the sun in the summer than in the winter.

   b. The northern hemisphere experiences longer days in the summer.

   c. The northern hemisphere is tilted away from the sun in the summer.

   d. The earth's tilt on its axis causes the rays of the sun to hit the northern hemisphere more directly in spring and summer than in fall and winter.

3. Which statement is the primary reason Pluto is no longer considered a planet?

   a. It does not orbit the sun.

   b. It is too small.

   c. It is part of an asteroid belt.

   d. It does not have a moon.

4. Describe two ways that trees and other plants contribute to the carbon cycle.

   _____

   _____

   _____

   _____

5. Match each of the natural resources listed with its correct label: renewable or nonrenewable.

RENEWABLE RESOURCE	NONRENEWABLE RESOURCE

   ■ water   ■ gas   ■ coal

   ■ wood   ■ plants   ■ oil

   ■ wind   ■ sun

6. Fill in the blanks of the following sentences using the list of words provided.

   ■ mountains

   ■ cliffs

   ■ oceans

   ■ faults

Converging tectonic plates create _____ or island systems. When tectonic plates diverge, _____ are created.

7. What is the correct order of the following steps in the carbon cycle?

   ■ All of these organisms release carbon dioxide back into the atmosphere when they breathe.

   ■ Plants convert carbon dioxide to sugars through photosynthesis.

   ■ Plants remove carbon dioxide from the atmosphere.

   ■ Bicarbonate ions (HCO_3^-) settle on the ocean bottom and form sedimentary rock.

   ■ The sugar in plants enters the food chain, first reaching herbivores, then carnivores and omnivores, and finally scavengers and decomposers.

   1._____

   2._____

   3._____

   4._____

   5._____

8. Describe what a natural resource is in your own words.

   _____

   _____

   _____

   _____

9. The passing of one object in space through the shadow of another object is called an *eclipse*. The orbits of the moon and Earth in relation to the sun cause both solar and lunar eclipses to occur. During a solar eclipse, the specific alignment of these three objects causes the moon to cast a shadow on the earth. During a lunar eclipse, the alignment causes the earth to cast a shadow on the moon.

The following diagram shows the sun and Earth. Where on the image would the moon need to be for a solar eclipse? Circle the correct place on the diagram.

10. Which of the following is true?
   a. The lithosphere gets thicker as it moves away from a mid-ocean ridge.
   b. The mantle gets thinner as it is subducted beneath a plate.
   c. The mid-ocean ridge is a collision boundary between two plates.
   d. The oceanic crust is thicker than the continental crust.

11. Compared to a planet with a stagnant atmosphere, the Earth's atmospheric circulation causes
   a. the poles to be cooler and the tropics warmer.
   b. the poles to be warmer and the tropics cooler.
   c. the poles to be cooler and the tropics cooler.
   d. the poles to be warmer and the tropics warmer.

12. El Niño is
   a. a current that runs from the tip of Florida and flows along the eastern coastline of the United States.
   b. when the sun's rays bounce off the earth's surface and are trapped in the atmosphere by greenhouse gases.
   c. very large, destructive water waves that are caused by earthquakes, volcanic eruptions, or landslides (not wind).
   d. a band of warm ocean temperatures that develops off the west coast of South America.

Answers and Explanations

Chapter Practice

1. b. The inner core is a solid mass of iron with a temperature of about 7,000°F; therefore, answer choice **b** is correct and choices **a** and **d** are incorrect. Most of the mass of the earth is contained in the mantle; therefore, choice **c** is incorrect.

2. d. The rocky mantle is ~1,750 miles thick and provides the largest contribution to the mass of the planet. The inner core is ~1,500 miles in diameter, the outer core is ~1,400 miles thick, and the crust is only 4 to 25 miles thick.

3. c. Metamorphic rocks form via heat, pressure, and chemical activity to some extent. Igneous rocks form via melting, followed by cooling and solidification. Sedimentary rocks are the type of rock found at the surface of Earth that are most likely to form through the listed processes of weathering, erosion, deposition, and compaction.

4. a. The ocean absorbs carbon dioxide from the atmosphere, rather than producing carbon dioxide; therefore, choice **b** is incorrect. While choices **c** and **d** are factual, they do not answer the question. Regarding choice **d**, evaporation is part of the hydrologic cycle, not the carbon cycle.

5. b. Nitrogen makes up approximately 78% of the gas in the atmosphere of the earth. Oxygen has the second-highest prevalence at 21%, and water vapor makes up 1% of the atmosphere. Carbon dioxide is released into the atmosphere in various ways but is not a significant component of the atmosphere.

6. a. Evaporated water condenses to form clouds, which then produce rain or snow. Condensation is the conversion of a gas to a liquid.

7. c. Earthquakes are caused by shifting tectonic plates. Choice **a** is incorrect because tsunamis can result from earthquakes but do not cause them. Choice **b** is incorrect, as global warming causes other natural disasters but not earthquakes. Choice **d** is incorrect because ocean currents do not cause earthquakes.

8. c. *Continental drift* refers to the splitting of the continents to form separate landmasses separated by water, which is not what is depicted here. *Convergence* is the opposite of what the image displays, as convergence occurs when tectonic plates come together. *Subduction* occurs when one plate slides underneath another. This image demonstrates *divergence*, in which tectonic plates separate from one another.

9. b. Choice **a** describes a tropical cyclone, or hurricane; a common misconception is that El Niño is a storm or storm system. Choice **c** describes an effect of subduction of plate tectonics. Choice **d** provides the definition of the Earth's lithosphere. Choice **b** correctly defines El Niño.

10. b. A nonrenewable natural resource is one that can be depleted. Oil is considered a nonrenewable natural resource because our planet has only a finite amount of it. Choices **a**, **c**, and **d** are all examples of renewable natural resources because they cannot be depleted.

11. a. The greenhouse effect is when the sun's rays bounce off the earth's surface and are trapped in the atmosphere by greenhouse gases. This results in increased warming.

12. Read the following scoring guide and the example of a 3-point response.

Scoring Guide for a Short Answer Question (from the GED® Testing Service Assessment Guide for Educators)

3-point responses contain

- a clear and well-developed explanation of how human behavior has contributed to the destruction of coral reefs across the globe.
- three specific examples of human activities that indirectly affect the health of coral reefs.
- complete support from the passage.

2-point responses contain

- an adequate or partially articulated explanation of how human behavior has contributed to the destruction of coral reefs across the globe.
- partial support from the passage.

1-point responses contain

- minimal or implied explanation of how human behavior has contributed to the destruction of coral reefs across the globe.
- minimal or implied support from the passage.

0-point responses contain

- no explanation of how human behavior has contributed to the destruction of coral reefs across the globe.
- no support from the passage.

Example of a 3-Point Response

Coral reefs are important for economic and ecological reasons. Yet human behavior is resulting in their destruction around the globe. Corals and the algae that help them live are very sensitive to changes in salinity, water temperature, and acidity. The effects of global warming and climate change can be seen in the destruction of coral reefs around the world. Increasing water temperatures can negatively affect coral reefs. The best temperature for corals is between 25°C and 31°C. In addition to warming the ocean, increases in greenhouse gases in the atmosphere have made the ocean more acidic (decreased pH by 0.1). Emissions from burning fossil fuels (e.g., cars, industry, coal-burning power plants) contribute to carbon dioxide in the atmosphere. This carbon dioxide is absorbed by the ocean, where it is turned into carbonic acid. This decrease in pH can harm or kill the small symbiotic algae that live in the coral and help it thrive.

13. a. Earth spins (rotates) on its axis once about every 24 hours. This causes day and night and makes most extraterrestrial objects seem to move around the sky in about one day.

14. A comet is a small, icy celestial body that may display a tail, caused by solar radiation and solar wind, when it passes close to the sun, and is composed of ice, dust, and small, rocky particles. Asteroids differ from comets in composition, as they are made of metals and rocky materials, and they also have no tail because they are not composed of ice. There are over 4,000 known comets, most of which are not visible to the naked eye. Most asteroids are part of the asteroid belt between Mars and Jupiter.

15. d. An exploding star core is called a *supernova*. A black hole might be the remnants of the core of the supernova. A *nebula* is a cloud of dust and gas that can gain mass to become a protostar. A *red giant* is the state of a star as its radius expands during heating.

16. a. As the chart of the moon phases shows, the last quarter half moon transitions into the waning crescent, which then transitions into the new moon.

Earth and Space Science Review

1. a. A solar eclipse occurs when the moon moves between the earth and the sun. Choice **b** is incorrect because a lunar eclipse occurs when the earth's shadow comes between the sun and the moon. Choice **c** is incorrect because night occurs as the earth rotates every 24 hours. Solar flares are large emissions of energy from the sun; therefore, answer choice **d** is incorrect.

2. d. The seasons are caused by the earth's tilt on its axis. Because the northern hemisphere is tilted toward the sun in summer, the rays of the sun hit that part of the earth more directly. A common misperception is that the seasons are caused by the earth being closer to the sun in summer (choice **a**) and farther away in winter. The days are longer in the summer (choice **b**), but that does not explain why the northern hemisphere experiences warming in summer. Choice **c** is an incorrect statement.

3. c. Pluto is part of the Kuiper (asteroid) belt and shares its orbit around the sun with many other large asteroids; therefore, it is no longer considered a planet. Choice **a** is not true; Pluto does orbit the sun, but it just does so within an asteroid belt. The question asks for the primary reason that Pluto is not a planet, so **b** is not the correct choice. As for choice **d**, some planets have a moon and others do not; this is not a requirement for being considered a planet. In fact, Pluto has five known moons.

4. *Sample answer:*
Plants remove carbon dioxide (CO_2) from the atmosphere and convert it to sugars through photosynthesis. During respiration, plants take O_2 from the atmosphere and release it with CO_2.

5.

RENEWABLE RESOURCE	NONRENEWABLE RESOURCE
plants	oil
wind	coal
sun	gas
water	
wood	

6. Converging tectonic plates create **mountains** or island systems. When tectonic plates diverge, **oceans** are created.

Tectonic plates can slide past each other, separate from each other (diverge), or come together (converge). At some plate boundaries, one plate slides under the other (subduction). Converging plates create mountains. When two plates diverge, energy is dispersed, earthquakes occur, magma is released, and over the course of ages, oceans can form. The Atlantic Ocean was formed by the separation of plates over millions of years.

7. 1. Plants remove carbon dioxide from the atmosphere.

2. Plants convert carbon dioxide to sugars through photosynthesis.

3. The sugar in plants enters the food chain, first reaching herbivores, then carnivores and omnivores, and finally scavengers and decomposers.

4. All of these organisms release carbon dioxide back into the atmosphere when they breathe.

5. Bicarbonate ions (HCO_3^-) settle on the ocean bottom and form sedimentary rock.

8. *Sample answer:*
Air, water, sunlight, topsoil, and plant and animal life are examples of Earth's natural resources. Natural resources occur and exist in nature in some form and are used by humans for every aspect of survival.

9.

In order for an eclipse to occur, the sun, earth, and moon must be aligned in a particular way. When the moon is positioned between the sun and the earth, the moon will prevent sunlight from reaching a portion of the earth. This is a solar eclipse. When the earth is positioned between the sun and the moon, the earth will prevent sunlight from reaching the moon. This is a lunar eclipse.

10. a. The **lithosphere** gets thicker as it moves away from a mid-ocean ridge.

11. b. Compared to a planet with a stagnant atmosphere, the earth's atmospheric circulation causes the poles to be warmer and the tropics cooler.

12. d. El Niño develops in some years as a warm band of ocean water off the west coast of South America. Choice **a** describes the Gulf Stream. Choice **b** describes the greenhouse effect. Choice **c** describes tsunamis.

GED® SCIENCE PRACTICE TEST

This practice test is modeled on the format, content, and timing of the official GED® Science test. Like the official exam, the questions focus on your ability to read and comprehend scientific information in the form of text, graphs, charts, diagrams, and more.

Work carefully, but do not spend too much time on any one question. Be sure you answer every question. Set a timer for 90 minutes, and try to take this test uninterrupted, under quiet conditions.

Complete answer explanations for every test question follow the exam. Good luck!

35 total questions
90 minutes to complete

1. Kenya is a country located on the eastern edge of the African continent.

The graph below shows the number of hours during which the sun is visible in Kenya each month.

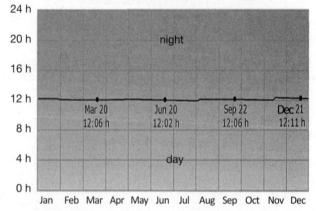

Which statement correctly explains the lack of variation in daylight hours over the course of the year?
   a. The length of the day is not dependent on daylight saving time.
   b. Kenya receives direct sun all year long because it is on the equator.
   c. Countries in the northern and southern hemispheres have opposite seasons.
   d. The earth's rotation places Kenya an equal distance from the sun during spring and fall.

2. The equation for photosynthesis is shown below.

$$6CO_2 + 6H_2O + Energy \rightarrow C_6H_{12}O_6 + 6O_2$$

Which of these correctly identifies the reactants in the equation?
   a. glucose, oxygen
   b. carbon dioxide, water
   c. oxygen, carbon dioxide
   d. oxygen, water, glucose

3. Circle the graph below that correctly depicts constant positive velocity.

(A)

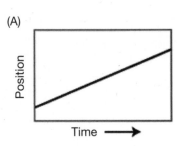

(B)

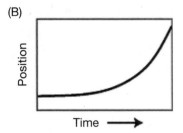

(C)

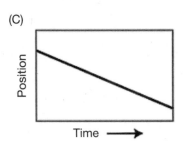

(D)

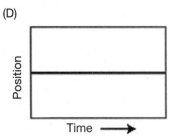

4. The diagram below shows the difference between an eye with normal vision and one with nearsighted vision.

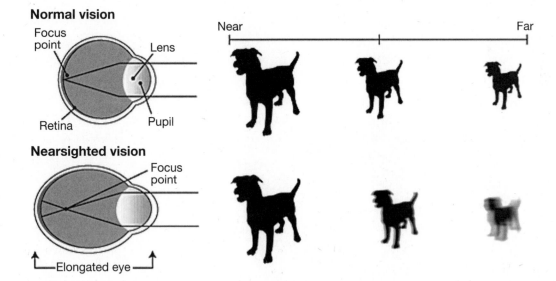

Which part of the eye is best described as a layer at the back of the eye containing light-sensitive cells that trigger nerve impulses to the brain?

a. lens

b. pupil

c. retina

d. focus point

5. Water moves easily across cell membranes through special protein-lined channels. If the total concentration of all dissolved solutes is not equal on both sides, there will be a net movement of water molecules into or out of the cell. The following diagram shows red blood cells in solutions with three different salt concentrations.

Red Blood Cells in Solutions of Different NaCl Concentrations

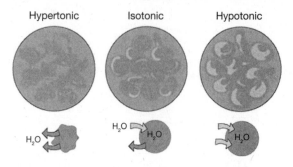

According to this diagram, when will homeostasis occur in red blood cells?

a. when the osmotic pressure of water is equal

b. when the concentration of salt is higher outside the cell

c. when the amount of water inside the cell is higher than outside the cell

d. when the osmotic flow of water out of the cell is greater than the salt solution inside the cell

Please use the following to answer questions 6–8.

Tetanus is a non-contagious infection caused by *Clostridium tetani*—rod-shaped, anaerobic bacteria. *C. tetani* affects skeletal muscles by releasing an endotoxin manufactured in the outer portion of the cell wall. The toxin infects the central nervous system and causes prolonged muscle spasms. Infection occurs through contamination of wounds and can be prevented by proper immunization. Most developed countries provide tetanus vaccinations as a standard of health care.

Tetanus is often associated with rust. Rusting occurs when oxygen, water, and iron interact in a process called *oxidation*. Over time, the iron mass will convert to iron oxide, or rust. A rusted surface provides a thriving environment for organisms with low oxygen needs.

Tetanus occurs worldwide but is most common in hot, damp climates with manure-treated soils. *C. tetani* endospores are widely distributed in the intestines of many animals such as cattle, chickens, and sheep.

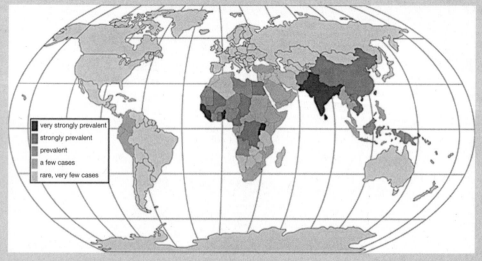

6. Explain how a non-contagious disease, such as tetanus, comes to be so widespread in certain parts of the world. Include multiple pieces of evidence from the text to support your answer.

Write your answer on the lines below. This task may take approximately 10 minutes to complete.

_____

_____

_____

_____

_____

_____

_____

_____

_____

_____

_____

_____

_____

_____

_____

_____

_____

_____

7. Anaerobic bacteria such as *Clostridium tetani* use the process of fermentation to obtain nutrition. The bacteria use organic compounds, typically found in the intestinal tract of animals, to ferment sugars for energy, and produce various acids and alcohol byproducts.

Identify the correct products in the fermentation equation below. Fill in each box with the correct term from the list below.

oxygen
water
ethanol
energy

glucose → [＿＿＿＿＿＿] + carbon
dioxide (+ [＿＿＿＿＿＿] released)

8. The diagram below shows some basic components of bacterial cells.

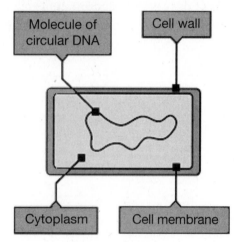

Diagram of bacterial cell

Based on the information in the passage and in the diagram, determine which cellular component is responsible for both the shape of *Clostridium tetani* and endotoxin production.
a. DNA
b. cell wall
c. cytoplasm
d. cell membrane

Please use the following to answer questions 9–11.

Bufo marinus, commonly referred to as the cane toad, can measure 6–9 inches long and weigh up to 4 pounds. The cane toad is nocturnal, breeds year round, and releases a toxin from the shoulders that is fatal to vertebrates. It eats crawling insects, small birds, mammals, and other amphibians, including smaller cane toads. It is native to tropical America but is permanently established in Australia. In the 1930s, sugarcane farmers imported the toads to Australia in attempts to control cane beetles.

Adult cane beetles measure about 13 millimeters long and are black, hard-shelled, dome-shaped flying insects with strong legs. They eat the leaves of sugar cane while their larvae hatch underground and destroy the roots. The flying beetles and burrowing larvae are difficult to eradicate. There is no evidence that the introduced cane toads have had any impact on cane-beetle populations. Cane toads have, however, had a significant impact on Australian ecology, including the depletion of native species that die when eating cane toads, the poisoning of pets and humans, and the decline of native animals preyed upon by the toads. While many populations of native species declined in the decades following the introduction of cane toads, some are now beginning to recover. One species of crow has even learned how to eat cane toads from the underbelly in order to avoid the venom.

9. Which of the following pieces of evidence supports the theory that the behaviors of other organisms are limiting resources for young cane toads?
- **a.** Adult cane toads often prey on juvenile cane toads.
- **b.** Cane-beetle larvae are buried underground and are inaccessible to cane toads.
- **c.** Adult cane beetles have heavy exoskeletons and the ability to fly.
- **d.** Cane-toad tadpoles can exist only in aquatic environments.

10. Based on the information in the passage, which of these terms best describes the effect seen in crows that eat cane toads?
- **a.** speciation
- **b.** adaptation
- **c.** development
- **d.** homeostasis

11. Discuss the impact that cane toads have had on the Australian ecosystem.

Include multiple pieces of evidence from the text to support your answer.

Write your answer on the lines below. This task may take approximately 10 minutes to complete.

_____

_____

_____

_____

_____

_____

_____

_____

_____

Please use the following to answer questions 12–14.

> In a marine ecosystem, there is a unique relationship between corals and the photosynthetic pro-tists that live on the coral reefs. The single-celled protists, called *zooxanthellae*, live in the tissue of corals and go about the business of transforming large amounts of carbon dioxide into usable energy. The photosynthetic products are used by the corals for metabolic functions or as building blocks in the making of proteins, fats, and carbohydrates.
>
> Although much of a coral's energy needs is supplied by these zooxanthellae, most corals also capture food particles with their stinging tentacles. Prey ranges in size from small fish to micro-scopic zooplankton. These food sources supply corals and zooxanthellae with nitrogen.

12. Based on the passage, corals and zooxanthellae demonstrate which type of symbiotic relationship?
   a. mutualism
   b. parasitism
   c. amensalism
   d. commensalism

13. Examine the trophic levels of a marine food web in the diagram below. The trophic pyramid groups organisms by the role that they play in the food web.

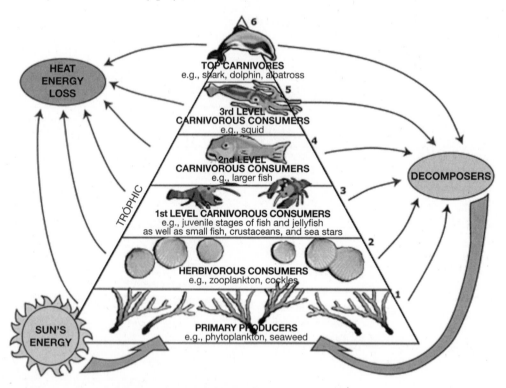

Write the appropriate answers in the boxes below.

Zooxanthellae are described in the passage as _____.

Based on the trophic levels identified in this pyramid, zooxanthellae would be classified as

_____.

14. The diagram below shows a marine food web.

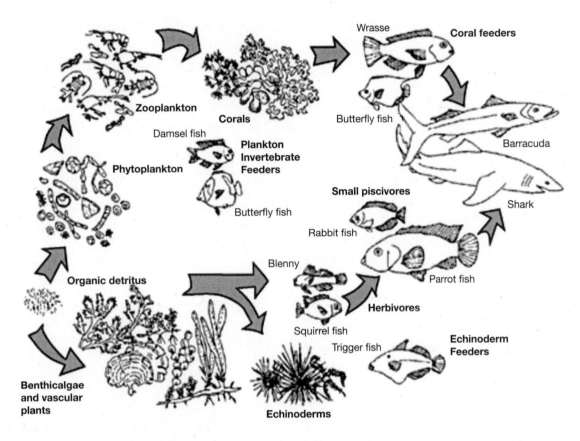

Using the information provided in the passage, identify the organism in the marine food web that supplies coral with energy. Circle the picture of the organism you want to select.

15. As seen in the following diagram, living things are highly organized, with specialized structures performing specific functions at every level of organization.

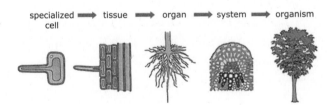

Select the correct sequence of cellular organization. Begin with the most specialized component.

a. red blood cell → blood → heart → cardiovascular system

b. cardiovascular system → heart → blood → red blood cell

c. red blood cell → blood → cardiovascular system → heart

d. heart → cardiovascular system → blood → red blood cell

16. The letters below show the genotypes of two parents.

Yy × Yy

The Punnett square below shows the possible combinations of parent alleles. Write the remaining correct combination of the parent alleles in the gray box.

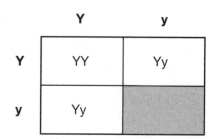

17. Work is a force acting on an object to move it across a distance. Inclined planes make work easier by providing a smooth surface for objects to slide or roll across.

Pushing a stroller up a ramp is easier than pushing it up a flight of stairs. When going down a ramp, the gravitational pull on the stroller may be all that the stroller needs to begin rolling and gain velocity.

The velocity of a moving object can be determined by the following formula:

$$velocity = \frac{distance}{time}$$

If a stroller travels with a forward velocity of 4 m/s for a time of 2 seconds, then the distance covered is _____ meters. (You may use a calculator to complete this question.)

18. Which of the following materials would be a good insulator?
   a. tile floor, because it transfers heat away from skin
   b. steel spoon, because it conducts heat from boiling liquids
   c. wool blanket, because it slows the transfer of heat from skin
   d. copper pipe, because it accelerates the transfer of heated materials

19. Every chemical reaction needs a certain amount of energy to get started, as illustrated in the graph below.

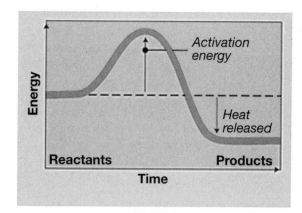

What type of reaction is shown?
   a. endothermic, because energy is required after activation to continue the reaction
   b. exothermic, because additional energy is needed in order to complete the reaction
   c. exothermic, because the energy level of the products is lower than the energy level of the starting materials
   d. endothermic, because the energy level of the final materials is higher than that of the starting materials

20. The amount of kinetic energy a moving object has depends on its velocity and mass. Kinetic energy can be calculated by using the following formula:

Kinetic Energy = $\frac{\text{mass} \times \text{velocity}^2}{2}$

Which of the following would have the most kinetic energy?
a. a truck driving 10 m/s
b. a bicycle traveling 10 m/s
c. a car stopped at a red light
d. a school bus parked on a hill

21. Carlos wants to make his home more energy efficient, and he wants an affordable and environmentally responsible solution. Carlos lives in the western United States. His house is located on a small lot in an urban neighborhood that is sparsely landscaped.

Which of these options would meet all of Carlos's needs and criteria?
a. Place solar panels on the roof.
b. Install a wind turbine in the front yard.
c. Replace an oil-fired furnace with a wood-burning stove.
d. Contact electricity companies to compare prices and negotiate rates.

22. The chart below presents information on ultraviolet radiation. It is divided into wavelength ranges identified as UVA, UVB, and UVC.

RADIATION	UVA	UVB	UVC
Main human effect	Aging	Burning	
Wavelength	400 nm to 315 nm	315 nm to 280 nm	280 nm to 100 nm
% reaching Earth 12 noon	95%	5%	0%
% reaching Earth before 10 A.M. and after 12 P.M.	99%	1%	0%
% reaching the Earth (average)	97%	3%	0%
NOTES:		creates Vitamin D	

People are most likely to be at risk of sunburn at
a. 10:00 A.M., because the UVA rays are the greatest.
b. 12:00 P.M., because more UVB rays reach the Earth.
c. 2:00 P.M., because UVC rays are least harmful.
d. 4:00 P.M., because the UVA rays have less strength.

23. Almost all of the weight of a carbon atom comes from which of these particles?

a. protons only

b. neutrons and electrons

c. protons and neutrons

d. protons, electrons, and neutrons

24. Examine the diagram of an atom below.

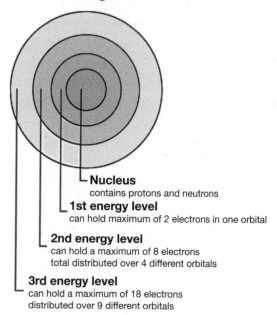

Nucleus
contains protons and neutrons

1st energy level
can hold maximum of 2 electrons in one orbital

2nd energy level
can hold a maximum of 8 electrons
total distributed over 4 different orbitals

3rd energy level
can hold a maximum of 18 electrons
distributed over 9 different orbitals

Which of these would be found in the 1st energy level?

a. 8 neutrons

b. 18 electrons

c. protons and neutrons

d. no more than 2 electrons

25. A cleaning service wants to offer a natural alternative to the industrial products it normally uses. Instead of bleach, the company uses a mixture of vinegar and baking soda. When the liquid vinegar and powdered baking soda combine, a bubbly gas is produced. What chemical property is observed?

a. flammability

b. color change

c. volume

d. reactivity

26. The following chart lists the mechanical properties of different metals and alloys.

TOUGHNESS	BRITTLENESS	DUCTILITY	MALLEABILITY	CORROSION RESISTANCE
Copper	White Cast Iron	Gold	Gold	Gold
Nickel	Gray Cast Iron	Silver	Silver	Platinum
Iron	Hardened Steel	Platinum	Aluminum	Silver
Magnesium	Bismuth	Iron	Copper	Mercury
Zinc	Manganese	Nickel	Tin	Copper
Aluminum	Bronzes	Copper	Lead	Lead
Lead	Aluminum	Aluminum	Zinc	Tin
Tin	Brass	Tungsten	Iron	Nickel
Cobalt	Structural Steels	Zinc		Iron
Bismuth	Zinc	Tin		Zinc
	Monel	Lead		Magnesium
	Tin			Aluminum
	Copper			
	Iron			

A jewelry designer wants to work with new types of materials. She needs a metal that is easy to shape, not easily broken, and resistant to tarnishing. Based on the chart, which material would be the best choice?

a. gold

b. nickel

c. bismuth

d. manganese

27. Hydrogen peroxide (H_2O_2) is stored in dark, opaque containers to slow the natural breakdown of the compound.

Write the missing number of water molecules in the box below.

The reaction is summarized by this formula:

$$2H_2O_2 \rightarrow \boxed{} H_2O + O_2$$

28. In a chemical formula, subscripts show the ratio of one kind of atom to another. For example, NH_3 shows that there are 3 hydrogen atoms for every 1 nitrogen atom.

Examine the following ratios:

- twice as many sodium atoms as carbon atoms
- three times as many oxygen atoms as carbon atoms

Which chemical formula correctly shows the ratios described?

a. Na_2CO_3

b. $NaCO_3$

c. Na_3CO_2

d. Na_6CO_{12}

29. The chart below displays solubility rules.

Soluble Compounds	Combinations That Are Not Soluble
Almost all salts of Na^+, K^+, and NH_4^+	
All salts of Cl^-, Br^-, I^-	Ag^+, Hg_2^{+2}, Pb^{+2}
Salts of F^-	Mg^{+2}, Ca^{+2}, Sr^{+2}, Ba^{+2}, Pb^{+2}
Salts of nitrates, NO_3^- chlorates, ClO_3^- perchlorates, ClO_4^- acetates, $C_2H_3O_2^-$	
All salts of sulfates, SO_4^{-2}	Ba^{+2}, Sr^{+2}, Pb^{+2}

Based on the chart, which compound would be insoluble?

a. $Mg(OH)_2$, because it contains magnesium

b. $NaOH$, because it is a hydroxide compound

c. KNO_3, because it is a potassium compound

d. $LiCl$, because it contains a group 1A element

Please use the following to answer questions 30–32.

Billions of barrels of oil are believed to be locked in soft, finely stratified sedimentary shale formations throughout the United States. Natural gas and oil companies are hard at work freeing these resources. Hydraulic fracturing, more commonly referred to as *fracking*, is a drilling process in which millions of gallons of fresh water, sand, and chemicals are injected under high pressure into a well. This cracks the existing rock and releases the natural gas and oil.

The fluids used in hydraulic fracturing, and the wastewater that comes back up the well, need to be disposed of. The safest, most cost-efficient method of disposal involves injecting the fluids into disposal wells thousands of feet underground. The wells are encased in layers of concrete and usually store the waste from several different wells. Each holds about 4.5 million gallons of chemical-laced water.

Sometimes injections of waste into these wells cause earthquakes. These earthquakes occur as crevices that previously contained oil are filled with water. The resulting pressure change needed to push the water underground can trigger a slip in a nearby fault line.

30. Based on the information in the passage, where are the natural-gas deposits that are targeted by hydraulic fracturing?

a. underneath sand

b. in shale formations

c. inside concrete wells

d. below the water table

31. On the following map, the circles indicate locations of earthquakes caused by or related to energy technologies. The larger the circle, the larger the earthquake.

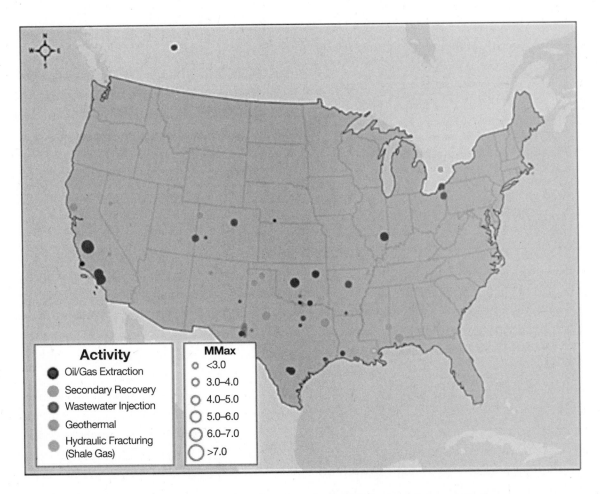

Activity
- ● Oil/Gas Extraction
- ● Secondary Recovery
- ● Wastewater Injection
- ● Geothermal
- ● Hydraulic Fracturing (Shale Gas)

MMax
- ○ <3.0
- ○ 3.0–4.0
- ○ 4.0–5.0
- ○ 5.0–6.0
- ○ 6.0–7.0
- ○ >7.0

Circle the activity in the key that results in earthquakes with the greatest magnitude.

32. According to the information in the passage, which of the following statements best describes concerns about the possible sustainability of hydraulic fracturing?

a. Ongoing fracking could pollute the air.

b. The potential for earthquakes is increasing.

c. Fresh water supplies in shale outcroppings are scarce.

d. Gas and oil surpluses cause less reliance on wind and solar resources.

Please use the passage opposite to answer questions 33–35.

Ocean acidification occurs when seawater absorbs carbon dioxide from the atmosphere. This causes the water to become more acidic. Dissolved carbon dioxide increases the hydrogen ion concentration in the ocean, which decreases the ocean's pH level. Calcifying organisms such as corals, oysters, and sea urchins find it more difficult to build shells and skeletons in acidic water.

Carbon dioxide in the atmosphere comes from many sources. When humans burn oil or gas to generate power, carbon dioxide is released. Carbon dioxide is also a greenhouse gas, which means it leads to warmer temperatures on Earth's surface by trapping heat in the air.

33.

Atmospheric CO$_2$ at Mauna Loa Observatory

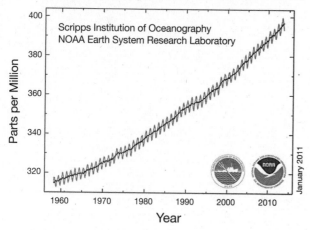

Based on the graph above and the information in the passage, what year presented the lowest risk of ocean acidification?

- **a.** 1960
- **b.** 1970
- **c.** 1990
- **d.** 2010

34. Based on the passage, which effect from carbon dioxide could have a direct negative impact on marine food webs?

- **a.** reduced calcification of coral
- **b.** increased air pollution from cars
- **c.** rising sea levels from melting glaciers
- **d.** warmer temperatures on Earth's surface

35. Which type of coastal erosion would be most impacted by ocean acidification?

- **a.** abrasion
- **b.** attrition
- **c.** corrosion
- **d.** hydraulic action

Answers and Explanations

You should aim to answer 26+ questions correctly on this practice exam in order to be well-prepared to pass the GED® Science test. If you score between 19–25 items correctly, you are on your way to passing, though you probably need a little more review before you take your test. If you answer fewer than 19 items correctly, take extra time to go over the review chapters and try some additional practice exams before you go in for your official test.

1. **Choice b is correct.** Kenya is located on the equator. The tilt of the earth's axis does not substantially change the length of daily exposure of equatorial countries to the sun. Thus, the length of the day does not vary substantially over the course of the year.

   Choice **a** is incorrect. Daylight saving time is the practice of advancing clocks during the lighter months so that evenings have more daylight and mornings have less. In equatorial countries, such as Kenya, there is little variation between daylight and morning hours, and there is no observation of daylight saving time.

   Choice **c** is incorrect. The difference of seasons in opposing hemispheres is due to the tilt of the earth's axis and the proximity of the hemisphere to the sun. In winter, the northern hemisphere is tilted away from the sun. During winter months, the hemispheres will also experience shorter daylight hours. Kenya, an equatorial country, experiences little variance in daylight hours.

   Choice **d** is incorrect. It is true that equatorial countries such as Kenya will not change position with relation to the sun in fall and spring as the earth rotates. However, this does not correctly explain the lack of variation in daylight hours over the course of an entire year.

2. **Choice b is correct.** Carbon dioxide combines with water in the presence of energy. These reactants produce glucose in addition to oxygen as a waste material.

Choice **a** is incorrect. Glucose and oxygen are products of the photosynthesis reaction.

Choice **c** is incorrect. While carbon dioxide is a reactant of photosynthesis, oxygen is one of the products, along with glucose.

Choice **d** is incorrect. Water is incorrectly grouped with oxygen and glucose, which are both products of photosynthesis.

3. **Choice a is correct.** Velocity is speed with direction, and it is calculated by dividing the distance traveled by the time it took to cover that distance. On this graph, time is increasing to the right, and position is increasing constantly with time. At any point on graph A, the position divided by time will produce the same number, indicating constant positive velocity.

Choice **b** is incorrect. The line on graph B is curving upward. This larger slope is indicative of a larger velocity. This shows a positive increase in velocity because the line is getting steeper, indicating acceleration.

Choice **c** is incorrect. Graph C is representative of an object that is moving with a negative velocity (as denoted by the negative slope). There is a constant, negative velocity (as denoted by the constant, negative slope).

Choice **d** is incorrect. If an object is not moving, a horizontal line is shown on a position-time graph. Time is increasing to the right, but the position does not change, so there is no movement. A straight-line graph, such as graph D, indicates an object at rest.

4. **Choice c is correct.** The retina is defined as a layer of light-sensitive tissue lining the inner surface of the eye at the back of the eyeball. The cells that are sensitive to light trigger nerve impulses that travel along the optic nerve to the brain, where a visual image is formed.

Choice **a** is incorrect. The lens is a transparent, biconvex body located in the front of the eye that focuses light rays entering through the pupil to form an image on the retina.

Choice **b** is incorrect. The pupil is a black circular opening located near the front of the eye, through which light passes to the retina.

Choice **d** is incorrect. The focus point, also called an *image point*, is the point where light rays originating from a point on the object converge. Although the focus is conceptually a point, physically the focus has a spatial extent, called the *blur circle*. The focus point differs based on the shape of the eye and elongation of the retina.

5. Choice a is correct. When the osmotic pressure outside the red blood cells is the same as the pressure inside the cells, the solution is isotonic with respect to the cytoplasm. This is the usual condition of red blood cells in plasma in a state of homeostasis.

Choice **b** is incorrect. When the concentration of NaCl is higher outside the cell, it is hypertonic. This results in an osmotic flow from the cell to the more concentrated solution outside the cell, instead of an equilibrium needed to maintain homeostasis.

Choice **c** is incorrect. When the solution outside of the red blood cells has a lower osmotic pressure than the cytoplasm inside the red blood cells, the solution is hypotonic with respect to the cells. The cells take in water in an attempt to equalize the osmotic pressure, causing them to swell and potentially burst.

Choice **d** is incorrect. The osmotic pressure of the solution outside the blood cells is higher than the osmotic pressure inside the cells. The water inside the blood cells exits the cells in an attempt to equalize the osmotic pressure, causing the cells to shrink.

6. The highest number of points you can earn on this short-response essay is 3.

A **3-point response** contains
- a clear and well-developed explanation of how tetanus endospores are transmitted and prevented.
- a well-developed explanation correlating the prevalence of tetanus in nations least likely to vaccinate with the high rate of occurrence, noting the favorable climate for tetanus endospores.
- complete support from the passage.

Sample 3-point response
It is probable that the countries with the highest incidence of tetanus infection are those least likely to vaccinate while also harboring the most favorable soil and climate conditions for C. tetani *endospores. Though* C. tetani *thrives on the low-oxygen surfaces of rusted metals, it is most common in the hot, damp climates of equatorial countries. Developed, vaccinating nations, such as the United States, Canada, and Australia, have low or no reported cases of tetanus. However, tetanus is strongly prevalent in third-world countries such as India and those found in Africa. Less developed, third-world nations are less likely to immunize people, thus the rates of tetanus infections are strongly prevalent, even though it is not contagious. Toxins from* C. tetani *enter unvaccinated bodies through open wounds, attack the central nervous system, and cause prolonged muscle spasms.*

A **2-point response** contains
- an adequate or partially articulated explanation of how tetanus endospores are transmitted and prevented.
- a partial explanation correlating the prevalence of tetanus in nations least likely to vaccinate with the high rate of occurrence.
- partial support from the passage.

Sample 2-point response
People can get tetanus if they are wounded by some kind of rusty metal object. They can also get tetanus from manure-treated soil. Tetanus is caused by a bacteria called C. tetani *and it can be prevented with a vaccine. Some countries in Africa may not vaccinate against tetanus.*

A **1-point response** contains
- a minimal or implied explanation of how tetanus endospores are transmitted and prevented.
- no explanation correlating the prevalence of tetanus in nations least likely to vaccinate with the high rate of occurrence, noting the favorable climate for tetanus endospores.
- minimal or implied support from the passage.

Sample 1-point response
More people in Africa get tetanus than in the rest of the world. It is hot in Africa and there are a lot of animals that have tetanus. People can get tetanus from soil or wounds.

A **0-point response** contains
- no explanation of how tetanus endospores are transmitted and prevented.
- no explanation correlating the prevalence of tetanus in nations least likely to vaccinate with the high rate of occurrence, noting the favorable climate for tetanus endospores.
- no support from the passage.

7. glucose $\longrightarrow$ **ETHANOL** + carbon dioxide (+ **ENERGY** released)

The first product is **ethanol**. In this item, the phrase "alcohol byproducts" clues the choice for the first product. Oxygen is clearly incorrect, as both the item and the passage indicate that the bacteria are anaerobic, thus cannot use oxygen to respire. Water is a factor in the anaerobic fermentation process in that anaerobes are commonly found and used in waste water treatments, but it is not a component in the simplified fermentation equation.

The second product is **energy**. In this item, the statement "the bacteria use organic compounds, typically found in the intestinal tract of animals, to ferment sugars for energy" indicates that the purpose of fermentation is to create energy to be released.

8. Choice b is correct. The cell wall provides rigidity to maintain cell shape. Additionally, endotoxins are produced in the outer portion of the cell wall.
Choice **a** is incorrect. DNA contains the genetic code for enzymes involved in respiration, along with other important information for the life of the cell. Endotoxins are produced in the outer cell wall.
Choice **c** is incorrect. Enzymes are made and chemical reactions involved in respiration are carried out within the cytoplasm of bacteria. However, endotoxins are produced in the outer cell wall, which is also the component that gives shape and rigidity to the cell.
Choice **d** is incorrect. The cell membrane is a non-rigid porous structure that allows gases and water to pass in and out of the cell while controlling the passage of other chemicals. Endotoxins are produced in the outer cell wall.

9. Choice a is correct. Adult cane toads could be a limiting factor for the juvenile cane toad population because large cane toads prey on other amphibians, even smaller cane toads.
Choice **b** is incorrect. Because cane-beetle larvae are buried underground, they are not accessible to the predation of cane toads. Furthermore, cane toads are such diverse predators that the unavailability of one prey species would have little to no effect on their overall population.
Choice **c** is incorrect. Adult cane beetles have heavy exoskeletons and strong legs fitted with spikes. They are difficult to prey upon. They have the ability to fly, while cane toads do not, so they are not a prey resource for the toads.
Choice **d** is incorrect. Cane-toad tadpoles do not limit the success of young, or juvenile, cane toads because they are confined to aquatic habitats, while juvenile cane toads can live terrestrially.

10. Choice b is correct. *Adaptation* is the evolutionary process whereby an organism becomes better able to live in its habitat or habitats. Over time, the crows learned a way to prey upon cane toads without exposing themselves to the toxins released from the cane toad's shoulders.

Choice **a** is incorrect. *Speciation* is the evolutionary process by which new biological species arise.

Choice **c** is incorrect. *Development* is a general term referring to physical growth and change in an individual organism.

Choice **d** is incorrect. *Homeostasis* is a property of a system that regulates its internal environment and tends to maintain a stable, relatively constant condition of properties such as temperature or pH.

11. The highest number of points you can earn on this short-response essay is 3.

A **3-point response** contains
- a clear and well-developed explanation of cane toads as an invasive species in Australia.
- complete support from the passage.

Sample 3-point response
Cane toads are non-native to Australia. They were imported nearly 100 years ago in an attempt to control the cane beetle, a pest that destroys sugarcane. Cane toads had no significant impact on the flying and burrowing beetle. However, they had a devastating impact on Australian ecology that includes the depletion of native species. Many species have been in decline for decades and are only recently beginning to recover.

A **2-point response** contains
- an adequate or partially articulated explanation of cane toads as an invasive species in Australia.
- partial support from the passage.

Sample 2-point response
Cane toads are not from Australia. They were brought from the Americas to eat cane beetles and are toxic to Australian animals. The only species they don't impact negatively is the cane beetle.

A **1-point response** contains
- a minimal or implied explanation of cane toads as an invasive species in Australia.
- minimal or implied support from the passage.

Sample 1-point response:
Some animals are killed by cane toads when they try to eat the toxic toads. Pets and humans have been poisoned. Only a few animals have learned how to eat the toads without dying themselves.

A **0-point response** contains
- no explanation of cane toads as an invasive species in Australia.
- no support from the passage.

12. Choice a is correct. The unique *mutualism* between corals and their photosynthetic zooxanthellae is the driving force behind the settlement, growth, and productivity of coral reefs. This mutualistic relationship is beneficial to the zooxanthellae by providing a host and expelled carbon dioxide for photosynthesis. The corals benefit when they use the products of the zooxanthellae's photosynthesis for metabolic functions or as building blocks in the making of proteins, fats, and carbohydrates.

Choice **b** is incorrect. A *parasitic* relationship is one in which one member of the association benefits while the other is harmed. Parasitic symbioses take many forms, from endoparasites that live within the host's body to ectoparasites that live on its surface. In addition, parasites may be necrotrophic (they kill their host) or biotrophic (they rely on their host surviving). Choice **c** is incorrect. *Amensalism* is the type of relationship in which one species is inhibited or completely obliterated and the other is unaffected. An example is a sapling growing under the shadow of a mature tree. The mature tree can begin to rob the sapling of necessary sunlight, and if the mature tree is very large, it can take up rainwater and deplete soil nutrients. Choice **d** is incorrect. *Commensalism* describes a relationship between two living organisms where one benefits and the other is not significantly harmed or helped. Commensal relationships may involve one organism using another for transportation or for housing, or it may also involve one organism using something another organism created after death.

13. Box 1: Zooxanthellae are described in the passage as **mutualistic photosynthesizers**. Producers are described as autotrophic, which means they are able to make their own food. Just like producers on land, producers in the marine environment convert energy from the sun into food energy through photosynthesis. Phytoplankton are the most abundant and widespread producers in the marine environment. **Box 2:** Based on the trophic levels identified in this pyramid, zooxanthellae would be classified as **primary producers**. Organisms in food webs are commonly divided into trophic levels. These levels can be illustrated in a trophic pyramid, where organisms are grouped by the roles they play in the food web. For example, the first level forms the base of the pyramid and is made up of producers. The second level is made up of herbivorous consumers, and so on. On average, only 10% of the energy from an organism is transferred to its consumer. The rest is lost as waste, movement energy, heat energy, and so on. As a result, each trophic level supports a smaller number of organisms—in other words, it has less biomass. This means that a top-level consumer, such as a shark, is supported by millions of primary producers from the base of the food web or trophic pyramid.

14. The correct answer is zooplankton. The passage states that "although much of a coral's energy needs are supplied by these zooxanthellae, most corals also capture food particles with their stinging tentacles. Prey ranges in size from small fish to microscopic zooplankton." The marine food web clearly depicts an arrow originating with zooplankton that points toward coral. This indicates that the flow of energy moves from zooplankton into coral.

15. **Choice a is correct.** The correct sequence moves from most specialized to higher levels of organization.

Choice **b** is incorrect. The correct sequence moves from most specialized to higher levels of organization; this choice moves in the opposite way.

Choice **c** is incorrect. The cardiovascular system is a higher level of organization than the heart.

Choice **d** is incorrect. The correct sequence moves from most specialized to higher levels of organization. Red blood cell should be the most specialized item at the far left, with cardiovascular system listed on the far right as the highest level of organization.

16. **The correct answer is yy.** In a Punnett square, the alleles combine, one from the side and one from the top, in each box. The two lower case "y" alleles combine in the bottom right box of the Punnett square, indicating that a recessive phenotype is possible when two heterozygous genotypes combine.

17. **The correct answer is 8 meters.** The formula for velocity, $v = \frac{\text{distance}}{\text{time}}$, can be rearranged to solve for distance. In this case, $d = v \times t$, which is 4 m/s multiplied by 2 seconds.

18. **Choice c is correct.** Materials such as wool are good insulators because they are poor conductors of heat. A wool blanket will slow the transfer of heat from the body so that it feels warmer.

Choice **a** is incorrect. A material that does not conduct heat well is an insulator. A tile floor would act as a conductor because it transfers heat away from the skin easily, causing the surface of the floor to feel cooler.

Choice **b** is incorrect. Metals such as silver and stainless steel are good conductors of heat. A metal spoon transfers the heat from the hot liquid to any surface it contacts, even skin.

Choice **d** is incorrect. A copper pipe is an excellent conductor of heat and electricity, making it a poor insulator.

19. **Choice c is correct.** The graph shows that additional energy is not needed to complete the reaction; energy is given off as the reaction takes place. As a result, the energy level of the products is lower than the energy level of the starting materials.

Choice **a** is incorrect. The graph illustrates an exothermic reaction because the energy level of the products is lower than the energy level of the starting materials.

Choice **b** is incorrect. While the graph does indicate an exothermic reaction, the rationale is incorrect in that there is no additional energy necessary to complete the reaction. The graph illustrates energy given off, instead of being used, after activation.

Choice **d** is incorrect. The graph does not show an endothermic reaction. This graph shows a product energy level lower than the reactant energy level.

20. **Choice a is correct.** While a truck and a school bus may have similar mass, the school bus is parked, indicating a velocity of zero. Thus the truck moving at any velocity will have the highest kinetic energy. Similarly, even though the bicycle is in motion, the greater mass of the truck will contribute to its larger kinetic energy.

Choice **b** is incorrect. A bicycle traveling at 10 m/s will have less kinetic energy than a truck traveling at the same velocity because it has less mass than the truck.

Choice **c** is incorrect. A car stopped at a red light has a velocity of zero, so it will have zero kinetic energy.

Choice **d** is incorrect. A school bus that is parked will have a velocity of zero, translating to zero kinetic energy.

21. Choice a is correct. Incorporating solar panels into his home would allow Carlos to use less fossil fuel energy while saving money.

Choice **b** is incorrect. While wind turbines could be an environmentally sound decision, they are not affordable, nor are they likely to be allowed in Carlos's neighborhood.

Choice **c** is incorrect. Replacing an oil-burning furnace with a wood-burning stove would cost a lot of money and provide no long-term savings or environmental benefits.

Choice **d** is incorrect. Changing electricity companies or lowering existing rates will not make Carlos's home more energy efficient.

22. Choice b is correct. UVB rays cause sunburns. The greatest percentage of UVB rays reach the earth at noon (12 P.M.), making it the most likely time of day for sunburn to occur.

Choice **a** is incorrect. UVA rays do great damage and are associated with the signs of aging. While they are in abundance from 10 A.M.– 2 P.M., they are not the cause of sunburns.

Choice **c** is incorrect. UVC rays do not reach the earth at any time of day and are not the cause of sunburns.

Choice **d** is incorrect. UVA rays are lessened by 4 P.M., but they are not the cause of sunburns.

23. Choice c is correct. Almost all of the weight of an atom comes from the protons and neutrons in its nucleus. Neutrons weigh approximately 1 atomic mass unit, and protons weigh 1 atomic mass unit (1.67×10^{-24} grams).

Choice **a** is incorrect. Protons are positively charged particles that weigh 1 atomic mass unit (1.67×10^{-24} grams) and are located in the nucleus. They account for the atomic number of the element, but the atomic mass, or weight, is a combination of the weights of protons and neutrons.

Choice **b** is incorrect. The majority of the atomic weight of an atom is determined by the neutrons and protons. Electrons are negatively charged particles that weigh zero atomic mass units and are located in the various orbitals of the energy levels outside the nucleus. An electron actually weighs 9.11×10^{-28} grams. This means it would take about 1,830 electrons to equal the mass of one proton.

Choice **d** is incorrect. An electron actually weighs 9.11×10^{-28} grams. This means it would take about 1,830 electrons to equal the mass of one proton, so they are too light to factor into the overall weight of the atom. Almost all of the weight of an atom is made up of the protons and neutrons in its nucleus.

24. Choice d is correct. The first energy level of an atom can hold a maximum of 2 electrons in one orbital. Each energy level is capable of holding a specific number of electrons.

Choice **a** is incorrect. Neutrons are found only in the nucleus of an atom.

Choice **b** is incorrect. The maximum number of electrons in the third energy level of an atom is 18, and they are distributed over 9 different orbitals.

Choice **c** is incorrect. Protons and neutrons are found only in the nucleus of an atom.

25. Choice d is correct. Reactivity is the tendency of a substance to undergo a chemical reaction, either by itself or with other materials, and to release energy. Reactivity with other chemicals was evidenced when the baking soda and vinegar combined and reacted to create carbon dioxide gas, as seen by the bubbles.

Choice **a** is incorrect. While flammability is a chemical property, it was not observed during the reaction between the baking soda and vinegar.

Choice **b** is incorrect. Color change can indicate a reaction, but it was not observed in this scenario.

Choice **c** is incorrect. Volume is a physical property of liquids, not a chemical property seen in this situation.

26. Choice a is correct. Gold is the best choice because it tops the list for corrosion resistance and will not tarnish. It is also malleable, so it is easy to shape but will not break easily because it is not brittle.

Choice **b** is incorrect. Nickel is not highly malleable, which would make it difficult to shape for jewelry design.

Choice **c** is incorrect. Bismuth is highly brittle and is not considered very malleable, making it a poor choice for jewelry.

Choice **d** is incorrect. Manganese is a very brittle metal that does not shape well and does not resist corrosion well.

27. The correct answer is 2.

The breakdown of hydrogen peroxide into water and oxygen is summarized as $2H_2O_2 \rightarrow 2H_2O + O_2$. The 2 balances the equation because there are 2 water molecules to equal 4 hydrogens.

28. Choice a is correct. The correct formula described is Na_2CO_3, which shows sodium with a subscript of 2, indicating twice as many atoms as the one carbon atom. Oxygen has a subscript of 3, meaning 3 times more than the single carbon atom.

Choice **b** is incorrect. The correct formula should have a subscript of 2 next to sodium because it is to have twice as many sodium atoms as the single carbon atom.

Choice **c** is incorrect. The 3 sodium atoms are more than the "twice as many sodium atoms as carbon atoms" described in the question.

Choice **d** is incorrect. This formula shows 6 times more sodium atoms than carbon atoms and 12 times as many oxygen atoms.

29. Choice a is correct. The rules of solubility state that all hydroxide (OH) compounds are insoluble except those of Group IA (alkali metals) and Ba^{2+}, Ca^{2+}, and Sr^{2+}. $Mg(OH)_2$ is insoluble because Mg is listed in the chart under the heading of "combinations that are not soluble."

Choice **b** is incorrect. NaOH is soluble, completely dissociating in aqueous solution. Sodium (Na) compounds are soluble, according to the chart.

Choice **c** is incorrect. Salts of K^+ and NO_3 are listed as soluble on the chart. KNO_3 would be classified as completely soluble by the general solubility rules 1 and 3.

Choice **d** is incorrect. Salts of Cl^- are listed as soluble on the chart, so LiCl is a soluble compound. The solubility rules state that all compounds of Group IA elements (the alkali metals) are soluble.

30. **Choice b is correct.** Soft, finely stratified sedimentary shale formations are home to billions of barrels of oil as well as natural gas. Choice **a** is incorrect. The natural gas and oil deposits are found in shale formations. Sand, chemicals, and water are used in extraction of the gas and oil through fracking. Choice **c** is incorrect. Concrete wells are used to house the disposed wastewater from the hydraulic fracturing process, after the shale formation is fractured. Choice **d** is incorrect. While the oil and gas can be located far below the water table, the best answer, as referenced in the passage, is "billions of barrels of oil are believed to be locked in soft, finely stratified sedimentary shale formations all over the United States."

31. **The correct answer is Oil/Gas Extraction.** The circles in the activity legend indicate the location of earthquakes that were caused or "likely related" to energy technologies. The larger the circle, the larger the earthquake. The largest circles on the map are black, which represents "Oil/Gas Extraction."

32. **Choice c is correct.** Water is scarce in the regions targeted by hydraulic fracturing, and the sustainability of fresh water must be addressed. When "millions of gallons of fresh water, sand, and chemicals are injected under high pressure into a well," the reality of the vast amounts of this resource being used comes to light. Choice **a** is incorrect. Air pollution is a concern, but it does not address the sustainability concerns. The primary sustainable resource used in hydraulic fracturing is water. Choice **b** is incorrect. The potential for earthquakes is not a sustainability issue. The resource that must be sustained in order for fracking to continue is water. Choice **d** is incorrect. Solar and wind resources are not the sustainability issue being raised in the process of hydraulic fracturing. Rather, the millions of gallons of fresh water used in the injection of the wells is the issue.

33. **Choice a is correct.** Ocean acidification occurs when seawater absorbs carbon dioxide from the atmosphere. The point on the graph indicating the lowest concentration of atmospheric CO_2 is 1960. Choice **b** is incorrect. 1970 shows more parts per million of atmospheric CO_2, which contributes to ocean acidification, than 1960. Choice **c** is incorrect. 1990 shows significantly more atmospheric carbon dioxide than 1960. Choice **d** is incorrect. More than 380 parts per million of CO_2 were detected in the atmosphere in 2010.

34. Choice a is correct. Increased acidification of ocean waters creates a poor environment for calcifying marine animals. Corals are primary consumers in marine food webs. When corals cannot properly function and begin to die, the secondary and tertiary consumers are negatively impacted.

Choice **b** is incorrect. Increased air pollution from cars does pour more CO_2 into the atmosphere, but this does not directly impact marine food webs.

Choice **c** is incorrect. Rising sea levels can be a result of overall global temperatures, which can be an effect of greenhouse gases. However, this does not have a direct effect on marine food webs.

Choice **d** is incorrect. Greenhouse gases increasing Earth's temperatures will indirectly affect many food webs, but it is not the best answer. The direct negative effect will be seen in coral calcification.

35. Choice c is correct. The process of corrosion occurs when materials with a low pH chemically weather cliff rocks with a high pH. The increased acidity of seawater significantly contributes to the way sea cliffs break apart. Choice **a** is incorrect. Abrasion is also called *corrasion*; this action is how sea cliffs erode. Various sizes of rock are carried by fast-moving waves that break against cliffs, wearing them down like sandpaper. Large pieces of the upper cliff face break or fall off because of gravity. Choice **b** is incorrect. *Attrition* is a type of mechanical weathering, in which rock particles are worn against other rock particles so they break up and wear each other down into smooth, round pebbles. This is usually caused by a combination of tidal action and coastal winds.

Choice **d** is incorrect. In *hydraulic action erosion*, air is forced into tiny fissures and cracks in large rocks by the breaking of large waves. This air pressure exerts enough force on these rocks that they eventually weaken enough to collapse.

ADDITIONAL ONLINE PRACTICE

Using the codes below, you'll be able to log in and access additional online practice materials!

Your free online practice access codes are:

FVENN4F5XWJAQ5DP1NDI

FVE6FY67LI20KP0EYVPN

FVEU0BUJP35IG34F553P

FVEY84I0C1HPUCGE3OFW

Follow these simple steps to redeem your codes:

- Go to **www.learningexpresshub.com/affiliate** and have your access codes handy.

  If you're a new user:
  - Click the **New user? Register here** button and complete the registration form to create your account and access your products.
  - Be sure to enter your unique access codes only once. If you have multiple access codes, you can enter them all—just use a comma to separate each code.
  - The next time you visit, simply click the **Returning user? Sign in** button and enter your username and password.
- Do not re-enter previously redeemed access codes. Any products you previously accessed are saved in the **My Account** section on the site. Entering a previously redeemed access code will result in an error message.

  If you're a returning user:
  - Click the **Returning user? Sign in** button, enter your username and password, and click **Sign In**.
  - You will automatically be brought to the **My Account** page to access your products.
- Do not re-enter previously redeemed access codes. Any products you previously accessed are saved in the **My Account** section on the site. Entering a previously redeemed access code will result in an error message.

  If you're a returning user with new access codes:
  - Click the **Returning user? Sign in** button, enter your username, password, and new access codes, and click **Sign In**.
  - If you have multiple access codes, you can enter them all—just use a comma to separate each code.
- Do not re-enter previously redeemed access codes. Any products you previously accessed are saved in the **My Account** section on the site. Entering a previously redeemed access code will result in an error message.

If you have any questions, please contact LearningExpress Customer Support at LXHub@Learning-ExpressHub.com. All inquiries will be responded to within a 24-hour period during our normal business hours: 9:00 A.M.–5:00 P.M. Eastern Time. Thank you!